The 12 COMMANDMENTS *of* SOCIALISM

Socialist Promises

A.Y Ph.D. and S.Y Ph.D.

WESTBOW
PRESS®
A DIVISION OF THOMAS NELSON
& ZONDERVAN

WestBow Press books may be ordered through booksellers or by contacting:

WestBow Press
A Division of Thomas Nelson & Zondervan
1663 Liberty Drive
Bloomington, IN 47403
www.westbowpress.com
844-714-3454

ISBN: 978-1-6642-0369-3 (sc)
ISBN: 978-1-6642-0368-6 (hc)
ISBN: 978-1-6642-0370-9 (e)

Library of Congress Control Number: 2020916400

Print information available on the last page.

WestBow Press rev. date: 10/07/2020

CONTENTS

GREAT THOUGHTS FROM GLOBAL LEADERS

DR. A.Y provides a unique viewpoint on issues of importance to the current political discourse in America, especially as it relates to the issue of socialism from a Christian and Biblical perspective. He was raised in an authoritarian socialist country, and, after completing his theological training in a free country, served for several years as a pastor, evangelist and Bible school leader in another major socialist country before being expelled and coming to America. His first-hand account of his experiences and those of his extended family, friends and ministry colleagues living in a socialist context, and his reflections on the current American political environment, are both provocative and compelling. His insights and analyses provide a valuable contribution to the current American debate about the role of socialism in our nation.

John F. Carter, Ph.D.

I want to congratulate Dr. A.Y and Dr. S.Y on this wonderful work about socialism and detailed analyses of real life in some socialist countries. I could not agree with them more about the limited freedom and many serious violations of human rights in many socialist countries. My family and I also experienced so many of those "socialist commandments" when I was put in various jails for a total period of 10 years and I was under 20 years of strict surveillances in a socialist country until my family and I were deported from that socialist country. This book provides much valuable information to readers about the choice of socialism and the great republic.

Rev. Dr. Paul A.

"Freedom is the heart cry of humanity and should be available to all people regardless of race or color. You will find this book to be a bright light shining through the darkness of false promises of socialism. The writers, Dr. A.Y and Dr. S.Y, pulls the mask off those with hate and disdain for America. We know the profound phrase, "Know the truth and the truth will set you free." Not only are these words spoken by Jesus Christ, but they are the driving purpose in the writing of this book. Read and know the truth."

Rev. Dr. J. W. Sloan

Please Make Your Decision To Read This Book Until The End!

The Many Victims Need You To Hear Them Out
The Victims Do Not Want You To Fall Into The Same Deceptive Path.
Kindly Help Others Know The Truth By
Making This Book Available to Them.

Many Heartfelt Thanks and Gratitude To the Millions of
Americans and People of The Nations For Receiving and
Embracing the Millions of Victims From Many Socialist Nations
and Regimes and Tyrannies To Your Lands Of Freedom.

Please Note That
Your freedom to read this book is at the expense of the
loss of freedoms and sufferings by millions of people
in socialist regimes, including the writers.

We hope that you would treasure the great freedoms
and the great protection of many human rights
that America and Americans do have.

**Please Send Us Your Stories So We Could
Learn From Your Experiences**
And We Would Share Your Stories In Our Next
Books If You Are Willing To Do So.
nationsrevivals@yahoo.com

SPECIAL APPRECIATION

This book could not be possible without the prayers, encouragements, patience, sacrifices, insights and wonderful support of our parents, spouses, children, brothers and sisters and many family and church members. This is their book, their experiences and their stories and we had the honor to put their stories together. We regret that many of their names could not be listed here now for security purposes.

We are indebted to the many supports, spiritual guidance, love, prayers and blessings of great spiritual leaders around the world and throughout the tough and great years that we do not often express our heartfelt gratitude publicly: Rev. Dr. Paul A. and Rev. Ruth A., Rev. Dr. Nate S. and Rev. Dr. Chris S., Rev. Dr. Richard S. and Rev. Jewel S., Rev. Lawrence K. and Rev. Nettie Y. and our board members Joe T., Mark M., Peter. B., Joshua D., Mary F., and their wonderful families.

We would like to say many appreciations to Dr. John F. Carter, our former excellent professor and President of Asia Pacific Theological Seminary and the Chairman of the Board of Asia Pacific Theological Association for his many academic, intellectual and spiritual investments in our lives. Without his precious critical thoughts, suggestions, advices and insights, the coherence of this book could not be possible. Thanks a lot also to Ma'am Bea Carter for your love, cares, supports and many prayers.

We would also appreciate Dr. David S. Lim, the President of the Asian School for Development and Cross-cultural Studies and the President of China Ministries International-Philippines, for his great academic insights on the subject matter of socialism that greatly challenged the writers to develop greater thoughts and discussions on socialism and the current situations.

We would like to express our many gratitudes to special people and their family members for their wonderful fellowship, generous support, great encouragement, bountiful care and love, and constant prayers: Rev. Dr. Mark H. and Dinh N., Joseph F. and Mary Y., John D. and Kitty D., John, Matthew and Mary, Rev. David K. and Tram U., Bang T. and

Loc D., Mindy N., Henry T. and Moon T., Rev. Jessie C., Stephanie P., Don N. and Phuong N., Thomas L. and Jenny L., Kathryn and Steve G., George L. and Orchid H., Tiffany D., Tan H. and Hannah Mom, Alex H. and Megan Mom, Rina B., Lisa L., Vinnie T., Hally T., Chau P., Chi H., Christine N., Vicky N. and Steve H., and many others.

This book could not be better and more beautiful without the many diligent and creative works of WestBow Press, a division of Thomas Nelson and Zondervan and staffs in their design, editing, marketing and distribution of this book and to make this book available readers worldwide. Thanks a lot to Eric Schroeder, the Senior Publishing Consultant, Joe Anderson, the coordinator of WestBow Press, Tim Fitch, Publishing Services Associate and Lucas Biery for content evaluation and many other staffs who made this book available.

Most of all we would like to give thanks to our Loving and Almighty God for all of His wisdom, blessings, protections and providences. Thank You, Lord, for Your many strengths, inspirations, thoughts and guidance throughout the process. Thank You, Lord, for Your many healings, deliverances, restorations, renewals, reflections, and powerful touches to every reader. Lord, may You also bless every reader and their family members abundantly and may You bring more encouragements, miracles, breakthroughs and peace to every home.

AMERICANS AND SOCIALISM: AN INTRODUCTION

Socialism found its way to the U.S. as early as the 18ᵗʰ century. "Then there were the labor activists who were mostly British, German, or Jewish immigrants who founded the Socialist Labor Party in 1877; with many of their descendants perpetrating the same ideology… And we see these people in today's labor unions such as the NEA, SEIU, Teamsters, and so on" according to Candie Suarez on the Daily Conspiracy.

Socialism was once popular in the United States of America in the 1910s. The Socialist Party was founded and saw the significant growth between 1900 and 1912 under the leadership of the socialist leader Eugene V. Debs who "led the establishment of the Socialist Party of America. Debs was the party's presidential candidate in 1900 but received only 96,000 votes" wrote Encyclopedia Britannica.

Socialism became known and accepted by more Americans when Eugene V. Debs continued to run for many of his presidential elections and criticized the economic power of capitalism, the flaws of capitalism and the traditional political concepts though he was not elected. "Between 1900 and 1920 Debs was the Socialist party's standard-bearer in five presidential elections" according to History. com Editors.

From the many threats of the Bolshevik revolution in 1917 to the rise of Soviet socialist nations, and till the end of the Cold War between the U.S. and the former USSR in 1991, the socialist movements also took part in fighting against labor and racial struggles in 1930s, social struggles in the 1960s, and 1970s and playing important roles in the civil rights movement with the New Left stated Wikipedia.

However, socialism in those seven decades since the decline of the socialist movement in 1920 in the U.S., was basically unpopular or at least it was forgotten from time to time in the U.S. because socialism pointed to the destructive Soviet type of socialism which was unfortunately filled with dictatorship, oppression, tyrannies, poverties and mass killings of millions of innocent people by the socialist leaders.

"According to Article 76 of the 1977 Soviet Constitution, a Union Republic was a sovereign Soviet socialist state that had united with other Soviet Republics in the USSR... the Soviet Union officially consisted of fifteen Soviet Socialist Republics (SSRs)." At the fall of former USSR, these former Soviet Socialist Republics are now independent countries according to Wikipedia on Republics of the Soviet Union.

The former USSR was the most powerful socialist state before 1991 and it grew as one of the most powerful nations of the day. The USSR just like other socialist nations did carried out the socialist agendas of social ownership and equality to the extreme. Unfortunately, the growth and groans of the socialist nations were at the grave sacrifices of millions of its citizen with failed reforms, famines and poverty.

The USSR was known as the Soviet Republics and it did mark its characteristics of Soviet-type socialism with militant leadership, big government, violation of human rights, corruption and limited freedom. It was once the nightmare of the Western World and million hopeless citizens in the socialist states and Soviet republics. Its history was tainted with countless streams of blood of million innocent people.

The USSR and Soviet-type socialism failed after seven decades of revolutions. "For most of its history, the USSR was a highly centralized state; the decentralization reforms during the era of Perestroika ("Restructuring") and Glasnost ("Openness") conducted by Mikhail Gorbachev are cited as one of the factors which lead to the dissolution of the USSR" stated Wikipedia on Republics of the Soviet Union.

Capitalism then won again the hearts of Americans and people of nations at the collapse of the former USSR, the powerful socialist nations in Eastern Europe, the Berlin Wall and other socialist nations elsewhere. Capitalism was still celebrated as it led America and Americans to go through economic crises and made America to be the top nation of the world with their economic, political and military powers.

The economic crisis in 2001 and 2008 brought many tragedies to the nationals and Americans were of no exception. In 2009, President Barak Obama was elected at the outbreak of this economic crisis or the Great Recession through his promising presidential campaigns on "Hope" and "Change We Can Believe In." Trillions of U.S. dollars were poured into reform agendas to revive the declining economy.

His achievements included "reducing unemployment and poverty, decreasing the number of Americans who lack insurance, focusing on clean energy, and reducing official discrimination against the LGBTQ group. In foreign policy, Obama is most known for the successful operation against Osama bin Laden, the Iran Nuclear Deal and improvement of U.S. relations with Cuba" according to Anirudth.

Unfortunately, the reforms and the huge spending of the Administration of President Obama through moderate tax, major stimulus package, comprehensive health care reform, banking regulation, did not bring much Hope and Change in income inequality, federal budget deficit, international trade and U.S. economy. Americans under poverty line increased from less than 800,000 to 40.0 million.

Michael D'Antonio wrote about the legacy of President Obama but he acknowledged that, "You've got a lot of lower wage, unfortunately, service jobs being created, not enough high-wage jobs for the people who want them, and at the same time you have this tripling of the stock market, and actually a rebound down real estate... but he didn't make the progress that I think he hoped he would on inequality, in part because there's only so much a president can do" stated WBUR.

Emily Stewart on Vox noted that, "The unemployment rate jumped from 6.1 percent in August 2008 to 9.5 percent two years later in August 2010. Millions of Americans lost their homes, their jobs, or both." By November 2012, the unemployment rate was 9.8 percent and the rejection of President Obama's advisers for large infrastructure projects led to the loss of homes of 10 million Americans.

The economic reforms did provide jobs but short-lived and thousands of companies closed their factories, moving their operations abroad. As the result, more jobs were lost than provided. Capitalism, not the top leaders or the democrats, was, every time, to be blamed for the economic crisis, economic instability, foreclosures of houses, high rate of unemployment to million Americans, and people of the nations.

Capitalism was again criticized for the failed economy. Capitalism was to be blamed for the inequalities. Capitalism was accused of for the unemployment. Capitalism was considered as the cause of wealth gaps and the elites. Capitalism was to be blamed for almost everything that failed when it was the failures and inability of the country leaders while President Obama is still praised as the great president.

"In the Obama years, the government let corporations get bigger and economic power grow more concentrated. Obama's regulators declined to push antimonopoly measures" against big corporations according to Farhad Manjoo on The New York Times. Interestingly, no mainstream media mentioned the failures of President Obama and his administration but the blames are on the economic crisis and capitalism.

Harold Meyerson pointed out that, "But the prime mover of millions of Americans into the socialist column has been the near complete dysfunctionality of contemporary American capitalism... the deregulated, deunionized and financialized capitalism of the past 35 years has produced record levels of inequality, a shrinking middle class, and scant economic opportunities for the young."

Farhad Manjoo emphasized that, "It's also true that over the course of his presidency, inequality grew, and Obama did little to stop it. While much of the rest of the country struggled to get by, the wealthy got wealthier and multimillionaires and billionaires achieved greater political and cultural power..." Then capitalism received all the dirt again for the monopoly of the wealthy corporations.

Thomas Frank reviewed in his book, "Listen, Liberal": that "Insurers remained embedded in the health care system. Wall Street retained its power in finances. Poverty was intractable, college students remained burdened by debt, and income inequality had worsened" reported Michael D'Antonio. Socialism once again found its way to re-emerge in American society and politics with its criticism of capitalism.

In 2008, there were about 28 million food-stamp recipients. The number of food-stamp receivers kept increasing under President Obama until almost 48 million recipients in 2013 and more than 44.2 million recipients in 2016 and that was "roughly 15% of the population—needed food stamps... It's another sign the recovery isn't reaching everybody yet" according to Heather Long on CNN Money.

"The number of able-bodied adults on food stamps doubled from 1.9 million in 2008 to 3.9 million in 2010 when Obama singed his stimulus bill and suspended a rule under the 1996 Welfare Reform Law that regulated how long able-bodied adults without dependents could collect food stamps." By June 2009, there were 36,029,506 persons participating in food stamp program reported Mary M. Olohan.

According to Matt Palumbo on The Political Insider, during the time of President Obama, the following areas kept increased such as student loans, food stamps, federal debt, money printing, health costs and black inequality. The following areas were declined such as labor force participation, home ownership and median family income rate that coincided with an increase in food stamp participation.

There were more than 10 million jobs added but 15 million jobs were also lost as companies and factories moved abroad. The unemployment rate was high and millions of Americans had no choice but facing with jobless, uncertainties, worries and pains. Should capitalism was to be blamed alone or should President Obama also be responsible for his failed policies and inability to revive the economy?

The Robert Tracinski on the Federalist pointed out that "President Obama has failed to live up to his promises and to the responsibilities of his office" because he didn't heal the racial divisions in the U.S., his stimulus didn't stimulate the economy but it was financed entirely with debt, his financial reform didn't reform. Congress voted for hundreds of billion of dollars for "shovel-ready projects" which Obama later discovered don't exist, and the money disappeared without a trace."

"President Obama has almost doubled our national debt to more than $19 trillion, and growing," Trump said. "Yet what do we have to show for it? Our roads and bridges are falling apart, our airports are in their worse condition, and 43 million Americans are on food stamps." "For all of the spending in Washington under President Barack Obama, the American people are not better off" reported Nadia Pflaum.

The mainstream media could not hide the truth any longer or to cover their failures and political games forever. The worse thing was, the many failures of President Obama, his administration, the democrats and the economic crisis were the main reasons why socialism took the attention of million Americans who were willing to embrace socialism with the hope of a better future without pressures and burdens.

Thus, the switch to socialism by millions of American millenials, by so many democrats and most of the democrat leaders since 2016 was **first of all** the cause of the failing economy and the disappointment of Americans under the presidency of President Obama. At the many criticisms of capitalism, Americans, then, were attracted to many freebies and offers of Sen. Bernie Sanders and the socialists.

"Today in the U.S., Berman says the support for Sanders and the idea of democratic socialism stems from the 2008 financial crisis and everything that succeeded it-including growing income inequality, declining social mobility and increased geographic divides particularly between young people based on whether they could afford college" reported Jeremy Hobson and Allison Hagan on WBUR.com.

Secondly, importantly, the rise of Soviet-type socialism in America was also the result of the successful plan of the leaders of American socialists to make Barack Obama the first Socialist President of the U.S. Millions of Americans may not know the fact that President Obama had a strong communist background and he was strongly influenced by socialism though he may not openly declared that.

Karin McQuillan noted the communist background of President Obama whose grandfather, mother and father and his many leaders, advisers, and supporters such as David Axelrod, Valerie Jarrett, Bill Ayers... who were either members or leaders of Communist Party or radical left. President Obama was also seen as a revolutionary Marxist in college according to John Drew, a Marxist student at Occidental College.

The current rise of Antifa, Black Lives Matter and the easy defund of police are the fruits of President Obama's works and the democrat leaders when he pardoned terrorists and serious criminals and put BLM militants in charge of police retraining. The democrat mayors and governors from Asbury Park to Boston, Chicago, Dallas, Los Angeles and all democratic states supported the riots of BLM and Antifa.

The growing support of Americans to socialism was also due to President Obama's supports to socialism as a socialist. According to Karin McQuillan on Life Site, "Obama chose communists and Marxists for the highest, most powerful positions in our land, including his closest political advisers and his head of the CIA. These facts are not in dispute. Most are openly admitted by the people in question."

Wikipedia on the history of the socialist movement stated an important fact that, the DSA strongly supported the Democratic presidential candidate Barack Obama in his race against Republican candidate John Mc. Cain in 2008. The National Director, Frank Llewellyn declared that, "over the past 12 months, the Democratic Socialists of America has received more media attention it has over the past 12 years."

"Obama tells us the radical socialist conferences he attended before law school gave him his road map in life... Obama's run for state representative was as the handpicked successor of a socialist state representative, who was publicly active in communist circles... Until he became president, Obama was a 20-year member of an openly Marxist church whose members had to take a pledge against the middle class" stated Karin McQuillan

Leon Puissegur concluded that, "our Marxist/Socialist/Communist President was not just supported by the Communist Party; he was "selected" by the Communist Party of the United States to replace the Communist, Alice Palmer when... What more proof is needed to show Obama's past is extremely deep in some sort of Anti-United States actions by the varied parties of Marxist, Socialist, Communist and maybe others that do not want the United States to succeed!"

Surveys of Rasmussen Reports, Pew and Gallup showed the growing support of socialism over capitalism during the administration of President Obama. Though President Obama and his administration denied that many of their policies were socialistic, yet, socialism grew significantly during his administration and it took the leap with Sen. Bernie Sanders with more than 13 million supporters in 2016.

This also explains the reason why the former Vice President Joe Biden who was under President Barack Obama and is now the top democratic candidate for the 2020 presidential election wholeheartedly embraces the destructive socialism and the socialist agenda. One could not help but to imagine the rise of socialism and the brutal reign of the socialists if he was to win the 2020 presidential election.

So, this switch to socialism could not be the issues or the failures of President Trump and his administration. The coronavirus pandemic affected all nations of the world but President Trump and his administration were quick to take measures against the coronavirus. Yet just like other pandemics, the issues could only be solved when vaccine for coronavirus is successful made and available to people.

The losses of million jobs took place in all major economies of the world. While nations are facing more job losses, the U.S. started to see the increase of jobs. Even more than 22 million jobs in the U.S. were lost due to the coronavirus pandemic since February 2020. 7.5 million jobs among the 22 plus million jobs were restored and workers go back to their jobs. 4.8 million jobs were added in June 2020 alone.

By May and June 2020, 7.5 millions of new jobs were added to the U.S. market. By July and August, the remaining 4 million plus jobs that were lost earlier are expected to make a comeback plus millions of new jobs. On July 1st, 2020, the USMCA went to effect and it is estimated to add about $70 billions to the U.S GDP annually and it also provides more than 170,000 jobs annually.

The U.S. economy will boom quickly again when millions workers go back to work as the foundation for the economic development is already laid in the last few years. It will be revived in no time and this is the greatest fear of his opponents. Thus they tried all means to maintain the lockdown and the close of businesses, and the riots to discredit President Trump so they could win the 2020 election.

Before the coronavirus pandemic, the U.S. economy was growing and strong during the first three years under the administration of President Trump. Thousands of companies and factories came back to the U.S. to start or restart their factories and business operations. This led to the creation of millions of jobs through tax cut reform, Pledge for American Workers and Special Economic Zones.

Jobs were plenty and the unemployment rate reached the lowest records in more than five decades. Job opportunities were more than the number of people who looked for jobs, and employers must increased the salaries to keep their employees. Millions of food stamp recipients under the presidency of President Obama were off from the list of food stamp dependency under President Trump's administration.

If the economy were not strong under the first three years of President Trump, most Americans would not think about the 2020 reelection of President Trump and there was no doubt that Sen. Bernie Sanders would be the democratic nominee for the 2020 presidential election as Sen. Bernie Sanders would defeat President Trump with his many appealing offers and freebies that people would want to have.

Yet, under President Trump's administration, millions of Americans began to realize that it was not the failures of the capitalistic economic system but the corruption, political manipulation, mainstream media distortion and deception, fake news and inability of the democratic leaders in the previous administration that led to the economic struggles of millions of Americans and the declines of the U.S. economy.

The success of President Trump in the first three years was not only about the economic successes, high employments and the revival of the U.S. economy and made-in-USA products but also his capability to deal with illegal immigrations, sex and human trafficking, terrorism, drugs and gang groups, and especially China issues that the previous administration failed to do so or was not willing to do so.

Thus, more and more millions of Americans supported President Trump because he kept well many of his promises and he even did more than what he promised though there are still only a few promises that he has not been able to finish and this was not because he did not keep his promises but because he faced and he is still facing so many obstacles, rejections and oppositions from the democrat leaders.

Importantly, the many successes of President Trump and his administration saved America and Americans from the disastrous consequences of socialism. The thriving economy under President Trump's administration undermined the many appealing proposals of Sen. Bernie Sanders. The many great record-breaking achievements of President Trump led to the end of Sen. Bernie Sander's 2020 presidential race.

Through the 12 commandments of socialism, millions of readers would realize the great contributions of President Trump and his administration in minimizing the influences, speed and destructions of socialism and American socialists to take over America and to save 330 millions of Americans and the neighboring countries from the many havocs of socialism and the Soviet-type socialists.

Thirdly, the switch to socialism was and is the ignorance of millions of Americans about the history of socialism and the disasters that the socialists had brought to humanity. Americans especially the millennials widely responded to and embraced socialism when Senator Bernie Sanders started to convince the people in 2015 that socialism would produce equality, stable job and income, wealth and great welfare.

Socialism then also found its way back to American society and politics and became popular again after one century of silence as Sen. Bernie Sanders, the socialist, ran his 2016 presidential campaign. American millennials did not know or did not care about the failures, the horrors and the limited freedom in the socialist nations, so they gladly supported and welcome the empty promises of the socialists.

Then, the Democratic Socialists of America grew fast from 6,000 members to 60,000 members by 2019 and "most of them in their twenties and eager to follow the socialist banner... Socialism is no longer a parlor game for academics but a political alternative taken seriously by millennials who are not put off by the radical DSA platform" said Lee Edwards, the leading historian of American conservatism.

For decades, the membership of the socialist parties in America grew little but the significant growth came in 2016 when the DSA had only 6,000 members. Wikipedia on Democratic Socialists of America noted that, "By the end of 2017, membership in the organization had risen to 32,000... As of September 2, 2018, membership stood at 50,000 and the number of local chapters had increased from 40 to 181."

Study of George Barna in 2017 showed that in every ten adults, four preferred socialism to capitalism. "That 40 percent of Americans now prefer socialism and capitalism could spell major change to the policies advanced by legislators and political leaders and to the interpretations of judges' ruling on the application of new and pre-existing laws" reported David Nammo.

Though the 2020 presidential race of Sen. Bernie Sanders was ended and it also ended the socialist dream for taking over the U.S. by election at least for now, the socialists did not give up their dream and they are now working with the leftists, leftwing democratic leaders, Antifa, local terrorist group, anarchists in hoping of removing President Trump and winning over the U.S. either by forces or violence.

These opponents of President Trump, of the Republicans and of the conservatives encouraged protesters and rioters organize the protests, riots and violence under the name of social justice to defund the police department and to remove the police task forces. They called for peaceful gathering to take over the U.S. in the name of freedom, yet those peaceful demonstrations turned into violence and deadly riots.

In just more than a month since the death of George Floyd, hundreds of people were shot and many people died in the name of Black Lives Matter. Hundreds of people were beaten hurt and wounded. Thousands of stores and businesses across states were damaged and looted. Houses, churches and communities were burned and billions of U.S. dollar was lost in the name of fighting against white supremacy.

The rioters, Marxists and radicals smashed people's cars and police vehicles. They used violence to oppress free speech and violated people's rights. They destroyed monuments and statutes of former great U.S. presidents and leaders who fought their lives in the war to protect and to free African Americans and people of all colors in America. They wanted to erase the great history of the U.S.

Brands, names, and pictures of products were asked to rename or redesign when they were considered as racist or signs of white supremacy or the reminders of slavery and shames. Almost everything is considered as racist and white supremacy according to the definitions of rioters and looters in order to justify their robberies, violence, arsons, rapes, lootings, lawlessness, shootings and murders.

These acts revealed the many characteristics of the Soviet socialists in the cultural revolutions that took place in many former socialist countries and that brought so many tragedies and sufferings to the socialist citizens as readers would discover soon. If the violent riots and protests do not stop, America and Americans would go through a full cultural and political revolution and it will be horrible and deadly.

Fourthly, the rise of socialism was the results of freebies offered by Sen. Bernie Sanders. He is winning the hearts of more millions including the democrats and the liberals with the great promises that could free the millennials and Americans from so much debts and financial pressures such as College For All, Universal Health Care, Debt Free for college students, Childcare Supports, climate reform and more.

Sen. Bernie Sanders and the socialists tried to offer as many free benefits from one's birth to the grave as they could in order to win people's hearts and ultimately their votes. If there were more free things that they could give they would be glad to do so because this was the only golden, the only and last opportunity for Sen. Bernie Sanders to realize his and the socialists' long-awaited dream here in America.

The weak economy, the high employment and the economic struggles of millions of Americans before President Trump came into the Oval office had created a longing desire of million Americans for a stronger U.S. economy. They longed for stable jobs so that their lives could become better, their families were to be taken care of, their debts were to be solved and their many burdens were to be relieved.

Sen. Bernie Sanders promised the great free stuffs that even many wealthy people would not say no. He proposed great offers that even the democrats would love to embrace the socialists in order to defeat their strong Republican rival, President Donald J. Trump. The democrats are willing to work with their long-opposing enemies, the socialists rather than their long-coexisting friends, the republicans.

To college students, Sen. Bernie Sanders' proposal for free college education would release 20 million students in the U.S. colleges, universities and graduated schools from burdens of tuition fees, boarding, pressures of works to pay for education expenses and from losing opportunities for higher education and thus better opportunities for golden jobs. Thus, many college students became his supporters.

To the graduates who are now working, Sen. Bernie Sanders' proposal for debt free would free them from the debts of their loans for education. They are indeed overload with many burdens and debts. They have to pay for their education loan, for their house's mortgage, for their car expenses, for children education and needs, for their insurances and for so many bills... They would be happy with debt free.

For common people, Sen. Bernie Sanders' proposal for Green New Deal would sound fantastic because every American would have stable jobs and high-paid wages. They would share wealth and they would have their shares, and they would have their voices in the leadership through social ownership. People would be equal and they would no longer poor and exploited by wealthy people or the bourgeoisies.

For parents of small children, Sen. Bernie Sanders' proposal for free children's care at free daycare centers would be ideal and perfect. Young couples do not need to worry about the costs for their children to be sent to daycare centers and they could be freed from all the headaches and pressures of taking care of children and spending their time for works and to improve their finances and living conditions.

For most people, healthcare in the U.S. is very expensive and many people may not be able to afford for many health services and drug prescriptions. Sen. Bernie Sanders' plan for free health services is the answer for everyone who needs to be free from the huge costs of medical cares, medical services for free check-ups, free medications, free surgeries and many more free things.

All of those plans were great and the struggles and pressures of people from all ages would be over with socialism. Is it possible for the socialists of America to provide all of these things for free? Please find more discussions in our book, "Be Free Or Not Be Free: Socialist Freedom." Unfortunately, Sen. Bernie Sanders' socialist Utopia was never realized in the 40 former socialist countries except failures and collapses.

Fifthly, the switch to socialism is also contributed to the betrayal of many democratic and leftist leaders to America and Americans. For political power, the leftist, socialist and democratic leaders have been willing to do everything possible to remove President Trump from the Oval office. They open the doors and allow socialism to be popular through education and media and to take over the U.S.

They tried all means to discredit President Trump and his many great breaking records. Though they knew that they could not win but they still impeached him to slow down his fast speed for the economic revival. They manipulated the coronavirus pandemic to prolong the economic losses and sufferings of people. They supported and sponsoring the rioters who brought many destructions to Americans.

Baxter Dmitry on News Punch stated that, "in large Democrat-run cities across America, radical leftists including Antifa and Black Lives Matter protesters are being coddled and encouraged by indulgent leftist mayors and city councils, as violent riots continue to spread like wildfire." At the greed of these leftwing leaders for powers, American lives are at risks, businesses are looted, communities destroyed.

Why are many democratic leaders willing to partner with their long-opposing socialists who were never kind to the democrats or any non-socialist partics in the socialist nations? It was just over a half century ago, the socialists were the real enemies that the democrats and the republicans worked hard together to destroy socialism and to protect millions of Americans from the great havocs of socialism.

That switch of the democratic leaders and millions of Americans to socialism was mainly due to the desperations of the democrat leaders and the democrat party to defeat President Trump and remove him from the office. The democrats and the liberals never expected that President Trump and his administration could accomplish so many changes and record breakings within the first few years.

Common Sense American Politics stated that the democrats hated President Trump a lot because he doesn't allow the democrats and their mainstream media to bully him, he says what's on his mind, he shows more support to the veterans, he's calling out failures in big cities that are dominated by the democrats, he called out both parties for not performing.

Terry Paulson stated, "Nothing works in derailing this president, and it's driving leftists crazy... He's delivered what many past Republicans have just succeeded in talking about. From cutting taxes and regulations to stimulating our economy and from appointing conservative federal judges to fostering energy independence... The left is frustrated that Trump has delivered a track record that's hard to beat."

Terry Paulson explained that, "He doesn't lets Democrats get away with their lies... Trump is piece by piece dismantling the socialist, entitlement transformation President Obama started to build... President Trump is taking on the task of getting rid of the "deep state" bureaucrats embedded in the federal government. The democratic stronghold of overpaid bureaucrats around Washington are afraid."

Many democratic leaders really betrayed America and Americans by covering the truth and releasing the fake news. They did not criticize or expose the failures of President Barak Obama because he was their choice so they would not dispose the issues and failures of their democratic leaders and Democratic Party. They did not reveal the truth of H1N1 pandemic that brought deaths to so many Americans.

They did not reveal the truth about the many breaking records that President Trump and his administration did. They always discredit his many great works. At the present, they still do not cover news about the violence, hurts and damages that the rioters have been causing across the U.S. but they praised the protesters and demonstrators for their peaceful demonstrations and fights for social justices.

They do not reveal the many threats of the socialists and the leftists which are now evident across many states of the U.S. with many protests and demonstrations that are manipulated by the democratic leaders and the socialist leaders who aim to take over the U.S. by any means even through violence and destructions as the socialists often did in so many former socialist nations.

The democrat leaders and the leftist leaders did not expose President Barak Obama because he is an African American and they knew very well then the sensitivity of racism. If they exposed him, they would lose their image, and it could also lead to chaos, protests and violent gatherings as it is happening now in America since the death of George Floyd and racist issues.

The democrats and the liberals never expected that President Trump and his administration could keep and carry out well his many signature promises in the midst of their much opposition. And President Trump still gained popularity and more supports from the majority of Americans due to great records of low unemployment, economic revival, America first policy and Made-in USA agendas...

They tried to remove President Trump from the Oval office but they are still not successful. They use the mainstream media to discredit President Trump in everything he did and does and will do. They used Russia conspiracy to attack him. They turned his phone call to Ukraine President Zelenskyy as evidence of quid-pro-quo to impeach President Trump though they knew that they could not win.

Many democrats and liberals accused President Trump as a threat to democracy but they manipulated the democracy for their power game and corruption. President Trump protects the Constitution and puts America and Americans first. But they employed coronavirus pandemic to attack and to put blames on him. They manipulated people and terrorist group to stir up protests and riots for their goals.

But President Trump and his administration overcame all the attacks and were becoming stronger and the democrats still did not have strong candidates to defeat President Trump for the 2020 election, thus they were willing to support Sen. Bernie Sander and the socialist agenda at that time with the hope that the appealing agenda of Sen. Bernie Sander may be able to compete President Trump.

Alexandria Ocasio-Cortez or AOC, a prominent leader of Democratic Socialists of America tweeted in May 20, 2020, "It's vital that Governors maintain restrictions on businesses until after the November Elections because economic recovery will help Trump be re-elected. A few business closures or job losses is a small price to pay to be free from his presidency." These could not be the words of a U.S. patriot.

AOC, the socialists and the leftists knew very well that President Trump and his administration did so well to revive the U.S economy, to create millions of jobs, to restore American values, to put America First and to Make America Great Again, to repeal their ungodly plans, to expose their corruptions and crimes, and to block their efforts for one-world government and they could not take to accept those facts.

These socialists and leftwing leaders are willing to put million lives of Americans at stakes by allowing the rioters and the radicals to ravage homes and cities. They are willing to sacrifice American businesses and securities for lootings and arsons. They allow violence and murders to take place to hold onto their greed and power. They are willing to paralyze the U.S. economy and prosperity for their political agenda.

For these leaders and AOC, the closures of million businesses, the unemployment of millions of Americans, and struggles of million Americans are just a small price to pay. For them, the closures of schools, and the education of millions of children and the development of children, students and their potentials are just a small price to pay. For them, the suicidal, the raping, and the murders are almost nothing.

My grandfather owned a bread shop and his business was very successful. Most of the concepts of the modern cakes and breads came from the Western world so he tried to learn how to make great breads from missionaries and Westerners. When the socialists took over the country, they came and ordered him to close down his bread shop because the breads were the products of the capitalists.

Was this just a small price that my grandparent paid to close down the business? How were they going to take care of their parents and their seven children and their many needs? How about the millions of businesses and business owners who are now struggling to pay the mortgages, the rents, the salaries, and the needs of their family members because their businesses were closed, destroyed and looted?

My parents also opened a restaurant and the business was great. Then the authorities came to the restaurant and they chased out the customers, and did a thorough search at our home without a warrant. They took things away and ordered my parents to close the restaurant. The readers could find this story and many stories of the socialist victims in our book, "The Boat of Destiny: Socialist Victims."

Was this just a small price that my parents and four innocent children must pay? Who would pay back our happy days? Who would compensate our losses, our pains, our hardship and our poverty? How about the millions of Americans and family members who are also struggling to survive? Do they need to pay those sufferings, struggles and strife at the political game of AOC, leftwing democrats, and socialists?

One night, the socialist authorities came to my grandparent house, they did not come to send gifts or send greetings, or to make friends or to understand the issues of the citizen, or to offer some help. They came to kill my grandfather, father of my mother. They entered the house with guns in their hands and with their killing faces. They broke the gate and then the door of the house and called everyone to line up.

If this does happen to AOC and her family when the rioters and radicals would break in her house and order everyone to wake up and to line up and to shoot her mother or father in front of her eyes, would she and the socialists and the leftwing democrats still think that is a small price to pay? How about hundreds of people who were beaten, injured, hurt and murdered since May to August of 2020?

My granduncle and his family members tried to escape the brutal attacks and the merciless assassinations of the socialists. They escaped not because they did anything wrong to the socialists or they tried to destroy the socialists and their regime. They escaped because of the "gratitude, appreciation and kindness" that the socialists repaid to the countless help of the capitalists by killing them.

My granduncle and his family got the whole family members and precious belongings on a truck then they drove the truck away from the rise of the socialists. They thought they were fine. Yet the authorities suddenly appeared and they stopped the truck, they dragged my granduncle out of the truck and they cut his throat open and he bled to death in front of all family members.

Just like millions of the capitalists in the past, my granduncle, my grandfather and the families provided many things and many financial supports to the socialists when they were not yet in power so that the socialists could build up their armies and their strength to make a successful revolution. When the socialists were in power they killed millions of wealthy people, bourgeoisies or capitalists.

This was because the capitalists and the wealthy people were and are forever the enemies of the socialists. The bourgeoisies or the capitalists are the sources and the causes of the sufferings and the exploitations of the common people and workers. They are the causes of the unstable jobs and unstable lives of the proletariats or the workers. They are the causes of the social inequalities and wealth gaps.

Thus the capitalists must be punished for their ideology and their acts of making people suffered the injustices and the inequalities. Thus the capitalists were either killed or they were tortured and imprisoned in the hard labor camps. Their properties and businesses were confiscated and their family members were sent to countryside or remote areas to do labor works.

The socialists' brutal killings of the capitalists or incarcerations of the capitalists in horrible prison and hard labor camps to death were not by coincident or the mistakes. They deliberately did so because the socialists and the capitalists could not stay together due to their clashed ideologies. They did not want the existence of the capitalists so no one could interfere with their agendas.

Now, the American socialists need the help and supports of the leftists, the democratic leaders to build up their influences and strength. When they are strong enough to take over the U.S. and Americans as they are trying to do that now, they would take over the possessions, properties, businesses of the wealthy people and they would annihilate those capitalists as they did in 40 former socialist countries.

Let us remind you that this fact could never be wrong because it did not just happen in one country but more than 40 countries and it is still happening in the remaining socialist countries but the socialists, the leftists, and the leftwing democratic leaders do not reveal those truths to Americans. They are still using their media channels to attract millions of Americans with their many lies, deceptions and empty promises.

Our families and relatives could have become wealthy and life would be great for us and we could be great blessings to many people but we suffered greatly because of the socialists. With their cruelties and brutalities, it is true that the many sufferings that our family went through seemed to be insignificant and unimportant to the Soviet-type socialists because they are so used to the brutal murders of millions.

So it is not a surprise when AOC and the many democratic leaders considered the sufferings that so many Americans are going through now are just a small price to pay. Millions of businesses were closed and thousands of business were destroyed and looted, and many people already died because of coronavirus and riots, and for AOC, that is just a small price to pay and that is the real nature of a typical socialist.

For AOC and many democratic leaders, leftists and socialists, the sufferings, the losses of people, the unemployment, the uncertain future, and the deaths of others are just a small price to pay at their political games and power. Americans, please wake up and protect yourself, your family and your control because millions of people would suffer when the socialists were to take over America and Americans.

In this book, we will also discuss some similarities between the Soviet type socialism and the leftists and American socialists in following session of the 12 Commandments of Socialism so that Americans would understand better what does it means to choose socialism and how is that decision of socialism would turn the U.S. into anarchy or regime and turn million Americans into nightmares and deaths.

The **last important but not the least reason** that more Americans are also in favor of socialism is because of the twisted meaning and half-truth of socialism presented by Sen. Bernie Sanders, the socialists and the mainstream media. Millions of Americans are not able to discover the ultimate plan and purpose of socialism and the socialists. What are the twisted messages of modern socialists?

The modern socialists, including Sen. Bernie Sanders, would never mention anything about the founder of socialism and socialist leaders.

Karl Marx was known with his Marxist socialism that bore his name. He "is the thinker behind the communist revolutions of the 20th century, and in some ways he is the shaping hand behind socialist economics in the 21st century" according to Bruce Ashford.

"American socialists based their beliefs on the writings of Karl Marx, the German philosopher. Many asked why so many working Americans should have so little while a few owners grew incredibly wealthy... They suggested that the government should own all industries and divide the profits among those who actually created the products" according to U.S. History.

Your Dictionary stated that, "Karl Marx described socialism as a lower form of communism and held the opinion that socialism was an intermediary step in moving from capitalism to communism... The two largest socialistic systems are the former Soviet Union and Mainland China. Each of these began with the ideals of socialism, but ended in becoming totalitarian in nature."

"Many Americans have forgotten the lessons of the Cold War and the disasters witnessed in the crumbling economies and failed polities of Communist and socialist countries in the 1990s. Communism was on its last leg, it appeared, and its little brother socialism was not far behind" commented David Nammo on the National Review. The cases of Cuba and Venezuela seemed to be insignificant to Americans.

American socialists are passionate to promote socialism but they do not mention the known socialist leaders such as Karl Marx, Vladimir Lenin, Joseph Stalin and many others. If the socialists told millions of people clear and loud that these leaders of socialism or democratic socialism were the causes of million deaths and tragedies to hundred millions of people, most people would not support socialism.

Besides, Sen. Bernie Sanders gave a false assumption of great socialist countries. Barnard College political science professor Sheri Berman said, "Sanders often talks about Scandinavian countries like Denmark as a model of democratic socialism. These countries have long-standing democratic socialist parties and some consider themselves a social democracy" reported Jeremy Hobson and Allison Hagan.

Sen. Bernie Sanders and socialists often used the Scandinavian countries as the excellent examples of the democratic socialism in their speeches. They talked as if these were the socialist countries with great social welfares. But, these countries are not the socialist countries. They are the democratic countries with capitalist principles. Please find more about this in our book, "**Be Free Or Not Be Free**."

"The collapse of Soviet communism has allowed younger Americans to identify socialism with the social democratic nations of Western Europe, all of which suffer from less economic inequality and its attendant woes than the United States" stated Harold Meyerson on the Guardian. The Scandinavian countries support strongly the operations of free enterprises and respect people's freedom and human rights.

The twisted message of Sen. Bernie Sanders ended here as the Prime Minister of Denmark confirmed in his remark at Harvard's Kennedy School of Government, "I know that some people in the US associate the Nordic model with some sort of socialism. Therefore I would like to make one thing clear. Denmark is far from a socialist planned economy. Denmark is a market economy."

The Scandinavian countries do not offer all social benefits or welfares for free as the socialists often said. The wealthy and the middle-class Scandinavians basically pay very high tax so that they could receive back what they deserve for social welfares. The Scandinavia countries are prosperous because of their hard works and free marker enterprises not because of the socialist economic system or big government.

In addition, modern socialists used the term social democracy and democratic socialism as if they were the same. Barnard College political science professor Sheri Berman said, "Because we've never had a party that has called itself social democratic or democratic socialist, the term is much more difficult to pin down" reported Jeremy Hobson and Allison Hagan on WBUR.org

Social democratic and democratic socialist are quite opposite in their meanings. These two terms describe the two different forms of governments. Social democracy encourages limited government and socialism fully supports big government. Democracy stimulates the privatization of businesses and industries while socialism prefer the government's control or social ownership to businesses and industries.

On theory, socialism could accept small government and free market operation but this is just because the socialists are still the minority. When the socialists become the majority or when they are dominating the political sector, they would make change to big government and eliminate other political parties so that they could hold on to power and control private enterprises and people.

Whether it is socialism or democratic socialism or Eco-socialism, their nature is still the same. The socialists always want to turn private ownership of lands, resources and businesses to social ownership. They want big government to control the mode of productions and means of distribution. As the results, people would have limited freedom and loss of many human rights and readers would discover this soon.

Moreover, the modern socialists talked as if every social benefit was the product of socialism. It is important then to keep in mind that the social benefits do not make a socialist country. Social cares and benefits did come from the biblical teaching which the Jewish people and later Christians applied to all nations of the world through charitable works. Social benefits indeed came from the charitable heart of God.

The Bible is indeed a great book about social works and social welfare to the widows, orphans, marginalized people at the command of God thousands of years ago that, "The righteous considered the cause of the poor, but the wicked regarded not to know it" (Proverbs 29:7). The Bible emphasized that, "Whoever is generous to the poor lends to the Lord and He will repay him for his deed" (Proverbs 19:17).

Many people may be familiar with the story of the Good Samaritan that the Lord Jesus Christ taught people more than 2000 years ago on how to take good care of the needs of anyone who is in need of help. Acts Chapter 2 told how the believers sold their possessions and properties to minister to the needy people. This is where Karl Marx learned and developed his concept of socialism, we believe.

Sen. Bernie Sanders said that, "Today, New Deal initiatives like Social Security, unemployment compensation, the right to form a union, the minimum wage, protection for farmers, regulation of Wall Street and massive infrastructure improvements are considered pillars of American society." But these did not come from socialism or socialists but the influences of Christian teaching and practices.

It is also important for Americans to remember that no socialist countries in the world could provide better social benefits than the U.S. does. For more than a century of its existence, the socialist countries never brought about better social welfare programs than America does. Many socialist countries indeed brought more inequality and wealth gap and many sufferings to their people.

Indeed, most nations that were and are strongly influenced by Christianity and biblical teaching and values would show more generosity, giving, benevolence and compassion for social welfares and social works. Socialism, on the other hand, is very materialistic oriented. Thus, the leaders and people are striving hard for self-gains and material wealth; and the weak ones suffer at the survival of the fittest.

More than that, Sen. Bernie Sanders promoted the Green New Deal, and the socialists often described the New Deal of President Franklin D. Roosevelt as the socialist agenda. They also projected President Franklin Roosevelt as a socialist. This could be the reason why American modern socialists came up with the Green New Deal to make the connection so that Americans could buy into the idea.

The socialists would say, "But Roosevelt avoided the socialist label because he understood the term's "negative resonance" in the U.S., Berman says. Though he never called himself a socialist, his policies echoed what social democrats were advocating for in parts of Europe during the 1930s." reported Jeremy and Allison. It was true that President Franklin Roosevelt was a democrat but not a socialist.

At that time, the Western world fought hard against the invasions and dominances of former Soviet Union and its socialist allies. It was impossible that former U.S President Franklin D. Roosevelt would adopt the policies or the ideology of the socialist rival if not the enemies of the Western world. Even if he did, Americans, the democrats, the conservatives and the republicans would not let him to do so.

The New Deal reflected the great influences and teaching about charity works of the Christian school where he attended years earlier. It was his application of the Keynesian economic theory, which was developed by the British John M. Keynes in the 1930s reported Kimberly Amadeo. There was no trace of socialism in his life. Besides, the former Soviet Union never had a positive impact upon him and the U.S.

Kimberly Amadeo explained on The Balance, "Keynesian economics is a theory that says the government should increase demand to boost growth. Keynesians believed consumer demand is the primary driving force in an economy. As a result, the theory supports expansionary fiscal policy. Its main tools are government spending on infrastructure, unemployment benefits, and education."

As Cass R. Sunstein pointed correctly, "Roosevelt's own goal was to save capitalism, not to overthrow it". As he once put it, "One of my principal tasks is to prevent bankers and businessmen from committing suicide…" Roosevelt created the Social Security program. He insisted on a minimum wage. He fought to protect the interests of the working poor. But FDR was firmly committed to private property and to free markets. Roosevelt-the nation's greatest progressive-was no socialist."

Sen. Bernie Sanders and the socialists also know how to stress the great benefits that socialism may offer rather than on the ideology of socialism. Thus, people just focus on the great benefits but they do not really understand much about the principles behind socialism. People only heard about the positive aspect of socialism but they do not really know the repeated failures and the consequences of socialism.

When he defined the meaning of democratic socialism in his 2019 speech at George Washington University, Sen. Bernie Sanders did not really define the real and core meaning of democratic socialism but he spoke about the free offers, the rights, and the same social issues of rich and poor, equality and inequality, failures of capitalism that the socialists said the same thing in various nations with new examples.

Sen. Bernie Sanders mentioned correctly the wealth gap in his speech but he never mentioned the truth and the fact that socialism did not work well anywhere in the world to bring about freedom and equality in its application in the last one century and more. He did not mention the truth that authoritarian regimes happened in all socialist countries where freedom and human rights are severely violated.

Sen. Bernie Sanders and American socialists never pointed out the fact that the wealth gap in the socialists and the wealth gap in the Scandinavian countries are also not different from the wealth gap in the U.S. In the socialist nations, most of the wealth of the country is basically in the government and the hands of the socialist elites and leaders who oppressed and exploited people to accumulate their wealth.

"It is obvious where such thinking abounds and continues to spread: in our college and universities. The ideologies of professors and educators have proven stronger than facts: The "benefits" of socialism and Communism are taught from the Ivy League to the local community college. A generation has been taught a lie, and they now believe it" said David Nammo. Unfortunately, the youth only see the benefits.

The millennials may not know that the socialist structure and hierarchy in the socialist nations breed too much corruption, abuses of power, injustices, oppressions and serious violations of human rights. Even many former socialist countries already change to democratic form of government, yet it still takes a long time for these nations to deal with these deep-rooted practices.

Last but not the least, even Sen. Bernie Sanders avoided to accept the core principle of socialism, that is, big government so that Americans could easily buy into his socialist agenda. Sen. Bernie Sanders even said that, "I don't believe government should own the means of production, but I do believe that the middle class and the working families who produce the wealth of America deserve a fair deal."

Oxford Dictionary defines "socialism is a type of government which states that the whole community owns and regulates means of production exchange and distribution." Merriam-Webster Dictionary defines socialism as "a form of government in which instead of individual people and companies owning industries, they are controlled by the government itself."

Generally, socialism is an economic and political system and philosophy that aims at developing an egalitarian society. It may require the strict or large control of the elected government over the modes of productions and the means of distributions or the government control of the resources of the economy. National resources are equally shared among the people or according to people's needs and contributions.

The core of socialism is social ownership and its form could be in public, collective, cooperative form or citizen ownership of equity where the surplus values would go to the working class and society as a whole according to Wikipedia on Socialism. This common core requires the workers to be in charge of the mode of production and the means of distribution; and the elimination of most capitalist principles.

The Green New Deal and social shares of cooperation would show that without big government, these agendas would not work. Without the centralized power, the government could not control private business and have power to distribute the wealth to people and thus equality would not be possible. Their goal is big government but American socialists do not want to make it clear to the public yet.

"His Green New Deal is a roadmap towards a future that is a public good, where nationwide programs could provide school meals that ensure no child goes hungry, Medicare for All makes healthcare a human right, agriculture is ecologically regenerate, internet infrastructure is publicly owned, and we collectively control our energy systems to provide free electricity for all" stated the DSA eco-socialists.

The DSA Eco-socialists continued to say, "This is a vision of an economy that decommodifies universal needs for survival, massively expands public ownership of resources, and reinvents our communities to serve people and planet-rather than private interests monopolizing control and destabilizing climate systems for short-term gains" and they declared:

"At the heart of Bernie's Green New Deal proposal lies insight that we share as socialists: that the climate and ecological emergency is a symptom of class warfare, and it will take a massive working class movement overcoming the capitalist class to save life on Earth... Bernie identifies the class enemies we must organize against and take down, from the fossil fuel industry to the military industrial complex and agribusiness... The face these capitalists deserve is clear: Fossil fuel executives should be criminally prosecuted for the destruction they have knowingly caused"

Socialist David Duhalde said, "Establishing democratic socialism means democratizing ownership of capital, our jobs and our personal lives... if you work somewhere, you should have a say in how it's run. Through unions, worker councils and elected boards, this is possible at the company level today. Furthermore, if your labor generates profit, under socialism you would have an ownership stake and a democratic say in how your workplace is run" reported Charles Krupa.

Socialist Thomas Hanna believed that, "A practical form of socialism in the United States in the 21st century would occur when democratic ownership displaces and supersedes the current, dominant extractive corporate model... full state ownership, partial state ownership, local/municipal ownership, multi-stakeholder ownership, worker ownership, consumer cooperative ownership, producer cooperative ownership, community ownership and sustainable local private ownership."

The Democratic Socialists of America made clear that, "The Pittsburgh Local of the Democratic Socialists of America seeks to facilitate the transition to a truly democratic and socialist society, one in which the means/resources of production are democratically and socially controlled." This means the DSA, if the socialists took over the U.S., would eliminate most private enterprises in favor of social ownership.

Thus, the socialism that Sen. Bernie Sanders and socialist members of the DSA tried to convince millions of Americans is the same with the Soviet type of socialism with social ownership of industries and resources, big government, central planning and little freedom of private enterprises. American socialists add a new adjective "democratic" to make it democratic socialism but its nature is still the same.

Each type of socialism may have different focuses to bring about equality to its members but whether it is the Market Socialism or the Utopian Socialism, Democratic Socialism, Liberal Socialism, Libertarian Socialism, Religious Socialism, Regional Socialism, Eco-Socialism, or Left-Wing Nationalist Socialism to be applied in any nation so far, no type of socialism produced what it promised.

The socialist ideologies cover Utopian socialism, communism, Marxism, anarchism, democratic socialism, eco-socialism, liberal socialism, regional socialism, religious socialism and syndicalism. "Types of socialism include a range of economic and social systems characterized by social ownership and democratic control of the means of production and organizational self-management of enterprises" and its political theories and movements according to Wikipedia on Types of Socialism.

Jeff Sanders noted the words of Stephen Crowder; "the DSA goes to great strides to distance itself from the totalitarian centralized control of Soviet communism and its offspring. It is difficult to do this when at the same time, under its "history" banner, it endorses the communist movements of Nicaragua, El Salvador, and Zimbabwe back in the 1970s and 1980s. It is also difficult to distance yourself from Soviet communism when you are still holding up Karl Marx as a good example of anything."

Sen. Bernie Sanders said, "It is my very strong belief that the United States must reject that path of hatred and divisiveness-and instead find the moral conviction to choose a different path, a higher path, a path of compassion, justice and love. It is the path that I call democratic socialism." In fact, Sen. Bernie Sanders should call this the Christian path because that is what the Christians do and only Christians can do.

Sen. Bernie Sanders said, "Now, we must take the next step forward and guarantee every man, woman and child in our country basic economic rights-the right to quality health care, the right to as much education as one needs to succeed in our society, the right to a good job that pays a living wage, the right to affordable housing, the right to a secure retirement, and the right to live in a clean environment" reported Tim Hains on Real Clear Politics.

Yet, many Americans still do not recognize the political goals and purposes behind the economic benefits proposed by Sen. Bernie Sanders and American socialists. Their goal aims at big government, central planning with full-state or partial-state ownership and the local private ownership is minimized at the local level and it is allowed to be just sustainable under the control of state or social ownership.

But with those nice slogans, promises and rights, American socialists are attracting the attentions of many Americans now. With the nice theory and flowering words, American socialists are captivating the minds and thoughts of millions of Americans now. With the appealing benefits and welfares, American socialists are now catching the hearts and passions of millions of Americans now. Will they be successful?

The democrat leaders and the democrats once opposed strongly socialism are now strongly supporting the socialist agenda by going too far left with the socialist ideology. Will socialism succeed in America or will the majority of Americans refute it? Will the liberals, the democrats and the socialists be successful by their far left agenda with so many free stuffs and free offers?

Social benefits are important but Americans would soon realize that life and security are more important to them than the risky and disastrous socialism. This is especially true to the millions of immigrants who suffered and ran for their lives to America from the socialist regimes or the regimes of their nations in order to find better life, freedom and security here. They would testify to the horrors of socialism.

The promises of the socialist ideology sound appealing to millions of Americans, but they would soon find out that the existing freedoms and human rights are more precious than the unreal freedoms and human rights offered by tricky socialism. This is especially true to millions of immigrants who lost their basic freedoms and rights in socialist regimes. They would say loud and clear, the terrors of socialism.

They would be the suitable people who could tell clearly and truly how life is and how people are being treated in socialist countries in comparison to human rights that they have here in America. They have been living in America or other countries for years but they are still haunted with fears, pains, nightmares and the horrible persecutions, imprisonments, near-death, deadly and deaths of past experiences.

I happened to read the following words of a former Cuban in responding to the article of Hunter Moyler, "76 Percent of Democrats Say

They'd Vote for a Socialist for President, New Poll Shows" on Newsweek. Her words are worth reading because those words came from the real heart and from a victim and a real witness of what a socialism and socialist country is all about. They are worth more than theories.

"Having lived under the Socialist system in Cuba, and reading now your comment, I like to tell you is that what is "Guarantee" is that we know the "painted picture" and the "reality." Once they take over, give about 70 years. Soviet Union 70 years, Cuba 61 years, Venezuela how long? If you only dare speak against your leaders, you go to jail with "no court." Look at North Korea. Accountable for their behavior? How naïve can Americans be?

Carmen Alexe from former Socialist Republic of Romania concluded that socialism creates shortages but capitalism advances private property and helps us be better individuals. "Individual freedom can only exist in the context of free-market capitalism. Personal freedom thrives in capitalism. Declines in government-regulated economies, and vanishes in communism."

She shared her experience in that socialist country; "I was born and raised in communist Romania during the Cold War, a country in which the government owned all the resources and means of production. The state controlled almost every aspect of our lives: our education, our job placement, the time of day we could have hot water, and what we were allowed to say."

Yet, Sen. Bernie Sanders and American socialists and democrats are still dreaming for a democratic socialist to be soon established in America from their ivory towers. Because of their political motive, ideology, power, immaturity or ignorance or whatever it is, they want to invoke horrible consequences upon almost 330 million Americans through socialist ideology. Please do not fall into that trap!

Since millions of victims took their adventurous, risky and deadly escapes from socialist nations to America and other free nations many decades ago, many former socialist countries at last denounced socialism since socialism could not deliver much prosperity but poverties and pressures of economic crisis. Socialism left these countries with much bloodshed, nightmares, sufferings and millions of deaths.

Some countries are still holding on to socialism and their idealistic promises of equality and prosperity, yet they could not deliver anything better than the painful experiences of other former socialist nations.

They were almost collapsed with socialism and socialist economist system so they have to change to the free markets to save the nation's economy, their political ideology, and their power.

Michael E. Telzrow on New American stated correctly that, "Socialism, the Utopian economic and political system that promises equality, prosperity, and universal peace through the workings of a collectivist state, has repeatedly been exposed as a colossal failure. Its history, marked by failed societies and brutal dictatorships, is quite literally littered with the bodies of millions of innocents."

Michael also lamented that, "and yet in the United States we stand on the brink of a socialist abyss, the edge of which looms ever closer as time passes... but despite socialism's historical failures, it remains attractive to those vulnerable to its false promises of egalitarianism and economic equality. Instead of being relegated to its own proverbial "dustbin of history," it continues to entice well after its failures and crimes have been laid bare for all to see."

The readers would soon find out the reasons that millions of people risked their lives to escape the socialist Utopia and hundred thousands of the people are still finding ways to leave those promised lands even though the policies of the nations are no longer welcoming them as they were a few decades ago. The readers would understand the socialist freedom through the 12 Commandments of Socialism.

We hope Americans in millions would read and share these books and learn from the painful and bloody experiences of millions of people in socialist countries who went through socialist regimes. It is important to know what is really happening in socialist countries so you would not be deceived by the unreal hope of socialists and the democrats for putting millions of Americans to be at risk with socialist ideology.

Let us begin with the socialist meaning of "truth" that is leading and controlling the life of millions of people in some socialist countries and even millions of people in the U.S. The life stories and experiences of the victims shared in this book, **Be Free Or Not Be Free,** or **The Boat of Destiny** and the reality of life in some socialist countries would reveal the truthfulness of the socialist equality and freedom.

THE PROVEN TRUTH

Growing up and coming out from socialist countries, just like the million victims of socialism, we do know the pressures, fears, the uncertainties, the injustices, the sufferings, the pains, the nightmares, and the horrors in living in socialist countries. We do know the oppressions, the persecutions, the cruelties, the corruption, the greed for wealth, and the thirst for power of the authorities in socialist countries.

The glory or the gloom, the happiness or the humiliation, the power or the pain, the prosperity or the poverty, the wealth or the weeping, the promotion or the pressures, the victories or the victims, the justices or injustices, the freedom or the incarceration, the life and death are being revealed in the fact that "you are with us or you are against us." It is not much about what we know but whom we know.

Equality? It is impossible or is it ever realized in any socialist country? Freedom of Expression and of Press? Yes, but it must be in accordance to the socialist ideology or the guidelines of the authorities. Welfares for all? It is just a luxurious and deceptive concept. With available information on the Internet, please see how many millions of people died of starvation and were killed in socialist countries.

More than 250 million people died in the socialist nations due to murder, starvation and wars. You may have never heard about this before, but now you are hearing about that truth. Does this number speak to you something about socialism?

Do you really understand what socialism is? Yes, you may only understand it theoretically that democratic socialism would make a better world to live with universal healthcare, free education, free tax… Yet, there is no free lunch here.

Do you really think that socialists' economic system would be more productive than the capitalistic economic system? If so, people in socialist countries should be rich and wealthy and the countries should be very powerful, but, in reality, they are not.

Do you really hope that socialism would bring about equality and happiness? People in socialist nations should then be happy to stay back in their countries to enjoy their happiness. But, why did multitudes of people escape their dreamlands?

Do you really know what it's like living in a real socialist country? If you really knew, you would not want to make America a socialist country, whether; it is a socialist country or democratic socialism of America or green socialism and America.

Do you really want to go through the serious violations and sufferings of human rights in socialist countries? You would "enjoy" those things in a very near future as the consequences of your own decisions today just as millions of us did.

Do you really experience the concept of freedom in socialist countries? I don't think so. If you have to lie to earn your freedom, if you have to hide the truth to purchase freedom, if you have to go against your consciences to get freedom, will you want it?

Do you think it is cool and exciting to carry out democratic socialism? Yes, you are no different with the excitement of the millions of people who shouted for it at the beginning and then regretted at the sufferings and pains for years it brought.

It is important for us to state here that the purpose of this book is just to share our real stories that our families and our relatives went through personally. We do not plan to criticize any particular socialist leaders, socialist ideologies, regimes or socialist nations in this book, and, we do not have any intentions to encourage people to overthrow the socialist nations or whatsoever.

Please take note that we will not, and we cannot mention the real names or even the name of the country where many of these stories happened and are still happening for the securities of the people relating. So, we will use the English names to avoid sensitive matters and protect us from harm. This is the beginning of the Freedom that you dream to have, the great Freedom you have been told partially.

What? You cannot even mention the name in publishing a book? This is how we protect ourselves and our family members or else injustices and tragedies may fall upon us at any time. How can people speak the truth? Truth must be redefined here. In socialist countries, people praise the socialist ideology, the leaders and their works even though we are forced to do so. And, that is the truth the socialists want.

When people speak negative things about socialist ideology and their wrongdoings that is not seen as the truth. When people speak about their weaknesses, failures, misuses of power, inhumane treatments, wealth gap, corruptions, injustices, persecutions and oppressions, that happened and are really happening, then those are not the truth, but "lies", and those lies must be punished severely.

Hundreds of thousands of those who spoke or spread those "lies" have been incarcerated, beaten, and tortured severely. Many could not endure tortures and died, others were beaten to death, and others just simply disappeared. Those who are still alive have been re-educated in horrible prisons and labor camps so that when they are out of prisons, they would perfectly speak "truth" not "lies" anymore.

Uncle George was put in prison for almost 17 full years. He was only 30 years old when he was brought to the secretive labor camp and prison in the far and deep mountains of the north. In his prison, there were about 300 prisoners who were mostly the officials of the former government just as he was. None of them went through court trials and they were there for their dying days as lifetime prisoners.

There were other prison camps nearby as prisoners could see some other camps from their place, but no one knew how many camps and how many people were put behind the bars in total. They were all from the south and they were placed in the north so that they could hardly find ways or connections to make escapes possible. They were there to suffer the cold weather, hard labors and poor living conditions.

They were there for their death sentences. Most of them could not make it alive due to the hard labors and exhaustions. Others died because of malaria and all kinds of sicknesses and diseases. Many were executed and the rest died because of severe tortures, harsh weather and hungers. Others committed suicides in frustrations. Their lives were only valuable as long as they had strength to do the hard labors.

They were mostly the talents of the nations but now they were suffering hades on earth. Early in the morning they were brought to the labor camps and went back late in the evening. They were fully surrounded with armed soldiers. After dinner, they had to attend the "Political Class" or "Political Meeting" where they listened to the great theories and marvelous things of socialism as long as they were still alive.

After the "Political Class" or reeducation or lectures, then the prisoners were asked almost the same questions every time about the greatness of socialism and the equality, freedom, and happiness. For years, the prisoners had to recite all the great freedom, great treatment and prosperity yet they knew well in their hearts, minds and experiences, those things were impossible at least to them, the prisoners.

How was it possible for them to have great freedom when they still the prisoners and victims who were under strict control and heavily guarded? How was it possible for them to have great prosperity when the majority could hardly survive the hunger? But for the sake of life they had to lie, pretend and speak against their consciences, beliefs and realities so they could survive each day.

For 16 years and 9 months, Uncle George miraculously survived malaria, various types of sicknesses and diseases, harsh weather, cruel treatments, hard labor, loneliness, loss of all freedom and human rights, and all the political tests. At least he still had the right to live so he ate everything possible to survive: from crickets to grasshoppers and rats, the luxurious meals of the prisoners in egalitarian societies.

People came and died in his prison. He was among the rare prisoners who survived the test of horrible prisons for such as a long time. He would have died in the prison and not many people would remember about him. But at last, he was allowed to leave his poverty, inhuman treatment, pains, bondage, and humiliation to a better place not by the socialists who promised equality, freedom and peace.

He was petitioned by the former allied nation and was released from his long years of miseries and nightmares with a ransom paid by the allied government. He was treated like an animal by socialists who promised great equality. The surviving prisoners and he were sold like objects by the socialists who said they fought for the well-beings of people but the socialists are the ones who made people suffer and die.

We asked him, "Why didn't you leave the country in those days?" He said, "I was not able to find my mother and my sisters and I could not just leave them behind." We almost cried at his answer. He paid a great price as a filial son. He suffered greatly for the love and care to his mother and sisters. Would any great ideology punish such a great man who cared not about his security but the well being of his mother?

The allied sent helicopters to pick him up. Every time the helicopter came, he gave chances to other people and Catholic priests who came and asked him to allow them to go. But he would not go. He just waited and hoped for the coming of his mother and sisters who was scattered everywhere as the new armies entered and invaded the city. Yet, his love for his mother and sisters cost him much and almost his life.

His hope was dashed when the policemen surrounded his home. His dream was cut short when the policemen handcuffed him. His desire to care for his mother and his sisters was diminished when they threw him into their truck. His life was rocky and uncertain as he was transported through the many rocky roads for days. His future was dim as they put a blindfold on his eyes and led him to unknown places.

For almost 17 years of suffering and hard labors in prison and labor camp, he was still taught and told to recite the greatness of socialism. For those 17 years of living in poverty and pains he was told of the great prosperity that the socialists brought. For those 17 years of humiliation and mistreatments, he was forced to speak of the equalities that only socialism could make it happen and brought to people.

In school, students are often asked to write essays about the prosperity and glory that their families have received under the wise and just leadership of the socialist party. If any student happened to write about the misfortunes of their families, then the teachers would immediately correct them and ask them to make up new stories to suit the "truth." Their misfortunes were not real, and, that is "truth."

"Truth" is then defined as: when people are not happy about the government, but they still have to praise them. "Truth" is when people suffer due to the injustices by the justice system or the corrupted leaders but people must keep quiet and obey the leaders. "Truth" is when people are being stripped of their rights but they are not allowed to talk about it due to the fears of punishment and incarcerations.

"Truth" is when people are hungry and dying of hunger but they still have to say thanks to the socialist leaders for the well beings and safety. "Truth" is when people are crying because of sufferings but they have to pretend to be happy about the great socialist ideology. "Truth" is when the party leaders led people into poverty and death and people still have to praise them for their wisdom and great works.

"Truth" is when the socialist leaders exploit the people and people are not allowed to say anything against them. "Truth" is when the corruption is so rampant and the leaders corrupt to the bones, and the newspapers must praise the integrity of nations and the leaders daily. "Truth" is when the government oppresses the people and the people still have to say thanks to them for the many freedoms.

Of course, this is not truth as people understand and perceive in the free worlds like America but it is called oppression and exploitation.

It is called the violation of human rights and it is called crimes against humanity. It is called lies, regime, autocracy, and dictatorship in its true sense. Yet, this is what millions of Americans want to embrace because they do not know the true face and reality of socialism.

As Americans really want socialism and now this kind of "truth" is also happening in the U.S. It is fine for every to say Black Lives Matter, but those who publicly said All Lives Matter or White Lives Matter might be attacked, beaten or shot to dead. The mainstream media denied and covered up the brutalities, lootings, arsons, lawlessness and violence of the riots and the rioters.

The members of Black Lives Matter, Antifa and millennials claimed that the many great American leaders of the past were slave owners and racists, thus they went around to destroy the monuments and to take down or destroy many historical statues. They disregarded the fact and the historical truth that many those leaders fought for their freedom and they even fought hard to make the blacks freed.

In the socialist countries, students are trained to "worship" the socialist party and leaders through singing and reciting written speeches. Parents also know that those speeches, songs and poems are not true but they have no choice but to make sure their children would sing the songs, deliver the speeches, or recite the speeches properly and perfectly for any performances to please the leaders. That's truth.

In fact, the millions of citizens in the socialist countries have been indoctrinated, brainwashed and deceived by the "truth" of the press in socialist countries. People have been told that socialist education is the best in the world, yet children of the socialist leaders are mostly educated abroad. People have been told that all famous scientists of the West are atheists, yet so many of them are Christians.

People are taught that the socialist leaders always love and protect the people but people soon realize that the leaders care more for their power, position, wealth and political ideology than they do us. People are indoctrinated that capitalism is so bad that they exploit the poor and we must fight against the capitalists, but, they soon discover that the socialists are a thousand times worse than the capitalists.

People are told that the capitalistic countries are very poor and the people are suffered at the extreme poverties, high taxes and inhumane exploitations of the capitalists, yet that is indeed the depiction and description of the socialist nations than the capitalistic nations that are known for prosperities, freedom, justice, and great respect for human rights. We were the victims of those deceptions for years.

That is also how "truth" or at least freedom is operated in socialist countries. This also proves how excellent Sen. Bernie Sander was and American socialists are in applying that socialist principle of truth here in America. They only tell many falsifying truths about socialism but the socialist "lies" or truths are being kept until the horrible days when the supporters experience the reality of socialism.

Ironically, this kind of deceptive truth is now happening in the U.S. where the mainstream media, many democrat leaders and the leftists praise the rioters and demonstrators for violent protests, the defunding of the police, and their demands but the mainstream media and the leaders never mentioned about the lootings the burnings of businesses and the murders of many policemen and innocent people...

People, who defensed people of white color and other colors are considered racists, are threatened, and beaten because only Black Lives Matter. So many white people even children were brutally attacked, hit, kicked, stabbed and shot as many African Americans were paid or encouraged to do so. Fears, lawlessness and uncertainties hover over the U.S. yet the mainstream media calls it peace and freedom.

Lee Edwards asked, "Would seven percent of millennials declare their willingness to live under communism if they knew the real costs of communism as practiced in some 40 nations over the past century-the denial of free speech, a free press, and free assembly, the imprisonment and execution of dissidents, no free and open elections, no independent judiciary or rule of law, the dictatorship of the Communist Party in all matters and on all occasions?"

If the millennials knew well that they are manipulated by the cunning leaders for their power and gain, then, America would not be in chaos. If Americans know well the 12 commandments of socialism, socialism will have no prominent role in this land of freedom of America. If Americans really understand the horrible experiences of socialist victims, Americans will still be saved from socialism and its disasters.

THE FREE WORLD OF SOCIALISM AND THE 12 COMMANDMENTS

You may be curious now to ask, "How about human rights and other freedoms?" "Why don't people fight for their rights?" Or, "Why don't you vote for new leaders?" Let us share with you some real stories in the following pages. In fact, these stories are just the tip of a large iceberg because it is not time yet for us to tell you more. We bet you will treasure better your precious and available rights and freedoms.

My... What happens? I find it difficult to tell the true story when I cannot even use the proper nouns that describe my relationship with this important person. Oh my goodness, I really want to use that noun before the word "My", but I will just leave it blank for now or else the family will be in great trouble again if I just write it down clearly. Is that the freedom of speech and freedom of press that you are looking for?

Ok. Let me put it this way. A very close family member of mine, Joseph, was put in prison and labor camp for more than 20 years. Thank God for his life and his survival because, without him, I would not have a wonderful family now. He was not a high-ranking government official and he was not a politician. He was not an intelligent agent. He was just a good and ordinary man. Why then was he arrested?

Did he go through trial by jury? Nope. He did not have a chance to go through trial by jury at court, but he went through trial because of his faith.

Did he kill someone? Nope. He is not that kind of person but he was targeted and planned to be killed by the socialists.

Did he commit any crime? Nope. He is indeed a very good man but he was given a bad name and bad reputation by the socialists.

Did he exercise his free speech to say bad things about the socialist leaders? Nope. He only spoke about the great morale of the Bible yet he was persecuted severely

Did he exercise his free press to criticize the cruelties of socialist ideology? Nope. He just wanted to be faithful to his faith and his God and his life was threatened.

Did he exercise his freedom of gathering to go against the government? Nope. He is indeed a very good citizen but he was discriminated and mistreated by the socialists.

Did he steal, kill, or destroy? None of those did he commit but he was incarcerated as the most serious criminal of the day.

He was charged and condemned with the most severe crimes of being a counter-revolutionary in those days just because he was a part-time seminarian. He was beaten and sent into the political prison and hard-labor camp just because he was an intellectual without any crimes or records of wrongs. He was incarcerated and discriminated just because he acknowledged himself as a Christian.

He was ill-treated and was incarcerated just because he called himself a true follower of Christ. He suffered and faced so many horrible things behind the ruthless bars just because he was not willing to deny God. He was mistreated and humiliated for the serious crimes and the unjust charges for things he had nothing to do with except his precious faith in God.

Do these things happen in America now? Not yet, probably, but may be soon. The First Amendment on December 15, 1791 stated, "Congress shall make no law respecting an establishment of religion, or prohibiting the free exercise thereof; or abridging the freedom of speech, or of the press; or the right of the people peaceably to assemble, and to petition the Government for a redress of grievances"

According to the Fifth Amendment, "No person shall be held to answer for a capital, or otherwise infamous crime, unless on a presentment or indictment of a grand jury... nor shall any person be subject for the same offense to be twice put in jeopardy of life or limb; nor shall be compelled in any criminal case to be a witness against himself, nor be deprived of life, liberty, or property, without due process of law; nor shall private property be taken for public use, without just compensation."

These protected rights and freedoms are the jewels and treasurers that Americans already have and are enjoying. Yet, many Americans are still dreaming for another unreal green pasture of socialist rights and freedom without knowing that the rights and freedoms offered in that green pasture of socialism are baseless and they are just unrealistic dreams that can never be materialized.

They do not know that millions of people in those forever-promised pastures can only see the dry, suffering and horrible pastures of human right and freedom. They forget that millions of the refugees and immigrants from all over the world have been running to America at any costs even at the cost their own lives in search of the great rights and freedoms for themselves and for their next generations.

The 2018 Index of Freedom in the World where the annual survey is made to measure the degree of civil liberties and political rights in every nation and region, (https://freedomhouse.org/report/freedom-world/freedom-world-2018) showed that socialist countries, especially in Asia, have the least points for civil liberties and political rights. The people were the pitiful victims of the civil and political rights.

There are no signs that civil liberties and political rights would get any better in socialist countries but it is the opposite. There are no positive signs that the religious freedom is well protected and the human rights are to be respected. There are no good signs that the freedom of speeches is granted. And, there are no possible signs that the free press is freely exercised in socialist countries.

Many socialist countries always declare that their countries and their peoples have all of freedoms of speech, press, peaceful gathering and religions... The leaders of socialist countries usually polish those concepts of equal wealth distribution, equal rights, equality, freedom, and happiness with nice and eloquent words. The calling of Sen. Bernie Sanders, reported Tim Hains, sounded very familiar as he said,

"And let me be absolutely clear: democratic socialism to me requires achieving political and economic freedom in every community. And let me also be clear, the only way we achieve these goals is through a political revolution-where millions of people get involved in the political process and reclaim our democracy by having the courage to take on the powerful corporate interests whose greed is destroying the social and economic fabric of our country.

At the end of the day, the one percent may have enormous wealth and power, but they are just the one percent. When the 99 percent stand together, we can transform society. These are my values, and that is why I call myself a democratic socialist. At its core is a deep and abiding faith in the American people to peacefully and democratically enact the transformative change that will create shared prosperity, social equality and true freedom for all."

Yet those are just great thoughts, idealistic offers and appealing ideals, but in reality, those are just lip services. Those words would carry out the similar destructive and deadly consequences that many former socialist nations experienced when millions of people took those words as truth to make the political revolution happened. Then they became the victims of the great and powerful words of the socialists at the end.

At that call of political revolution, millions of people responded and the socialists succeeded to establish new socialist nations. Then, they took over the wealth and properties of corporates, businesses, wealthy people and landlords in hoping of creating shared prosperity, social equality and true freedom for all people but wealth must be produced in order to provide the needs of the multitudes.

Unfortunately, the political revolution that Sen. Bernie Sanders talked about never brought about peacefully and democratically changes for equality and true freedom for all, but it already brought and continues to bring about chaos, injustices, misuses of power, riots, limited freedom, violations of human rights and deaths. It also led people to the loss of free press in socialist nations.

1ˢᵗ Commandment
"THOU SHALL HAVE NO OTHER PRESS"
Free Press

Pakistan Crusade.

In July 2020, suddenly groups of policemen came and surrounded the house of Anna and then they took Anna and incarcerated her with the reason that she engaged in prostitution at her home without any evidences and trials at court. Anna did not even know that she could have such a charge. With her old age, her last stage of cancer and her current look who would possibly be interested in her?

Yet, that was how the socialist leaders tried to insult her and destroy her image, credentials and dignity publicly. She was the former professor and the adviser of doctoral students of one of the top three universities in the country. She was known with her many great writings. Then, she was fired from the university and she was refused from any teaching position, and from any invitations for giving lectures.

For many years, she was under strict surveillances of the socialist authorities and she was not allowed to travel abroad. This was all due to some of her famous writings. She did not object the socialist country, the leadership or the political party, she just wrote her recommendations and her views about the advantages of this socialist country in allowing people for free press, free speech and freedom.

Her books were published at home before and abroad and she was praised by writers worldwide but her writings, her articles and her books were later rejected and were not welcome at home. Her writings were considered as negative criticism on the country and the leadership. Those kinds of writings were not and are not welcome in socialist country and the writers would be punished severely.

In America and nations with free press, the citizens can publish a book, a journal or a pamphlet if they are able to and want to. One may purchase an ISBN number on-line or Amazon and publishes his or her book. One may choose any publishing house to produce their publications. Writers can freely express their views and thoughts in their books, journals, and websites without the fear of political incorrectness.

In the free world, writers may share their views on life, education, religions or any areas of life without the fear of being monitored and warned with the content of their writings. Writers or common people may respond to any philosophies, social issues, and government policies without any fear of being incarcerated. People may freely post information of their concerns without fear of being threatened.

In socialist countries, a writer must go through a publishing house and the content of the book will be checked to see if the content is proper before a book is published. Yes, people may write and post anything but the golden rule is that the content must have nothing to say against the political party, the political leaders and government policies. Any content that is against those things is considered counterrevolutionary.

In other words, most people in socialist countries cannot write or make a critic about the weaknesses and failures of the political party and the ideology. People cannot share about the bad qualifications, corruptions and the wrongdoings of the political leaders. People cannot point out the flaws and negative sides of government policies. Those areas are to be praised if one wants to have free press.

The press in socialist nations is filled with great plans and successes of the political party and the socialist leaders. It is filled with glories and congratulations for many achievements. It is filled with great reports and great prospect of the future. Yet when the projects are carried out, local people would be on strikes due to corruptions, violations of human rights, but the press would not cover those news.

 A.Y Ph.D. and S.Y Ph.D.

Unfortunately, as socialism is the main political ideology and the only ideology, it covers all disciplines and areas of life so the best golden rule is that nothing should be written against the ideology. In socialist countries, the government can only accept the praises and not the criticism and the leaders can only accept the lies and not the truth. The ideology can only welcome the supporters and not the critics.

In America, journalists or writers may use social media, podcast, and websites to post their articles or to do live stream to express their views. People may speak on any topics they want to. This is not so in socialist countries. Although there is more freedom now to use social media, not all social media are accessible and certain topics must not be discussed in opposing the ideology and government views.

Basically, there are no independent presses or journalists in socialist countries in Asia. The government controls all the news and information released. If there is independent press, then news and information are also strictly controlled. How free is it when people cannot express their different views and when local, international press and news agencies are not accessible to the general public?

In the socialist countries where we used to live, there is no press or social media that dares to oppose the top leaders of the countries. Those press and media may sometimes write against certain leaders because these leaders are deserted by the current top leaders so the leaders could cover up corruptions, immoral convictions of the leaders or political party. In most cases, they are just the scapegoats.

No press dares to oppose the leading political party because the political party is the shining star and sun leading the people and the nation to freedom, equality and prosperity. The press would explain the failures and terrible consequences of capitalism, other regimes or other ideologies. The press proves how great socialist countries are and their lies are believed and applauded by millions of people.

When social media was not yet available to the general public, the press in our socialist country often talked and published pictures about the poverty and the exploitations of the Western world. The citizens were not allowed to listen to radio stations from abroad so that our mind would not be polluted by Western ideology and dangerous thoughts.

Many people who knew the truth about the prosperity and freedom of the Western world still tried to listen to radio broadcast from abroad secretly. But when they were caught by the government authorities, they would be put in prison or they would be sent to the labor camps, reeducation camps, or new economic zones as punishments. That was the freedom of the press that people had.

The press would propagandize the glory and wealth of the socialist countries but the people knew nothing about the failures, poverties, struggles, hardships, and deaths that these former socialist countries encountered because people were not free to know the truth. Thus, millions of people believed the deceptions of the press as truth when the socialist countries and the people were very poor and suffered.

When first we read CNN news, ABC news, New York Times or USA Today and other media, we were very surprised because writers and journalists could freely express their views, disagreements, objections and even mock at the presidents, twisting the words of top country leaders, senators, government policies. This could never happen in the mainstream or independent media in socialist countries, even now.

The social media in the U.S. could even have the rights to refuse to make Ads for President Trump and his presidential campaigns. Facebook company could sensor and delete certain ads or post of the top country leaders. Twitter may even dare to close the account of the leaders if they violate company's policy. This kind of freedom of press in America could not be found in the socialist nations.

This could never happen to the leaders of the socialist country because people all know that the leaders have power to shut down or to take over the company of that social media. Though many media channels in the Western world are partisan in their content and information but the people could exercise their free press when in the socialist countries, only the socialist leaders could exercise that freedom.

According to FreedomHouse.org, many socialist countries are not free and are the worse in the Press Freedom Status. The legal, economic and political environments are at the worse levels. It "remained one of the most repressive media environments in the world in 2015. The state-controlled domestic media produce propaganda with the aim of ensuring absolute loyalty" to the top leader of the country.

"Although the constitution theoretically guarantees freedom of speech and of the press, all reporting that is not sanctioned by the government is subject to severe restrictions in practice. Under the penal code, listening to unauthorized foreign broadcasts and possessing dissident publications are considered crimes against the state that carry serious punishments, including hard labor, prison sentences, and the death penalty" reported FreedomHouse.org.

You may say, this country is an extreme case of a communist or socialist country. How about America's neighboring socialist countries like Cuba or Venezuela and others? Do you think that these countries have better freedom of the press than America? By nature, the socialist countries are all the same. When the leaders are in power, the people will lose their power and freedom and voices.

Socialism is believed to be perfect in its ideology, form of government, mode of economy, policies and ways. All the problems and failures of the country have nothing to do with the socialist ideology. The problems are with the fallen people, the corrupted subordinates, the traitors and betrayers of the countries. The socialists have to protect their ideology by all means to hold on to power and wealth.

The socialists would not take time to ask, "If socialism is perfect why do all the socialist countries fail their the economic reforms and wealth distributions through the socialist economic system?" The socialists would not dare to question their leaders, "If socialism is great why there are so many corruptions, injustices and inequalities?" If they dare to questions the leaders, they would loose everything.

When the Chairman, the President, or the top leaders speak at a press conference or conferences, all media outlets such as TV networks, newspapers, radios, social media would broadcast their messages wide and far. Journalists and media then quickly release the news with good comments, great supports and incredible praises to those speeches or policies, and the wisdom of the political party.

Does any media have the choice and power to stop broadcasting or publishing the messages delivered by the leaders? All media are controlled by the government and they are the instrument of the government, thus, that is not likely to happen. The media and the staff consider it an honor for them to cover the previous messages of the leaders and it is an opportunity for promotion and rewards if they do well.

Even the independent media would not dare to does so. If they do, the operation would be closed down totally. The leaders must make public apologies and corrections must be made before the operation is to be closed for good. The journalists and people involved in making those decisions would be punished severely for the crimes of counter-revolutionary and false accusations of the leaders.

Books, journals and articles are allowed to be published, but, the publishing houses will make sure that there is no counter-revolutionary content, there is no sensitive political issue, there is no content that goes against the government, leaders and political party. News, information, facts, events are censored before they are released in the press to make sure that they are politically correct.

When those censors are being carried out, the information and the thought are no longer objective. The content would no longer reflect the reality or the truth of the situations or the stories. The ugly side of the socialist leadership is only revealed when a socialist leader is punished, mostly with corruption charges. But, common people would never know the real truth about internal conflicts of the leadership.

There are people who spoke the truth through available alternative media today, yet their endings are never happy. For the sake of security, job, living, benefits, family, future, the majority just follow the order and guidelines. Depending on the sensitivity of the content, the writer or the editor or the publisher may receive warning, or discipline, or removal from the position, and even imprisonment.

When a human rights activist or political activist was punished or sentenced to prison by the government or powerful leaders because he or she opposed the leaders or government, no local press dared to voice out the injustices or unfair judgment, or injustices upon that person even if he or she is not guilty. The presses would cover almost the same stories as the judges said. The appeal would not work.

The best way to change the sentence and the situation is to acknowledge that the right thing that he or she did was his or her wrong. The more one opposed the government the worse was their scenario. Many activists were released from prison and the country thanks to the help of international human right agencies, yet, the activists must suffer years of imprisonment first before they were set free.

In America, the situation is quite different. Human rights activists, political activists and people have various presses to support or disagree with their views. They could freely criticize the government policies or the policies and views of any government leaders. Readers may freely react to what these activists said. In socialist countries, this may happen once in a blue moon or when the leaders approve the matter.

While human right activists and political activists in America and the free worlds are highly praised, appreciated and funded for their operations because of their stand and their fight for human rights and freedom, human right activists and political activists in socialist countries are criticized, humiliated and persecuted. They are fighting for the human rights and freedom of others, but theirs are being deprived.

History is also rewritten to suit the purposes of the socialist ideology and to consolidate the power of the socialist leaders. The press never reveals exactly how many millions of people were killed by the communists, socialists, the soldiers and leaders. The press never discloses exactly how many million people died because of starvation, of imprisonment, of new economic zones, and of labor camps...

The press never shares information about the true number of political prisoners, civil rights and human right activists, freedom fighters, and religious workers who have been tortured, arrested and killed. The press never shares the injustices, the oppressions, and the corruption unless it is for the building of their good image or threatening others. Is this the free press freedom that you are looking for?

The printed and digital materials that are allowed to be used in all levels of education in the socialist countries must be approved by the authorities. These materials are mostly written by the socialist scholars to make sure that the contents are in line with the socialist ideology and political party. This is how the socialist leaders could brainwash people's mind and keep people loyalty to the ideology.

Yes, there is "Free Press" in socialist countries but it is used differently in socialist countries. The "Free Press" is used to protect the political party and the political leaders and their abuses of power. It is the political party and the political leaders not the common people who freely use the "Free Press." It is the governments and their agencies who use the "Free Press" for their purposes and agendas.

They have the power to Press the innocents and the powerless.

They have the power to Press freedom fighters and demonstrators.

They have the power to Press civil right workers and justice seekers.

They have the power to Press human rights activists and peacemakers.

They have the power to Press different political dreamers and commoners.

They have the power to Press the truth to vanish and lies to become the truth.

They have the power to Press black to become white and vice versa.

They have the power to Press the light to become dark and vice versa.

They have the power to Press the facts to become fakes and vice versa.

They have the power to Press the evidences to become nothing and vice versa.

The recent detain of doctors who suspected the emergence of a new virus in January 2020 was the most recent example of the restriction on the free press in a socialist country. These doctors only shared their suspects and findings with friends through alternative media and yet they were called to the police office and they were warned not to share the truth of the situations to anyone else.

They were forced to sign the paper to make sure that they would not reveal the matter again. When the virus became known, anyone who shared the information about the virus on the media was blocked. When the matter was out of the control with the many cases of death and infections, then the leaders began to put the blame and the wrongdoings on someone else and the doctors were quickly released.

If the truth were told earlier, then the situations would not be as terrible as it is right now where thousands of people died and millions of people suffered. If the truth were told earlier, one of the doctors who was detained may not have died, and, the people would not be so upset that they now were victims and were cheated by the fake news of the press that has led to the turmoil and sufferings of nations.

This does not mean that media monopoly does not happen in the West. Yet, sooner or later, the real situations would be discovered because different presses would find out the real information from different sources and media outlets. In the socialist nations, the real information could hardly be found because the press and sources only update the information according to the government guidance.

Though freedom of press is still available for many Americans, yet the contents of the mainstream media are basically partisan and are no longer objective or even accurate. The press could be independent but due to the purposes and intentions of the press organizations or the sponsors, the information released by many presses in the U.S. are longer reliable or even true.

The mainstream media in the U.S. are very critical of President Trump because President Trump is among the first rare U.S President who openly pointed out the lies and inaccuracy of the mainstream media.

One could hardly find if any mainstream media did or does release news about the great accomplishments of and the revival of the U.S. economy under President Trump and his administration.

A very relevant example of the media corruption in the U.S was the hoarding of H1N1 outbreaks in 2009. It took President Obama at least 6 months before he declared a State of National Emergency over the outbreaks H1N1. In fact, the declaration only came after three major outbreaks; 22 million people became infected; 98,000 hospitalized and 3,900 deaths due to H1N1 by October 17, 2019.

Yet, President Barak Obama was always hailed as the great president for the great things that he and his administration did including their combat against H1N1 flu. Harvard School of Public Health carried out the monthly poll to discover how did Americans respond to the health services and the government actions toward H1N1 pandemic, and Americans' responses were always positive.

"A majority of adults (59%) rated the overall response of public health officials to the H1N1 outbreaks as "excellent" or "good." Conversely, 39% rated the overall response as "fair" or "poor" according to Harvard School of Public Health Poll on January 20-24, 2009. In reality, President Obama and his administration and the mainstream media did well to cover the real truth about the H1N1 situation.

Samantha Chang on BPR stated, "In 2009, Barack Obama waited six months after the swine flu had infected millions of Americans and killed 1,000 people in the U.S. before declaring it a public health emergency. In contrast, President Trump reacted to the coronavirus within four weeks of it first being observed in China... Naturally, the Left did not criticize Obama for his delayed, limp-wristed reaction to the pandemic."

No mainstream media criticized President Barack Obama for his late declaration of the National Emergency. No media talked about his late responses and the deaths of many thousands of people. No media said that he would not be elected for his second term. No media gave him many bad names. But, President Trump received all the complaints and criticisms even though he acted quickly to coronavirus.

Right from the beginning of his office, President Trump tweeted on February 17, 2017 that, "The FAKE NEWS media (failing @nytimes, @NBCNews, @ABC, @CBS, @CNN) is not my enemy, it is the enemy of the American people." Former President Richard Nixon once said, "The press is the enemy. The press is the enemy. The press is the enemy. Write that on the blackboard 100 times."

Though there were so many great things that President Trump and his administration did but the mainstream media only discredited him in every way due to the monopoly of the democrats in the mainstream media in the U.S. Though there are still alternative and social media that could provide different views or both sides, but they are still weak in their coverage, news, and information to the public.

The media control in socialist nations not only monitors the top operation but also the users in alternative media. Even though, we only shared preaching and scriptures through social media, but our personal accounts on social media were closed by the authorities many times. Every time the accounts were closed we just opened the new ones and then the new accounts would be closed again.

Of course, our content and information had nothing to say against the government, the country leaders or the political ideology. Our content in the social media is always about godly morality, loving and caring for others. Our content is about helping and forgiving one another, praying and encouraging people for better lives. It is all about the salvation and transformation in the Lord, Jesus Christ.

People may send the information through social media, but when one's social media is getting more people subscribed, followed and watched, then that account would be monitored. If the content of that account is only about entertainment, it is fine but if it is about politics, education, human rights and religions; the account may be closed soon when the content is sensitive and the host may be jailed.

When there is an attempt to develop a Christian channel or television, the authorities would try to shut it down as soon as possible. The host may be given a warning or called for interrogations or persecuted. This is because the government leaders would try their best to minimize Christian influences in the country and religion freedom is still limited and religious workers are still being persecuted.

The sentence of 10 years in prison for blogger Tammy was a case in point of bloggers who dared to use the free press and freedom of speech to talk about sensitive social issue against a socialist regime. She used her blog to talk about her concerns about the mistreatments of poor patients in hospitals, land issues and illegal or unfair land confiscation, police brutality and corruption.

She was arrested the first time and charged for abusing the democratic freedoms. She was released when she agreed with the local authorities to abandon her blog and when she promised to keep quiet. But she continued to raise her voice about those issues again after sometimes. She was arrested again and was charged for 10 years in prison because she spoke the truth and the rampant injustices of the land.

Her expression of the truth and social issues through social media was not appreciated by the socialist leaders who have been corrupting wealth and natural resources. They also abuse the power to destroy the powerless people. Tammy was not seen as a hero but a dissident, a dangerous anti-State instigator, a rebellious anti-political party criminal, and she must be punished.

Just like many people who were incarcerated for using social media or printed materials to call the government leaders' attention to the corruptions and injustices in the land, she was also put behind the bars leaving her two small children and an elderly mother at home. They all suffered for the truth they spoke while the corrupted and wicked socialist leaders are still enjoying their lives and powers.

Please take not that under the reign of the socialists and the socialist party, the free press would not be available anymore to the general public. The socialist press is to serve the purposes of the socialists to spread their socialist agenda and to indoctrinate and brainwash the citizens. If Americans and people of nations want to keep their free press and freedom of speech, socialism is never the right choice.

Another characteristic of the socialist nations is the severe persecutions of the people of faith. The socialists may talk very well about freedom, equality and democracy but they demand people total submission to their leadership. The socialist leaders only want people to worship their socialism and their socialist leaders and no one else. This leads to many oppressions on religious freedoms.

2nd Commandment
"THOU SHALL HAVE NO RELIGION"
Freedom of Religions

Many people may say, "I see many mosques, temples, church buildings, and religious places of worship in socialist countries." Yes, people may see huge and newly built mosques and church buildings in socialist countries, but, that was the result of the significant growth of Muslim and Christian populations in the last few decades. The Christian revival and missions especially reached out to people everywhere.

About 2 or 3 decades ago, people hardly saw those buildings. If they did, they would only see the old buildings and church buildings that were emptied or only a small number of believers were seen for the services. Former church buildings were forced to close down and many church buildings and properties were turned into museums, coffee shops, schools, government offices or business complexes.

Among the list of the 50 top nations that are persecuting churches and Christians on World Watch List 2019, the socialist countries are among the top list. According to the Open Doors, these socialist countries are among the most dangerous countries for Christians. (https://

www.opendoorsusa.org/wp-content/uploads/2019/01/WWL2019_FullBooklet.pdf).

Open Doors USA also revealed that 245 million Christians are being persecuted worldwide in 2019. One in nine Christians experience high levels of persecution worldwide. In the top 50 countries, 4,136 Christians were killed for faith-related reasons, 1266 churches or Christian buildings were attacked and 2,625 Christians were detained without trial, arrested, sentenced and imprisoned.

There appears to be free religious freedom in socialist countries; people may see thousands of people flocked together inside mega churches. Yet, a closer look reveals that people are not very free in their religious practices and rights. Religious gatherings outside of the state-churches are prohibited and people would be fined, detained and imprisoned to practice their faith outside of the state-churches.

The socialist governments announce loud and clear that there is freedom of religion, yet that freedom is allowed and limited in the places that the government designated for worship. Beyond those four walls of the church buildings, religious gathering and preaching are illegal. Cameras are installed and recording systems are set up inside the buildings to monitor all the church activities and the believers.

Before online services became available, the audio recording system was already set up in the church buildings. The recording and the transcription were not for the good purposes of sharing the sermons or for the purposes of Pastors' evaluation of their preaching, but, the recording and the transcription were and are to be submitted to the authorities to see if the preaching is in line with political guidance.

In many state churches, sermon scripts often had to be approved before the preaching and the preaching was being recorded by the government religious workers for monitoring purposes. Many so called "Pastors" receive salaries from the government openly or secretly. Many church offerings are basically not used for Christian missions but it is used for purposes ordered by the higher authorities.

During the socialist rule in former Soviet Union, the cries for religious freedom were unbearable with so many severe oppressions, persecutions of churches and horrible executions of religious workers, though, the majority of the people were Orthodox believers. This was a typical example in the past about religious persecutions and it is still the current situations of socialist countries toward religions.

Socialist countries severely persecute the people of faith because the socialist leaders do not believe in the existence of a God who created the universe. They consider religion as opium and the belief in a God is destructive. God for them is just a product of human imagination. They do not like to have a God who saves, delivers, blesses and prospers people because socialism wants to be the only agent to do so.

This is why the atheists and socialists try hard to remove Christian education from schools. This is why they try hard to remove prayer from schools and workplaces. This is why they ban Bible classes, worship and prayers from schools, workplaces and government offices. This is why they persecute people of faith. This is why churches are being raided, the crosses burned and church buildings demolished.

This does not mean that there isn't any religious persecution in the U.S. such as some hostile attitudes of the non-religious people to people of faith, or Johnson's Amendment, or the bans on religious exercises such as prayer in public places, or many cases of losing jobs due to religious exercises. Yet, those incidents are no way to be compared to the severe religious persecutions in socialist countries.

Millions of Americans now see that some church buildings were burnt. Members of BLM and Antifa vandalized churches and disrupted believers, the services and the worship places. They now publicly burned the Bible and the cross. They even hurt the believers and ridiculed street preachers. Religious persecution is common in socialist countries, when will Americans totally loose their religious freedom?

The socialist governments may show to the public the religious laws, policies, and regulations to prove that there is real freedom of religions. They may show the number of church buildings, Bible schools, houses of prayer, seminaries to support their claims. Do they show how many Pastors and believers that were and are still in prison? Do they show the numbers of churches that were forced to close?

Do they show the unlimited times that the policemen and religious workers raid the worship places? Do they openly allow physical examinations of the dead bodies of those they claimed dead due to various sicknesses or accidents in prisons, labor camps, detention centers? Do they admit or just deny all the causes of these deaths due to horrible tortures and physical punishments?

Do the socialists show how many spies that are planted in churches on their lists? There are always spies in churches and religious settings. Many of the top Christian leaders for example are often the high-ranking political party members and numerous numbers of Senior Pastors across the land are also the party members. Even so, there are always spies in the churches to monitor what the Pastors are preaching to send reports to their leaders.

Months before I was arrested at a place where I conducted Sunday services, there was a lady who came to our Sunday services. She was there for the morning and afternoon services. She always came early and prayed wholeheartedly. The afternoon service was especially for those who were hungry for the presence and the power of the Holy Spirit. You may call that the Spirit-filled service if you want.

This lady prayed fervently and she also spoke in tongues. Everyone could see her devotion through her prayers and worship and hunger for the Word of God. She told me that if I can make arrangement for her to serve, she was willing to do so. Since she was still new, we wanted to observe her for a while. To make the story short, the policemen suddenly walked in one day and ordered us to stop the service.

I asked the policemen to go out and wait for me outside and I would meet them when the worship service was over, but they did not give in to that suggestion of mine. They rushed in, took over the microphones and commanded everyone to sit down as other members of theirs confiscated our Bibles, computers, and cameras... Other policemen forced me into their van and brought me to the police station.

In many cases like this, I always had miraculous deliverances or escapes from the back doors, but, this time, they came all of a sudden and so many of them surrounded the building from the inside out to make sure that I would be caught on spot, this time. On that day of June 2017, more than 120 policemen and security members came and surrounded and raid our places of worship to arrest me.

Then they registered the name, ID number, home addresses, jobs... of each church member as they often did in cases like this. Before they released the church members to go home, the authorities would inform church members to go to state churches because the underground services or home church services were illegal and they warned each member to not go back to this "illegal service."

Usually the authorities would interrogate some members, and then they may take many of the key leaders to the police stations for further interrogation. But this time their focus was on me so they just let everyone leave the place and they told some of my co-leaders to meet with them the following days for "tea times," which is the term church leaders often use for interrogations by the authorities.

I will share more of my stories as the situations allow later. Let me go back to the story that I was sharing before. When the policemen and the security members came, one of my co-workers, Grace, happened to hide in another room. This room had a big glass window and one could see easily everything inside of that room through the glass window. The policemen did go and check that room.

Yet, it was indeed a miracle that the policemen did not discover Grace in that room. God did that miracle so that I could have this story to share with you. From that window, Grace could see that lady who came faithfully to the church services and who prayed in tongues; she was the last one to show her ID and then she congratulated the policemen, "well done" as they shook hands and laughed.

Let me tell you the truth; do not think that there are no spies in the major churches across the States of America. I do not know about other countries, but I am sure that many socialist countries also send religious spies to their national churches in America. They may even hold important positions in the churches. This may sound strange and funny to people in the free world but that is for real.

In fact the socialist spies are almost everywhere in American societies. They are there in the political arena. They are there in schools and education institutions. They are there in the labs and research centers. They are there in the companies and corporations. They are there in the media corporations and news agencies. They are there in the law firms and government offices.

Just think about this, there must be a strong reason why so many politicians, lawyers, researchers, educators, scientists, media agencies, business people and the likes are so supportive to the deadly and destructive socialism? Why do these people and agencies talk so nice about socialism when it is not? Thousands of these people are literally "bought" by the socialists.

For years, I had regular weekly "tea times" with the authorities and their knowledge about the churches and mission organizations abroad was very impressive. They knew the major current religious events. They knew very well the religious leaders who preached against them and they watched closely the preaching, activities or the social media of those leaders and pastors as they are still doing that to me now.

Or, you yourself could be a spy for the liberals, secularists, atheists and anti-Christian activists, because you know the hostilities of these people toward your church and God, but yet you still want to be one of them. You know better that they are anti-Christ and they are for abortions, wrong genders, abominations, and yet you still vote for them. Are you that spy? You probably were but now you are not.

In socialist countries, spies are everywhere. In the religious setting, the spies could be the common people or Pastors, or they could also be the high-ranking religious leaders. At the funeral of Pastor John, a Senior Pastor of a prominent church in the city and a top leader in the religious ministry, many believers were shocked to find out that the funeral service was not performed according to Christian ceremony.

Indeed, there was nothing to show that the one who passed away was the highly respected Pastor and a famous religious leader. The reading of his biography did not even mention his role as a Pastor or religious leader. There was no prayer, no Christian songs, no preaching, no mention of God or the Bible except the hail of his achievement in his political career and his sacrifice for the political party.

Yes, he was a religious leader by profession but he was indeed a high-ranking political leader to direct religious leaders to follow the political direction. He was a Pastor by assignment, but, he was also a government official who preached what he was told and allowed to speak. He was a Christian by name but he was indeed an atheist who led the religious people to be obedient to the political ideology.

This was mainly the reason why the underground church movement was born and why many Pastors, leaders and believers did not and still do not want to be part of the state church. They were forced to close down their home churches, cell groups for Bible Studies, prayer meetings and they even faced severe persecutions, tortures and life-threatening sentences. They want to hear the truth and preach the truth.

They want to preach about the miracles and the supernatural power of God, which is forbidden to be mentioned in the state church because those things are not scientifically proven. They want to teach about the second coming of the Lord Jesus Christ, which is not allowed because it is like a fairytale. They want to share about the works of the Holy Spirit, which is not acceptable because it is superstition.

They want to declare salvation by faith in the Lord Jesus Christ, which is not highly encouraged because the socialist ideology is the light and the sun for the people. Nothing but socialism can save people from inequality, superstition, tragedies and suffering. The gospel of love is mainly taught in the church because it is the best way to indoctrinate believers to become submissive to the leadership, even the regime.

They want to preach against evil things happening in the state-churches but that could be an offense to the leaders. They want to preach against corruption, yet, corruption is very rampant here. They want to follow The Way, The Truth and The Light but they are told to follow the commands, the lies, and the darkness. They want to follow God's will, but they will be persecuted by the orders of men.

By the way, there are also plenty of religious spies in the U.S. too.

Many Americans see that President Trump really made America Great again and the U.S. economy became better with high records of employment and increasing wage before coronavirus, yet, they just discredited his records. Many Americans see that the corrupted leaders made up the stories to impeach President Trump and they are still trying to remove him from the office even now, yet they just keep quiet.

Many Christian Americans may see clearly that President Trump is really a strong fighter for religious freedoms and values. He made the words "Merry Christmas" to become popular again across the U.S. when the greeting, "Merry Christmas," for so many years, was an offense to many people due to its political incorrectness and religious meaning. Yet they still do not care much to support him.

President Trump supports and stands with Israel more than any previous presidents because he follows God's word to protect and pray for Israel as Israel is the chosen people and the nation of God and the central point of many Christian prophecies, events and the second coming of the Lord Jesus Christ. He moved the U.S embassy to Jerusalem when many previous presidents only promised to do so.

President Trump fought hard against abortion and stopped the Planned Parenthood from using taxpayer money for their abortion agenda leading to the closing of many abortion clinics. He removed All Gender toilets, and opposed the legalization of gay marriages. Yet many people still considers him as an immoral person and they are moral because they supported all the things that are detestable in God's eyes.

President Trump tries to repeal the Johnson's Amendment that put restrictions on religious freedom and religious speech at the threat of tax-exempt removal. He appointed 200 conservative judges and more later to protect the Constitution, the precious freedom, rights and to restore godly values. Yet people still prefer to elect ungodly leaders who want to change the Constitution and promote immoral values.

President Trump fought to protect religious business people so they could operate their business against the orders that are against their convictions and religious beliefs. He invites God to be the Lord of the White House and of the United States. He brings back the Bible and prayer to the White House, public places and schools, yet, many Christians still vote for the ungodly leaders who are against the Bible and God.

President Trump called for the special National Day of prayer and called Christians to pray in so many important events of the nations. He famously said, "America do not worship the government but God." He is the most outspoken president of the U.S. who talks more about God in all of his speeches. Yet many people think that he is a fake Christian, when "the so-called-true Christians" dare not talk about God.

Though President Trump is not perfect just as all of us are imperfect, a true Christian and Bible-believing Christian must vote for President Trump who ensures religious freedom and biblical values are to be protected and practiced. A true Christian cannot elect an ungodly politician who vows to go against all the biblical teaching and values if he was to be elected as the President of the United States.

Though coronavirus outbreak affected the U.S. economy and the lives of millions of people and it is beyond the expectations of anyone, President Trump made many quick actions to prevent the spread of the coronavirus and to protect lives instead of hiding the information for political purposes. He knew well that his declaration of the State of National Emergency would affect his 2020 reelection.

But President Trump and his administration care more about the lives, health, safety and securities of millions of Americans than election or politics because he puts America First. He and the Congress also passed economic stimulus packages to help Americans and businesses overcome the situations. President Trump should be praised as one of the greatest American President instead of being downplayed.

Why are people of faith being persecuted in most socialist countries than others? **First of all:** it is the clash between ideologies. Socialism is atheistic in nature and it does not want to accept the existence of God or religion because, for them, religion is superstitious and is opium.

They believe God is not real and God is only the product of human imagination. God is not needed because they are gods.

Socialists cannot agree with theistic views, the supernatural and doctrines that are being taught by religious leaders because they claim that they are very scientific and everything must be proven. Thus they neither believe in life after death nor the existence of supernatural beings. They refused to believe in the existence of God, the creation of God, the spiritual world, and the reality of hell and heaven.

In reality, they cannot explain scientifically why they strongly persecute Christians and yet there are more and more Christians in their countries in the end. They cannot explain scientifically why with so many hospitals, labs and research institutes with scientific equipment, but only when Christians pray that the blind receives sight, the lame walks, and the mute speaks and the deaf hears.

They cannot explain why their scientific methods cannot transform the lives of countless drug addicted people, evildoers and prisoners, but the Bible (the book that they burn and destroy) can do so. They cannot explain scientifically why the demon-possessed people were so violent in their scientific treatment that they had to give up on them, yet, the demons were subject to the power of the Name of Jesus.

Because many socialists and the atheists cannot disprove scientifically the facts and evidences of millions of people who received healings, deliverances and restorations in socialist countries, many of these former atheists at last has come to the scientific conclusion that the presence of more Christians and their transformed lives indicates the presence of the true, powerful and living God.

So, they also came to accept God as their personal Lord and Savior because their lives and their transformations are also the living evidences of the existence of God. Many of them are willing to give up their political power, positions and benefits to follow God when they are under the pressures of the higher authorities to follow Caesar or to follow their new-found faith and salvation.

Secondly: socialists worship their ideology and power not deities or God. When someone or an organization refuses to pledge allegiance or loyalty to socialism, the socialist government feels and considers that as a sign of rebellion and a threat to their existence. The larger the organization or the larger the number of people who disagree with the socialist government is, the larger the threat the socialists feel.

Socialism and socialists are very insecure when their ideology and power are being challenged because their ideology and power are all they have to control people. They use power to suppress the people to maintain social order, their power, authority and wealth. So the socialists must put a stop to any growing movement when they feel that their power and positions are being threatened and challenged.

Socialism cannot stand to accept other views because they believe that socialism is the higher form of government and ideology. Socialism is the best in everything and it offers the best form of government and the best mode of economy, so why do they need others. If they think they are the best, then there is no cure for them because they would not open up to new ideologies but they would oppress new ideologies.

The socialists could not accept God or any savior of the world because according to the socialists, socialism is the sun and the light. Socialism is the answer to human issues. Socialism is to be hailed not God or any other leaders except the socialist leaders. Thus, people are taught and told to idolize the socialist leaders and in many places, people even worship the founding socialist leaders.

Last but not the least: socialists cannot bear to listen to the moral teaching of faiths especially Christianity. They cannot bear to hear the preaching of sins because they realize that they are the worst sinners but they don't want to accept that. They realize that they are the most corrupted leaders but they don't want to admit that. They realize that they are immoral people but they don't want to confess that.

This is also really true to the many atheists and ungodly leaders in the U.S. today. They cannot bear to hear moral preaching because they are so used to immoral things. They cannot bear to hear prayers that talk against the detestable things of abortion, gay marriages, incest, and unnatural sexes in the Congress and political meetings, so, they walked out of the meetings.

When they agree or accept the religious teaching, they may lose everything they have. The socialists say there is religious freedom, but when any of them in the government is known to become a Christian believer particularly, he or she will be warned and will even be disciplined. That believer may still be allowed to work, yet the chances for promotions or higher positions are very slim.

One of my evangelistic team with almost 20 members was arrested in a city and all the members were then brought and detained at a police station. Usually, the policemen would take one member after another into different rooms for interrogation and it might take a few days for them to do so. They would ask each member their long list of questions again and again while note taking.

The policemen usually want to find out the reasons why the team is there in this place? Who are the leaders? Who lead them to Christ? Who are sending them to this place? Who are inviting the team to come? What is the connection with the local people? Who are the financial supporters? And many related questions. Then they would read their long written reports and force the people to sign.

Then it came the time they would threaten each person. They would tell about the illegal activities of preaching the Gospel. They would outline the laws and policies and tell the team the consequences of imprisonment and the bad future as the result of becoming a criminal. Then it came the time they would lecture how good it is to believe in socialism and they would give people the chance to renounce our faith.

Then they contacted the local government where each member lived and told the local government and policemen about the situations based on their reports. They confiscated the instruments, sound systems, computers, and phones. In most cases, they gave back the phones and sometimes the computer after getting information they needed, but not other items even though we were not guilty of anything.

But this time, the situation was totally different from how we were often treated before. The policemen did not ask what the team members did nor interrogated any member of ours. They just detained all the members in different rooms. When our members prayed aloud as we usually did in these situations, the policemen did not stop us. When the members sang songs in worship, the policemen did not scold us.

When the members danced, rejoiced and shouted in the detaining rooms, the policemen did not even come to order them to keep quiet as they often did. Instead, they brought meal boxes and bottles of water for the team during lunch and they did the same with early dinner. After the early dinner, the policemen just asked the team to leave before it got dark. What happened?

The team members were surprised and asked the policemen, "Why didn't you interrogate us?" Indeed, the team members were expecting to be interrogated and they were prepared on how to give the answer in these important times. This was the chance for team members to share the Gospel to the policemen personally as they had been prepared to do in persecuted situation like this.

Yet, the policemen just smiled and this was what the policemen said, "we know that you Christians are good. If all the people here become Christians, we have no job to do here" as they said good-bye and wished the team well on their mission trip. Their words brought a lot of encouragement to the team and to those who believe that the Christian missions are still bearing fruits and impacting lives.

Another important point here is that even the socialists and the atheists know that Christians are good and indeed Christianity and Christians contribute much to the enhancement of social morality and peaceful living, yet, they do not want the existence of Christianity. Christians also contribute much to social development, yet they still persecute Christians. Is this the ideology that you are looking for?

Dr. Jack Graham rightly said, "Can you name one socialist country-communist or otherwise- that is open to religious liberty? There is none. Opposition to God is at the very root of this system called socialism. It is agnostic, atheistic, and aggressive to believers in Jesus Christ." Let us pray that God continues to do miracles and that missionaries would be sent out from socialist countries to nations of the world.

When it seems impossible with men, with God, everything is possible. If God could heal the sick, He could heal the hearts of people. If God could turn around the life of Saul who once persecuted Him to become His faithful servant and hero of faith, God could also transform the lives of socialists and atheists to testify about Him. If God could raise the dead to life, He could also raise up this nation for Him.

By the way, you are most welcome to worship and serve God with the local Christians and to feel the freedom of religion in these socialist countries. Most people asked us, "Is it safe for us to join your service?" All we can and still say is, "We can assure you the freedom to worship God, but no one could assure you the safety and security you would face here in the socialist countries."

Of course, we cannot assure you the safety either because we could not even assure our own safety and security. So, how could we assure yours? We are also victims of that "freedom of religion." Personally, I was "invited" to leave the socialist nation by the grace of God. This is why you could read these words that we wrote here in this book and other books about the reality of socialism to enlighten you in some way.

Yet, the fact that we wrote this book also put many people, our relatives and ourselves at risks when the authorities find out our identities, because, we are not supposed to speak openly about these matters according the golden rule. People in socialist nations could not just freely speak the many things they want to speak as people do in the free word because their freedom could not protect them.

In most cases, the freedom activists would be given warnings, threatening, or some lessons with physical attacks by the local authorities. In many cases, the freedom fighters were imprisoned or they just simply disappeared. In special cases, their throats were cut open so they could take their freedom of speech to the grave. You might be shock to know about this and this is the fact.

There are always unhappy ending or negative consequences to people who do not keep the golden rule. So if you still want to choose socialism, you better learn to say nothing negative or unhappy things about the socialist government, their leaders, political party, ideology and their policies even though what you want to say are true and it is important for you to voice out the concerns about those things.

But that is how you think and should act in most of the Western world and many people in the U.S would appreciate you and praise you and the various media channels may even invite you to be their guest on their special shows or programs. The U.S government may also listen to your great idea and may respond to your truthful and insightful comments or solutions.

But that mostly happens in the free world but in the socialist countries, what the common people have is merely a promise of the freedom of speech. How do people in many socialist nations exercise that freedom of speech? Are there any human right activist and political activist praised and appreciated by the socialists? Do the freedom fighters are encouraged to fight for freedom in many socialist countries?

3rd Commandment
"THOU SHALL NOT SPEAK OTHERWISE"
Freedom of Speech

It was raining cats and dogs on that day and streams of water flowed down from the nearby mountains flooding the neighborhood where my uncle Paul lived. The same thing happened from year to year and the issue could easily be solved by building a drainage system at the many suggestions of the local people. But, the local socialist leaders did not take actions to build the drainage system.

When this happened, the house would be filled with water destroying many things. When the waters retreated after many days, the house and the garden were filled with mud and it took time to clean up and money to fix the house. There was no insurance to cover all those cost and there was no help from the local government. Their voices were too weak to be heard and they just suffered the annual floods.

That year, the rain was hard and the waters poured down from the mountains flooding the house. My uncle Paul was fighting hard against the flood to move precious things to higher place, yet, the water levels kept increasing. He was tired and exhausted. He could not do anything more about the flood and the water. He could only sit down and look at the house and things destroyed by the flood.

Suddenly, he ran out of the house and went to the main street as the strong rains poured all over his face and the strong streams of water flowed through his knees. He suddenly shouted, "Why do people suffer so much under socialism and why don't they do something good for people?" He poured out his anguishes against the socialist leaders who did not care for the many people who had to suffer like him.

The family members quickly stopped him and pushed him back into the house. He felt better after speaking out the things that were kept and pressed in his heart and mind for years. If he could not release the anger that kept burning inside of him for so many years, he would have become more frustrated and he would even become crazy. But, what he spoke was dangerous and was not acceptable in the country.

Readers may say that what Paul did is very normal and every American has the right to say and to complaint or to say against the government and the leaders especially when the authorities are the causes of the people's sufferings and tragedies. Americans even have the right to ask the local government or to demonstrate to ask justices to be done for them but this is not the same in socialist countries.

All the family members just hoped that the rain was so hard and that no one heard what my uncle Paul spoke for they were indeed very worried about that. The next morning, the local policemen came and took my uncle to the police station and interrogated him about the incident. My uncle answered shortly that he was so frustrated by the flood and he did not mean to say anything against the government.

They let him go with the warning that he should be careful with what he says. They let him go because of his "repentance". But, they let him go probably because they worried that unhappy things may happen to them if they put him into the dead end because, they took away his big land recently and that really frustrated him and the flood was only an opportunity for him to show his frustration and desperation.

You may ask, "But he is talking about the reality. Why can't he talk about the truth? Why can't he be allowed to express his true feelings?" All the people in the socialist countries want to express their true thoughts and feelings but that freedom of speech is still very limited and it comes at a great cost because the socialists only like to hear praises not criticisms. Please remember the golden rule.

The socialists do not want people to say that socialism does not work well to bring about equality and prosperity even though many countries have already collapsed due to socialism. They do not want people to say that the control of one political party is unfair, but, it is really unfair. They do not want people to speak about the social gaps, the wealth gaps, and power gaps at their failures to deliver equality.

Does this help you to think twice about your choice of socialism so far for the U.S.?

By the way, you may also wonder what do we mean by stating that the members in the evangelistic team were eager to be interrogated by the policemen. Of course, in normal situations, none of us want or would like to be interrogated by the authorities because it is not really a happy encounter. It is stressful to be asked so many questions. It is serious and scary as well.

Yet the interrogation is unavoidable in socialist countries where freedom of religion is quite tricky. The interrogation may begin any time when the persecution takes place. The church leaders did not let the persecution and the interrogation intimidate them but they took these as good opportunities to share the Gospel to the authorities as the Apostles did when the early church was persecuted.

Policemen may enter peoples' places at any time to check to see if there is a prayer meeting, Bible study or worship service going on at home, factory, restaurant, hotel, office or even bed room. So, Christians are often taught to be prepared to share their testimonies of salvation, healing, deliverance, and restoration or life transformation to the authorities. This is how Christians could share the Gospel to them.

Years ago, my mentor and spiritual leader, Rev. Dr. Paul developed a course called, "If One Day." This course was required for all students who wanted to be equipped to serve the Lord. This course was not about if one day someone became rich or famous but, it was about what happens if one day, one was caught by the authorities while preaching the Gospel, what should he or she say to the authorities then?

Basically, the students were taught to share why they came to accept God, what were their lives before knowing God and what God did in and for their lives or how were their lives after experiencing God. Students were also taught how to use the Bible stories to give the answers to common questions that the authorities often asked in the interrogation process and how to then seek God for the answers.

So when the team members were brought to the police station, they were praying and waiting for their turn to share the Gospel to the authorities. But this time, the situation was different and they ended up just giving glory to God at what the policemen said. So, they just thanked the authorities and encouraged them to dedicate their lives to God as they already knew what God had done in their areas.

In the free world, people are trained to become effective and fluent speakers and they are encouraged to freely speak their mind and freely share their feelings. In the socialist nations, people are taught automatically how to control their thoughts and hide their feelings towards the wrongs caused by socialism, and, they are taught to say nothing about the corruptions, injustices or abuses of power of the regime.

The following is a funny conversation between a co-worker of mine, Lydia and the spies. During a conference that my ministry and I organized, some spies came to attend the event. The spies attended different seminars and made friends with the participants and tried to get more details about the information. Lydia quickly discovered their intention and this was how she answered their questions.

The spies: "By the way, how do you know about this event?"

Lydia: "I saw the information online before."

The spies: "Why do you come here?"

Lydia: "God spoke to me that I should come here to pray for the peace and prosperity of our country, the protection for our country leaders and people".

The spies: "Do you know who organized the event?"

Lydia: She said nothing but pointed her finger upward.

The spies: "Are the organizers on the second floor now?" (as they interpreted the way she pointed her finger upward)

Lydia: "No. I mean God is the organizer of this event."

The Spies: "Where does the money come from to organize this event?"

Lydia: "Please go and ask the Lord Jesus. God is the Provider"

Then the spies just pretended to laugh and they went away to look for others. In most cases, the spies would hear similar quick answers because many leaders and coworkers could quickly discover the intention of the spies during the conversation, and, they did not want to talk much for someone else to be endangered. Some leaders may pray for the spies and preached the Gospel to the spies in their prayers.

But it was not that simple and easy during the real interrogation. There were times the authorities would listen to the testimonies. There were times they just cut short the stories that the believers tried to share with them. Many authorities would stop the believers immediately when the believers mentioned the Bible. Even so, many Christians would share something about God to the authorities.

Unfortunately, in most cases, the authorities would dictate what the people should say at the end. Why? Because those who did not listen to what the socialists wanted, they would be tortured and people would face more severe charges against them. In the free world, like the U.S., people have the power and real freedom to speak. But in socialist countries, most people say only what they are allowed to say.

It is very common here in America that people can say almost anything they want to say without any fear of being apprehended. In the socialist countries where we lived, we have an expression saying, "Shssss, don't talk about it, the ants would know." Yes, we may talk freely about the foods we like or dislike, the fashions, the movies, and the sceneries, but there are certain things that people cannot talk about.

There are certain things when people talk the ants would know. When people are not cautious with the content that they spoke, their words would be reported to the local authorities. That person would be invited to the police station for lecture times and warnings. The citizens are taught to speak constructively about the government, party and leaders but they were not to speak anything bad or against them.

One day the policemen came and knocked at my door. When my wife opened the door, they asked if I was at home. In fact, they already knew that I was at home. They asked me to go to the police station quickly. Of course they did not need to show me a warrant and they did not need to bring one to order people to go with them. As I was changing clothes, I heard what they were telling my wife.

They said that my wife and I were intelligent and good people but the issue was that I was very stubborn, they said, and that my wife had gotten married to the wrong person. My wife just smiled and kindly replied, "Yes, my husband is a very good person and he is great to me." The reason they said I was stubborn was because I did not follow their orders to stop the mission works.

They said that because I was stubborn and did not listen to them, I would be the cause of suffering for the family and that they would separate me from my family as punishment. Upon hearing that I prayed and asked God to give me wisdom on how to respond to what they said.

Then they took me to the police station and they told me in the car again that I was the cause of suffering to the family.

Then I said to them, "that is not the real suffering." They were shocked and asked, "Isn't separation from family a real suffering?" I told them, "You know that with our educational background and our ability, we could go almost anywhere and we could still enjoy our great life. Yes, persecution is a suffering and separation is not the thing that I want for my family. Do you know why we are here to suffer?"

"Do you know why we stay here to suffer the air pollution? It is because we want to see the sinners become saints. Do you know why we stay here to suffer water contamination? It is because we want to see the hopeless to have hope. Do you know why we stay here to suffer food poisoning? It is because we want to see the prisoners of sins become the preachers of salvation."

"We are here to suffer the persecutions, the interrogations, the monitoring and the surveillances because we want to see the victims of drugs become the victors of darkness in the Name of the Lord Jesus Christ. We want to see the lost to become loved by God, the sick people to become singers of praise for God's supernatural healing, and the demon-possessed to become the delivered person in God's power."

Those were the words from God for me in that situation to respond to them. They were really shocked at those words and they said nothing to those words. I believed that God spoke to them at that moment. Yet, unfortunately, many of them just shook off the words God spoke to them and continued to follow the command of the authorities for the sake of security and life or else their lives could be in danger too.

During the first few months of "weekly tea times" with the authorities, I felt tired and pressured. They were not very rude and tried to scare me with many threatening as they did the first few times. They were kind and punctual with the weekly three-hours "fellowship." I was pressured and tired because I had to be very careful with every answer I gave them in response to their lists of questions.

They would ask the same questions again and again from weeks to months. They compared my answers and questioned if there were any differences. I was very careful with what I said because my answers posed some threats to the safety and even imprisonments of other people. They always reminded me that God's servant must speak the truth and I did, though, I gave half-truth answers most of the times.

I prayed and asked God what should I do because I could hardly go on with the "regular tea times." I heard God's answer, "Preach the Gospel to them." I was scared at that thought. "What if they put me into prison because of preaching the Gospel to them?" But I just obeyed God and that was when I experienced the secrets of freedom of thousands of God's servants when they faced tough persecutions.

When they asked a question, I would shortly answer their question and then I would relate that content to Bible stories or history or current great things that Christians did and give lectures on the topic as long as I could. I did not feel tired or pressured anymore but I felt motivated and passionate to share about the things God did for me, for others and what God could do for them as well when it was possible.

Before, I really did not like going for the weekly "tea times," but now I felt better because I took these regular meeting as the cell group where I was the leader who could really share the words of God and I got many chances to share the Gospel and to ask their opinions about the love of God, about miracles, about good attitudes of Christians, and about many Christian contributions to the country and about others.

Of course they would kindly stop me from time to time. Even though this "small group" never grew in term of membership though there were "newcomers" coming sometimes, I preached and shared so long that most of the times, the authorities would remind me, "Pastor, it is 5pm." They reminded me that it is enough for that day and they needed to go home and I was happy to go home as well.

Every time I said goodbye to them, they always reminded me that I should not talk to other people about our conversations. I did keep my free speech quiet for decades in socialist countries. I can now exercise my free speech in this land of freedom, but, still, I cannot fully speak freely because of the safety of other people. Want to exercise your free speech in a socialist country?

I think you better study first, the course, "If One Day," that my spiritual father and mentor Rev. Dr. Paul developed so that you could be more prepared if you happened to be interrogated. The course provides you with common questions asked during interrogation, and how you could respond to the authorities with Bible stories and your stories. But, your real experiences will teach you better how to respond.

I think this course is very needful in America and many free nations of the world today because, it would let Christians know that persecutions for the sake of the Gospel, and objections to the Gospel are real, scary, and yet fun. The beauty of the course is how to trust God for the answers from the Bible and revelations to the many questions asked and, it would let Americans appreciate the freedom they have.

Rev. Dr. Paul was in prison for ten years because of the Gospel and he was under strict surveillances for more than two decades. In the many restricted prisons, he still preached the Gospel to hundreds of prisoners and planted churches in the prisons. He also planted hundreds of churches and trained thousands of leaders in a socialist country. Don't forget to invite him to inspire you and your congregations.

As we look back at the many moments of God's interventions, we just give thanks to God for His many protections, miracles and deliverances upon our life and His servants. We thank God for His wisdom to proclaim His words in Gospel-restricted places and to bring His healings and restorations to wounded people and to the lost world, as well as training thousands of leaders and believers to preach the Gospel.

We thank God for His many servants who really faced tough interrogations, tortures and persecutions and yet they are still faithful to serve God regardless of the unfavorable treatments they received. We thank God for the many words of wisdom, knowledge and courage to respond to the many tough and tricky questions of the authorities while sharing God's love and plan of salvation to the authorities.

What are the topics that people should not talk about or should not get involved in or discuss if they don't want troubles to fall upon them and their families? They could not say against the political party, political ideology, or anything that the government and the leaders are not happy about. These are the forbidden things or taboos that one should not support and should not spread information about.

Whenever people want to speak against the corrupted practices of the political leaders, the bad, the policies, wasting expenses or agendas, the abuses of laws by the authorities, the unrealistic ideology of socialism, the persecutions of religions, the authoritarian of the government, the internal politics, the luxurious country leaders, one better keep quiet about those topics if he or she wants to live happily ever.

Some people may think that those people who dare not speak about those obviously wrong things are just cowards and that those wrong things should not be allowed to continue. Yes, everyone knows that those things are not right, but, their quiet keeps them safe from all the injustices and tragedies that could happen to them. You are most welcome to come and speak against those things if you have the guts.

Last November 2019, the president of a university announced that if any student was caught talking, sharing or forwarding videos, pictures or writings, which were related to the recent protests that had been taking place many months in a major city in Asia through social media or writings, they would be expelled from the university. That is the freedom of speech in socialist countries.

The detention centers and prisons in socialist countries are always ready to welcome people who dare to speak against the countries or criticize the leaders. Welcome to your freedom of speech and then you will find out that those prisons are not empty. The bad news is that prisoners are not free to speak their minds but they would be re-educated on how and what to speak. Want to try your freedom?

The medical student, Lisa, was arrested and put into the Labor Camp for reformation and re-education because her friend happened to read her dairy and found out that Lisa wrote some sentences that criticized the socialist party. Her friend immediately reported the case to the authority. As for the consequence of her free expression in her hidden note, she was put in the Labor Camp for 24 years.

Her study was over in just a click and her dream to become a medical was never realized. Her youth and her talent were wasted in prison, labor camp and hard labors. Her right to pursue happiness and a family of her own were taken away. Her life was totally destroyed and she suffered with so many humiliations, loneliness, mistreatments, poverty, sufferings and more.

Where were the human rights for Lisa when the socialists declared her sentence? Where were the freedoms and equality for Lisa at the great shouts of the socialists for her incarceration? Where were the justices and happiness for Lisa when the socialists locked her up? It sounds ridiculous and impossible, right? Yet the situation matches nothing to the sound promises that socialists made to many people.

How are the freedom of press, freedom of religion, and freedom of speech in the U.S. recently? Are Americans being persecuted for exercising these freedoms? The bad news is that the oppression of freedom of press, freedom of religion and freedom of speech are also happening now at the rise of the Soviet-type socialism in the recent riots, protests and vandalizing of members of Black Lives Matter and Antifa.

The truth is now coming out when many leaders of Black Lives Matter and Antifa are revealed as the Marxists, Marxist-trained leaders, and hardcore communists. These leaders and the socialist leaders and members of terrorist organizations are working together to take over America and to destroy America and Americans and they have been causing many chaos and destruction since the death of George Floyd.

Court briefings from police in Oklahoma showed that, "Several people were carrying flags that were identified as belonging to the following groups: Antifa, Soviet Union (communism), American Indian Movement, Anarcho-Communism (solid red) and the original Oklahoma flag... currently adopted by Oklahoma Socialists" reported by Law Enforcement Today. They are turning to violence and riots.

They demand to defund the police and remove the police so they could freely do what they want. They are looting businesses and stores and they are burning churches and communities. They are shooting people from young children to seniors. They are now also armed with guns and weapons and they have become the threats and fears to so many Americans in various cities and states.

In the midst of those struggles, uncertainties, tragedies, and losses of lives, more Americans get to know the true face, the violence and the destructions caused by these Soviet-type socialists, the anarchists and the terrorists. More Americans start to realize the loss of their freedoms, human rights, properties and even lives when these socialist and radical members are to take over the U.S. and their lives.

President Trump, his administration and many patriots have been fighting hard against the plans and the plots of various groups of socialism, and the leftwing democratic leaders who tried to remove President Trump from the Oval office so they could take over and carry out their socialist agenda. But President Trump and the patriots would not let the mobs to destroy the U.S. and Americans.

Some local authorities are now taking actions to stop the violence, the riots and the destructions, yet governors and mayors in most of democratic states just let the mobs, the radicals, the anarchists, the terrorists and the violent socialists to ravage people, homes, towns and cities and their mainstream media even praise those riots, lootings, and destructions in the name of freedom and social justice.

The quick dismantle of CHAZ or CHOP and the violent protests in Seattle is a strong evidence that peace and order could be reestablished when the democratic leaders uphold the laws not lawlessness. Oklahoma Country District Attorney said, "When you act like a terrorist, you will be treated like a terrorist. This is not Seattle. We're not putting up with this lawlessness here" reported by Law Enforcement Today.

In the last three months since May 25, 2020, Americans and organizations must be extremely careful in using, saying or writing the phrase, "White Lives Matter" in the public places or in the press because the mobs, anti-white supremacy people and violent members of Black Lives Matter and Antifa could use any reason or anything to accuse people as racist or white supremacy.

They could use that phrase or business brands, advertisements and even statues of leaders that they interpret as white supremacy or slavery memories to threaten people, to attack people, to rob people, to humiliate people, to torture people, to shoot people and to murder people. This is the historic beginning of the oppression of the freedom of speech and of press in the U.S., the land of freedom.

People could freely say Black Lives Matter but when it comes to White Lives Matter or All Lives Matter, the freedom seems to be lost in places where the members of BLM or Antifa are attacking and destroying businesses, communities and churches. Some Americans lost their jobs because they protect their view and their lives that "White Lives Matter Too." So many people were hurt, wounded and murdered too.

This is the only oppressive freedom that the socialists could ever offer to people of the nations in the last one century of their existence though they have been promising Americans and people of the world the utopia freedom which is only available in dictionaries and their sweet talks. Unfortunately, so many people of the world and Americans are still falling into the socialists' empty promise.

Even though the socialist movement has been on the rise again in the recent years, they are now showing their nature of oppression, greed, power-oriented, and brutal killing. Americans could have been naïve earlier but this is the time for Americans to wake up from their socialist utopia and to protect America, Americans and their precious freedom and human rights that no socialist countries could ever offer.

In 2017, when the socialist authorities severely persecuted churches, an influential and Senior Pastor of a state mega-church voiced his disagreement about the demolition of the crosses and church buildings. Shortly after that, he was removed from the position as Senior Pastor. He was put under house arrest, surveillance, and then into prison in 2017 for misappropriation of a very small amount of funds.

Please take notice that he was charged with something different from what he wanted to say about the persecutions of churches and the leaders. This is what the socialist governments and leaders would do to those who did not follow the political direction and leadership. They would not charge people with things that are related to people's freedom and rights because that would hurt their images and promises.

But they know well how to use other reasons to charge disobedient people and in turn take away their rights and freedom. In socialist countries, regardless of how powerful one may be at the present, one's position, power and wealth may be gone overnight when he or she says something against the government even though what he or she said was true. Thus, freedom of full speech is impossible.

In fact, people only have freedom of half speech. The freedom of half speech means the citizens can freely speak anything good and great that the leaders did and do. The citizens can freely speak about the greatness and the glory of the political system. The citizens can freely speak about the efficiency and effectiveness of the government policies when those are not true. This half speech is highly encouraged.

In America, it is common that one may stand at the corner of a street, a park or a public square to speak freely for hours about the government leaders and the policies with "full speech." They can freely speak the other half-truth concerning the failures of the policies or the corruption of the leaders. The speaker sometimes may be mocked and ridiculed by the bystanders, but their arrest by the policemen is rare.

But that freedom of speech for Americans might be at loss and fallen into the hands of the Soviet-type socialists or the radicals, the terrorists or the leftwing democrats if Americans do not protect well their freedoms and rights. They are also using their powerful media to support their plans and to keep millions of Americans from the truth with their many fake news.

In socialist countries where we are from, there are many courageous Christians who still go from place to place, from house to house, from village to village to share the Gospel in the public. Most of them are doing so through personal evangelism and others are doing so publicly through preaching, literature distributions, prayer, music and all of them have to face the risks of torture, detention or prison.

These preachers did not preach against the government or the leaders or the political party. They preached about doing good. They preached about loving one another. They preached about living a moral life. They preached about forgiving one another. They preached about helping one another. But they were and are persecuted severely because the government does not welcome them to do so.

If you think that socialist countries give you freedom of speech, why don't you do this simple experiment by yourself; you will find out the truth immediately. Just go to North Korea or any socialist country nearby. Upon your arrival at the country, look for a local person who may speak English on a subway or a bus and talk to him or her openly about the protests, the failures of socialist reforms.

Ask about the trade war, the sanctions, the local issues of the economic situations, persecutions of the churches, the 100,000 million killed by the socialist leaders, the revolutions, and the injustices... What will be his or her response? If they are kind enough they would tell you that these topics are sensitive and they would not reply to your questions or just walk away for security sake.

If you are brave enough, you may find a public place you feel comfortable with, then talk publicly about what you think about those topics. What will happen to you? The level of punishment is depending on which socialist country you are at. You may be put into prison, you may be deported out of the country, you may be interrogated, or you may receive a warning before you are forced to leave the country.

I was deported from the country in 2017 and I have been away from home and the country since. When I came to the U.S. in 2018, friends and people with goodwill suggested that I should contact the U.S. Department of States or many other human right organizations to help me out so that my family and I could be united quickly after knowing why I was deported alone but, I chose to keep quiet and pray.

I chose that way because I understand the golden rule. Now you will understand more the reason why we were hesitated if we should write this book to let you know the reality of socialism. It is not our intention to say anything against or oppose any current leaders or government and we don't want to do that. It is safer to say socialism in general and the name of the country or people won't be mentioned.

For those who are curious as to why I was deported, I will speak to you, your organizations, or churches in person if you want to know more.

All I can tell you right now is that I do not violate any civil or criminal laws. I do not rob any bank or anyone. I hurt no one. I am neither a political activist nor a counter-revolutionist. I am neither a drug-addict nor a drug dealer. I am a Christian called to serve God.

I am a Pastor and a former university professor and I was being persecuted because of my Christian faith and my call to serve God. I was punished because I did not stop the mission works and mission trainings. I was interrogated because I did not close down the Bible Schools, Seminary, training centers for leadership, church planters and missionaries, evangelistic trips and crusades, revival and mission conferences...

Yes, those were and are the works that I had been doing and I am still doing though there are so many obstacles. There were many Pastors and leaders who were deported or ran away from the countries with religious reasons like me and it took them 7 to 21 years before their families were united. Others may never make it to see their family members again because they violated the golden rules.

They went abroad and they shared their stories on radio, television, and newspapers. This might be fine if they did not mention the names of the country, the name of the president, the leaders, the province, the city, and town. I am not saying that these leaders are wrong in doing so. Even I didn't mention any name of leaders or location but this book may still put my family and related people at risks.

I would not put cold water into their faces because the logic is quite simple. If Americans who talked against a socialist country and they may not be allowed to enter a socialist country because of what they said against the country, then the case would be more serious to a citizen and their family members who are still living in that socialist country. I hope they would understand my good intention!

For the sake of my family members and co-workers and ministry, there are still many challenging things that I had been experiencing for years, but I still cannot use that freedom of speech to share those experiences to you. Maybe I can do that in the far future when the situation is getting better. When? I don't know but maybe soon. My friends, is this the kind of socialist freedom you are passionately looking for?

But if America were to become a socialist country, then our families must move to another country if we still want to write more about socialism. But you might not need to read more stories like we share now because you would experience and understand more the meaning of limited freedom in socialist country then. You want to run to another free country, but it may too late for you then.

It might be difficult for people in the free world to accept the censoring and monitoring of the authorities because people in the free world are so used to the exercise of their human rights, freedom and privacy. But if socialism is to take over America, then it is certain that not only the freedom of press, or speech or traveling would be limited to you and the people of the Democratic Socialism of America.

We hope that you would treasure the great freedom and precious rights that you have here in the U.S. We could tell you that the freedom and rights that you are freely exercising here in the U.S. are the things that hundred millions of people in the socialist countries are longing for. They also long for the freedom to travel without being censored as Americans do have.

4th Commandment
"THOU SHALL NOT GO OUT OF THE FOLDS"
Freedom of Traveling

On the surface, it seems that people from socialist countries except people from North Korea, can travel freely around the world and that is allowed if people just go for holidays or vacations. Yet, when it comes to religion, human rights or politics, the traveling of those peoples and public servants are strictly monitored, censored and even forbidden especially travelling abroad or even domestically.

Many public servants today are not allowed to travel without the permission from the agencies they are working for. After their travel, the organizations where they are working would "help" them take good care of their passports. When they want to travel abroad, they must apply for a permit before the passports are released to them, and, they have to submit their passports to the leaders upon returning.

In 2019, a family member of mine was removed from the high position of a political leadership because my family member did not report to the organization that her child went to study abroad. It is still good that she is still allowed to work at the same organization with a lower role, but, she dare not ask permission to go abroad to visit her son now or else she would lose her job, benefits and everything.

She has to wait for years to do so. When? Who could tell about the political situation? Maybe when her child graduates and goes back home then they would see each other. Is this acceptable in the U.S? It does not sound right and humane, but, that is just a small thing in many socialist nations. Is this the freedom Americans want when America turns into a socialist country sometime in the near future?

There were so many meetings and conferences at home and abroad that the Pastors, leaders and believers tried different ways to attend to their spiritual edification. And they have had to use various reasons to explain to the local authorities upon their return so that they would not be punished; especially when they went to certain church or revival meetings that the government did not want them to attend.

In July 2017, thousands of leaders and believers were not allowed to go to an Expo Convention Center to attend the Send Out Conference that we organized. Thousands of the leaders received direct phone calls and warnings from the local policemen about the possible consequences if they went to the event. Top leaders were called to the local police stations to give information about the event.

They were told to stay home and even their co-workers and church members were not allowed to attend the event. A few days before the event, many leaders and my co-workers were stopped at the borders and they were not allowed to travel abroad since then. And days later, so many leaders and church workers were stopped at the border if they were suspected of going to the Send Out Conference.

Foreseeing the significant drop of the attendants, we quickly changed the arena to a conference hall in the same Expo Convention Center. Thank God, thousands of leaders, church workers and believers across the land still came to the event in the midst of the opposition and threats of the authorities. It showed the cries and passions of the Body of Christ for the salvation of the lost and the nation.

They came because they wanted to be part of the Great Commission to preach the Gospel to every corner of the world. They came at the call for world missions and the reaching of the nations. They came as they were called to be sent to the lands of the nations. They came because they were so hungry for the many things of God that they often experienced at this annual conference.

They came because they wanted to receive more teachings of God's Word, more passion for the lost, healing power, anointing, and manifestations of the Holy Spirit, which were so evident at the conference. They came even though they knew that there were many spies who were watching them and giving them hard times upon their return. They came to be empowered and challenged for missions.

They wanted to go and to attend event and place that they desired to go and to exercise their freedom of travelling but that freedom is not always appreciated and allowed where their lives were and are still being monitored by the socialist regime. People who are able to make it to other nations or the conference that we organized, they are not totally free from the monitoring of the Soviet-type socialists still.

There were so many spies that came our event and to stir up issues. They told the attendants that the purpose of the event was to go against the government so they better return home. They argued with the attendants about theologies, worship styles, speakers and they gave so many complaints to stir up the strife. Then, I asked the leaders who knew these spies and invited these spies to come for a meeting.

Then we spoke to them saying, "you already know us for many years and we never do anything against the government except what the Bible teaches us." Then we asked them to stop causing arguments and we assured them that we only prayed for the country and the leaders, and we only spoke well about the country as we have been doing that for years, and there was no words or content against the country.

We told them that we would do live stream so their leaders at home may watch the event and their leaders would not be worried about the potential riots that they thought would happen. We asked our co-workers to buy more than 30 phones and we immediately opened more than 30 different accounts to do live stream so that their leaders across the provinces may see what was happening at the conference.

After the first two days with so many arguments and strife, peace was restored and everything was great for the next 5 days of the event. These spies looked very happy and were more relaxed as each day went by. At the end of the event, they even came to congratulate us for the success of the event and they offered to help organize this conference next year. Of course, we welcomed them and said many thanks.

Maybe you are asking, "Why don't we just stop the spies from attending the event?" For years my co-workers and I always encountered the spies we knew, the spies we suspected and many spies we never knew. If we did not allow one to enter, there were still others inside our meeting anyway. If we made anyone of them upset, things only got worse when they gave a bad report about us to their leaders.

The main reason we were kind to them was not because we were afraid of them but we are called to love them and we are called to preach the Gospel to them as well. They were also sinners who needed God's grace and salvation. As they joined us in worship and listening to the Word of God, there would be more opportunities that they would be touched by God and their lives may be transformed forever.

This was also the case of Bishop Judah. He was sent to the seminary to study. When he was in the seminary, he was seen as a great student and a potential religious worker. After the graduation, he really dedicated his life to serve the church and the people. Then he was ordained and for years he was always among the top candidates to be elected for prominent position due to his character and dedication.

Just like so many church leaders who went through great persecutions, Judah was also arrested and imprisoned. He was also beaten and tortured and when he could not bear the tortures, he talked to the authorities that he was also one of the socialist members and that he was sent to church to serve as undercover agent. The authorities asked who was his superior and they checked the information.

But the authorities could not find his superior according to the information that Judah provided, so they thought that he cheated them and they tortured him more because of his lies and deception. He asked the authorities to contacted his superior again, but they could not find his superior. The authorities thought Judah fooled them and as the result, Judah was incarcerated for almost 20 years in labor camps.

He suffered all the hardships, hard labors, sufferings, mistreatments, and poverties as millions of prisoners went through in those days. At last he was released from horrible incarceration and hard labors. He was greatly welcome to the church, loved and praised by leaders and believers for his strong faith through years of sufferings and persecutions because people did not know his real identity yet.

Judah was then appointed as Bishop and he continued to serve for many years in that position. Bishop Judah was really loved by people because of his faith, his faithful service and his life. No one knew his struggles, his shames and his guilt for many years. When he was about to die, he shared the truth to a church leader who was the granduncle of my in-laws. He shared his true identity as a spy.

He said that he already abandoned that identity in prison and he decided to serve God if he was still alive or when he was released from prison and he did keep that promise. Yet, he dared not share his secret to anyone because he was afraid that church leaders and members may reject him and they would consider him as a traitor and that would be the end of his ministry.

Out of anguish, he asked his leader if God would forgive him and if the leaders and church members could accept him. Our granduncle quoted him a Scripture in I John 1:9, "If we confess our sins, he is faithful and just and will forgive us our sins and purify us from all unrighteousness." Shortly after that Bishop Judah passed away peacefully and he still gained the respects and love of so many believers.

We would never know that many spies might come to the Lord when we are kind and take opportunities to share the Gospel and God's love to them. Though they are spies or undercover agents, they are still human beings and sinners who need God's love and God's grace. I could also see the great changes in the lives of the authorities that I regularly had "teatimes" with them weekly and sharing God's words to them.

Besides, we did not do anything wrong and we just preach about God and the good we are supposed to do to save lives, edify people and to restore broken lives so we should not be afraid of their presence. This does not mean that we were careless with our words and plans, but we refused to let the fear to govern us and to trust God or else we could hardly share the Gospel in the Gospel-restricted countries.

Importantly, by nature, the socialists were very insecure as we often mentioned. So we prayed hard and we tried to let them know that our hearts are pure and we are only serving God and people, and, Christians always love the country, so that they may treat us better. Yet it is really hard to know what the socialists think and what are they going to do to us regardless of how kind and sincere we are.

In saying so, we do not mean that the principle we applied here may be applicable to all situations in socialist countries and Gospel-restricted countries. This may never happen because every forest has its own tiger, and different places have their ways. There is almost no right or wrong approach here in the unpredictable nations of the socialists. We need to be sensitive to the leading of the Holy Spirit for every move.

For example, one day, Aunty Hannah, our prayer coworker went to the park and shared the Gospel to the people in the park. The policemen came and stopped her from sharing the Gospel. She kept on preaching the Gospel to these policemen telling them to repent and accept the Lord Jesus Christ. As she did not listen to their command, they arrested her and escorted her to a very big police station.

She kept speaking to them about the Lord Jesus and how God transformed and healed so many lives as they were on the car going to the police station. She was then escorted to an interrogation room. The policemen asked her to sit down on the chair that was designated for the convicted or suspected criminal and the leader sat down in the chair designated for the judge.

At that moment, she immediately spoke to that police leader and she commanded him, "stand up and sit on this side." All the policemen were puzzled and really did not understand why she said that, so, they explained to her that this seat of the suspected people and the criminals was for her because she was committing crimes and the other seat was for the authority to judge her case.

She boldly said, "I do nothing wrong and I am not a criminal. I am a child a God who was forgiven from all sins. You are the sinners who need God's forgiveness and mercy." Then she talked to them how Adam and Eva committed sins against God and then sins entered the world and human beings were controlled by sins and Satan and human beings were separated from God.

She continued to say, "I am no longer a sinner. God changed my life and I am doing the good things for people, but, you are the sinner and rebellious against God and you must sit at this chair. I will sit at the other chair and I will tell you how your sins are to be forgiven." At the power of her word, the police official just stood up and gave her his seat as he sat down in the chair that they had planned for her to sit on.

She sat down at his seat and she began to preach the words of God and how sinful people were. She preached about the Creation and the Fall. Whatever they asked her she answered quickly and kept on preaching. They asked her to stop talking about religion but she kept on preaching about God's plan for salvation and the Cross and the Resurrection. She talked about God's love and men's response for salvation.

The policemen could bear no longer her preaching and they begged her to stop but she kept on preaching until late in the afternoon. At last, they gave up on her and they decided to release her and then asked her to go home. She said, "I'm not a criminal, you took me here by car so you have to take me home." They knew that she was not joking so they drove her home as she continued to share many more stories.

I forgot to ask her then if she gave those policemen an altar call. If she gave an altar call at that time they may also had prayed the sinners' prayer. Her approach worked in that situation as God was leading her to do so, but it may not work in another situation. But one thing that never goes wrong is that Christians should not be ashamed of the Gospel because it is God's power to save the lost and transform lives.

The Apostle Paul said we have to preach the Gospel whether it is in season or out of season and because anyone who calls upon the name of the Lord will be saved. People will not call on God if they do not believe in Him. They would not believe in Him if they do not hear about him. They cannot hear about him if no one preaches the Gospel to them. Let us be bold to preach the Word of God in all situations.

Dear American friends and people of nations, please treasure the freedoms you have in your nations. In the U.S, you may go anywhere you want to with your freedom of travel. Do not take for granted what you have and remember that the founders of the U.S., God-and-Bible believing people, had risked their lives to sail across the Atlantic Ocean and to make this freedom of travel available to you all today.

But that freedom of travel is limited to many people in nations. Religious people are limited to go to churches and religious events. Policemen and the security members even stood in front of the houses or the residential areas of many Christians and stopped them from going to churches on Friday nights or Sundays. Christians are strongly persecuted when they go out and share the Gospel in the public place.

So many Christians, pastors and leaders were and are still under arrests or surveillances because they want to exercise their religious freedom by going to different places to disciple believers or to train mission workers. They are also persecuted and monitored when they go to small groups, discipleship training, Bible study groups or prayer groups or Bible schools.

In socialist countries, for sure, Pastors and leaders from the state churches must have permission from the government if they ever plan to travel abroad for a conference, a Christian event, or even for a holiday. It is still easier for house church leaders and Pastors to travel abroad because the records at the Customs and Borders may not show their identity as religious workers or Pastors.

But there are still so many pastors and leaders who are not allowed to have a passport. If they got the passports earlier, they may be asked to submit their passports back to the authorities. Many others apply for their passports but there is no definite answer as to when they are going to receive it. Currently, the freedom to travel is getting harder for Pastors and leaders and they are restricted to do so.

If they are criminals or suspected criminals, it is understandable that their travels would be under restriction or monitored. If it was for top security reasons, it is acceptable that they are not allowed to go to certain places. Yet, these Pastors, leaders and believers are the good citizens and good people. They wanted to go to places where they could freely worship God, but Pharaoh did not let them go.

In socialist countries the majority of the Pastors and leaders prefer to go around by transportations owned by private owners, motorcycles or cars so that they do not have to register their identification when they purchase tickets to avoid being followed by the policemen. In case we have to travel by airplanes or fast trains due to the long distance, we often purchase the tickets on spot.

Though the ticket is so expensive in that case, yet for the security of everyone, that is one of the prices we have to pay. Even so, intelligent agent of the government is very good in finding out quickly where we are going. There were times when I purchased the tickets a few days earlier due to peak seasons; my "weekly-meeting friends" called me one day ahead of time to kindly warn me not to go to the next day's event.

If you would like to have "invisible secretaries" to tell you if you are allowed to go certain meetings, welcome to socialism! If you are human rights workers, religious workers, freedom fighters and political activists of a political party that is different from socialist ideology, or the hosts of those areas on media, your talks and your movements would be strictly monitored by the socialist government for sure.

In most of our travel for leadership or mission training or mission mobilization, we would take a bus first and stop at a certain station where our co-workers would pick us up from as we communicated the location on the way. We drove to the city or town where the training was to be done. Upon arriving at the place, we would get into another car, which the local friend would use to take us to the location.

Some may ask, "why don't they just give you the address and then you can go directly to the place?" Yes, an address with directions is a must in the free worlds but that poses more risks to everyone here when the address is given through text. The policemen would find out the meeting place immediately. The place of meeting must be kept in secret and would be changed in seconds for the sake of security.

So, how did people or the invited leaders get to the meeting place? A few local leaders would be responsible for picking up the leaders who were invited to the meeting place. Even though we knew well who was coming and the new coming leaders were also invited by leaders who knew them well, we never knew which leader could possibly be a spy. So upon their arrival, all phones were collected.

Once they were brought to the venue, no one was allowed to go out of the training place until the training or the meeting was over. All the collected phones were put in different places to avoid the situation where the venue was being detected through phone signals. If any leader who had some urgent needs to buy something, we had people to take care of their needs. Does this sound like detective movies?

I still remembered before I was deported out of the country, the situations were so tight, yet, we still needed to make some important visits to arrange for the up-coming 'Send Out Conference' on July, 2017 for thousands of leaders as mentioned earlier. Our plan was that every city would partner with one country of the world for world missions and we needed to meet many more leaders to carry out the plan.

It was impossible for me to go by any public transportation because my travel documents were kept by the securities and I was under radar, so, my co-workers and I drove almost non-stop for 5000 kilometers or about 3100 miles across many provinces within a week to meet many leaders that we needed. We only stopped for the meetings mostly at local restaurants for safety and to refill our hungry stomachs.

To avoid unnecessary security issues to local leaders and to save time, we did not sleep at their places. We took turns to drive and slept in the cars. And, I had to reach home on Thursday for the weekly "tea time" that had been going on since 2012. These things are still happening now in socialist countries as you are reading these words. Want to try your freedom of travelling there? You are most welcome.

In responding to God's call for churches in the socialist nations to reach the goal of 20 percent of the population to come to know the Lord Jesus Christ as their Lord and Savior and to send out missionaries to the nations to preach the Gospel, and to bless the nations, church leaders were and are still being strictly monitored by the socialist authorities because the authorities does not want those goals to be realized.

At that call for revival and world missions, the churches and leaders became very active to secretly prepare and mobilize churches to accomplish the Great Commission. To carry out the plan effectively and feasibly, every city was assigned to form a world mission team and every city would train and send out 20 missionaries. Every city would pray and partner with one country for missions.

For local missions, we also did similar things of forming mission teams and sending out church planters in many provinces. Basically, our ministries already connected many cities in the country for world missions and many cities had been praying for the country they wanted to partner with. The plan was working and the vision was well received as leaders and churches had been praying to take action for it.

We started bringing mission teams to more than 20 nations and organized crusades, conferences, charities, mission exposures or networking. Supposedly, we could have connected home church leaders from all cities of a socialist country by 2018 and city leaders of a few more nearby socialist countries by 2020. But, just like the freedom of travel may be obstructed and have twists and turns and so it is with vision 20%.

But neither strict surveillances could stop the movements nor severe persecutions could hinder the growth. As deep waters naturally keep running under grounds in the midst of the storms and earthquakes, the underground church movements and the vision for church revival and world missions keep moving with the supernatural power and manifestations in the midst of oppressions and persecutions.

Many foreigners often asked, "Can we come and minister to your students in the Bible Schools or leaders if possible? And is it safe?" Yes, as the saying goes, "where there is a will, there is a way." The opportunities to do outreach and mission works in socialist countries are plenty. One thing we cannot do is to promise security to anyone. That is beyond our control as we said earlier.

If you dare to trust God together with us for safety then you are most welcome here. If you come to teach at our underground Bible School, my co-workers will take you to the Bible School or the leadership training location at night with a cap on to avoid the attention of the neighbors and the authorities. Then, you will stay inside for a few days or a week to teach until you finished teaching and we take you out at night again.

It is easier with home fellowship so you are most welcome to minister to people through your teaching, discipleship training, songs or testimonies in Bible study groups, prayer meetings, or worship. If "unexpected friends" come for "a special visit," we would quickly change the meeting into a dinner fellowship or a birthday party, or anniversary celebrations or welcoming party or whatever available.

For those who are interested in charity works, it is even easier to do charity works in socialist nations as doors are still open and there are still more freedom to travel to do these humanitarian works in the countryside or in the mountainous areas. Teams, organizations and individuals are welcome to do wheelchair outreach, clean water outreach, building of Gospel bridges, gift distributions, livelihood projects...

Want to Try? You are most welcome. If you could not come, you are most welcome to partner with our organization to makes vision 20% a reality in socialist countries. We are requesting each of the 2,000 churches, organizations, companies or sponsors to support one church planter so that the Gospel-restricted countries would be transformed and saved as the Gospel is being preached. Will you say Yes?

If you are not able financially, kindly pray and help connect Global Missions Vision to your churches, your pastors, your friends or business owners who you know that they would be able to support Global Missions Vision to bring hope and freedom in Jesus Christ to the millions of the thirsty souls whose lives could only be better when they experience the love, the salvation and the breakthrough in Christ Jesus.

In recent months, a socialist government made use of coronavirus situation to especially stop believers from going to churches as the persecutions are becoming more severe. Church services on zoom or social media are also being monitored and interrupted by the authorities. State-churches are totally under the control of the government and the government tries hard to crack down the house churches.

Yet, millions of believers are still faithful to meet together for church services, prayers, and Bible studies in small groups even though this is extremely difficult during the lockdowns, quarantines and severe persecutions. The majority of the believers would have small groups, ministries and outreach at homes or through zoom, phone calls or other social media available.

Since March 2020, businesses, services and church gatherings have been seriously affected by the coronavirus pandemic in the U.S. The anti-church and anti-God leaders also try to manipulate the pandemic to stop churches from conducting services and believers from going to churches or places of worship. Church service is declared to be non-essential service and it is required to be closed.

While coronavirus pandemic is still spreading, the ungodly leaders once again took the advantage of the death of George Floyd to mobilize people for protests and demonstrations that led to riots, violence and lootings that have been damaging so many businesses, communities, policemen and people. The rioters even destroyed churches and burnt churches to scare believers from going to churches.

Robert Spencer on Jihad Watch reported many cases of churches such as St. Patrick's Cathedral or St. Paul's Episcopal Church and synagogues such as the Reform Jewish Congregation or Congregation Beth Israel and others that were sprayed with graffiti, defaced with obscenities, destroyed or burnt including the famous St. John's Episcopal Church, known as the Church of the U.S President.

Many Americans may now feel insecure to travel recently due to the recent protests, riots, unrests, lootings and killing that have been taking place in hundreds of cities over the death of George Floyd. The freedom of travel of millions of Americans is now at great risk because many politicians and terrorist groups are trying to manipulate the situations to create chaos and to take over the U.S. by forces.

The protesters and rioters stopped cars on the highways, business areas. They beat and hurt innocent people on the streets and business areas. They spread fears among the people with their violence, lootings and crimes. Many cities and streets are now unsafe at the absence of policemen and security task forces. The protesters freely broke stores and businesses, and enter homes to rob and to hurt people.

The leftist politicians, the terrorist groups and the deep state are working together to create lawlessness situation in the name of freedom. Yet that is how they could claim places and they want to establish a new country or at least new leadership. Many Americans are so innocent now and they would not realize that they would loose their freedom and rights when the militants and the anarchists are in power.

While mainstream media hailed the activists for the establishment of CHAZ or CHOP in Seattle where the activists surrounded the Capitol Hill neighborhood, set up barricades, and sprayed graffiti on businesses and local communities, the residents were terrified and insecure at the absence of policemen and task forces but the presence of the armed guards of the far-left groups and anarchists.

As the results of the hailing of lawlessness and militancy over laws and orders, violence broke out, shops were looted, businesses were smashed, cars were crashed, rapes increased, and innocent people were hurt. Only the anarchists, the terrorists and the political leaders were happy as they thought that they won but the people were always the victims of the political and power games of the few leaders.

It is called the Free Capital Hill and the people are free from the policemen, security protection, laws and orders to do whatever they want. How long that freedom would last with the lawbreakers and militants? People thought they are free now yet it is the beginning of new bondages and brutal oppressions as people in the socialist nations experienced after the successes of the political revolution for freedom.

The fact that no mosque was affected by the riots is a clear indication that the rioters are anti-Christian, anti-Church and anti-Christ people. The leaders of Black Lives Matters revealed that they are trained Marxists and they are carrying out Marxist movement. As Marxists, they are going after schools, families, communities, churches, and Christians as this happened in many socialist nations.

If American believers and patriots are not willing to stand up to protect their freedom, many precious rights, their freedom to exercise those rights might be taken away from Americans by the Soviet-type socialists, terrorists and anarchists soon. It is the great time and the right time to stand with President Trump and the conservatives to protect the U.S and Americans from the socialist disasters.

By the way, if you are still planning to make socialism a reality in America, make sure that you better make your travelling plans now to go to places that you really want to visit first, because, you never know when you would be able to travel freely one day in the near future. Are you ready for more limited freedom? How about the freedom of trial by jury? Is it really going to work in socialist nations?

If socialism ever became a reality in the U.S., Americans better took time to adjust to the new government and the limited freedoms provided by the DSA when Americans' freedom and rights were no longer available because their freedom of trials by jury could never be their right any longer but it was the right of the socialist leaders to make the trials of Americans' life available and real.

5th Commandment
"THOU SHALL NOT NEED TRIALS BY JURY"
Freedom of Trial by Jury

Rev. Dr. Paul, my spiritual father and mentor, was put in prison for almost 10 years because of his faith in God. He was one of the founding members and Pastors that God used to bring about the home church movements and the revival. Through his ministry, hundreds of churches were planted and thousands of leaders were trained. He was behind bars of one prison to another. Did he really have trial by jury?

In most cases, there was not even the need to talk about that because trial by jury was just a show, if it did happen at all. The freedom of trial by jury was more applicable to the political leaders and powerful people so that their charges would be reduced every time they made an appeal, but, for the common people, human right workers and religious leaders, the charge would become heavier every time.

It may seem odd and weird to you, as you may be able to find some good advice on YouTube on how to prepare oneself for a sudden imprisonment, and, what are the things one must have as his or her belongings if one day someone was suddenly arrested and put into prison. These were the special advises and experiences of people who suffered the injustices of socialist countries.

Dr. Paul testified that he was arrested so often in a socialist country that wherever he went or even when he slept at home, he always had a ready bag beside his bed. When the policemen entered his home and took him away, he just needed to get that bag, which was filled with a mosquito net, toothpaste and toothbrush, tower, suitable clothes and a blanket for prison... Got yourself a bag when socialism come?

You may promptly react, "that is not legal and policemen cannot just take people away like that without a warrant or without the freedom of trial by jury." Remember what we often said, that, you are living in a free world and so many people are not living in a free world though the socialists often said so. If we were against them, they would charge us more severely. They are the law and they are above the law.

Americans are mostly well protected by the legal system and they are so used to many freedoms with little interferences from the government. Many Americans will hardly accept or understand the ways things are especially in socialist nations or regimes. If American millennials could really understand the real meaning of big government, they would understand better how things work in those regimes.

Many millennials often identify the role of big government with many free benefits for the people. They simply understand it as the government control of the modes of productions and the means of distribution so that the rich would not become so rich and the poor would not be exploited much. But what they may not see is that if the government has much power to control the rich, then, they could do so to the poor.

They may not see that if the government has so much power to get even the wealth of the rich then the government could easily get more things from the poor. They may not see that if the government has so much power over the people then people will definitely lose their power. They may not see that if the government has so much power, the government no longer needs to listen to the voices of the people.

They may not see that if the government has so much power, then, the leaders will begin to manipulate or abuse the power. This is human nature. They may not see that if the government has so much power to control, the leaders will begin to corrupt, and as they corrupt they must use power to protect themselves. This explains why big government soon turns a country into a regime or tyranny.

Then the people must listen to their commands. Then the people will lose their freedoms. Then the people will be abused, exploited and people will become the victims of the big government. This explains the reason why the freedom of trials by jury is really needed or if it really works for the people in socialist nations or regimes where big government controls every aspect of life.

When the 14 leaders in our networks disappeared on February 14, 2018, and I would be among them if I were there, did they have that right of trial by Jury or Grand Jury? I am sure you know the answers. Do you still want that "freedom?" Can Americans bear this limited freedom if America were to become a socialist country? Please do not take for granted the great freedom you have in the U.S. now.

Family members do not know where they are and if they are still alive at the moment. No one knows how they were taken away or who took them. No friend knows if they travel somewhere else. The 14 co-workers do not have the last chance to meet their family members. They are the servants of God and they just want to freely worship God and serve Him, yet, the socialists took away their freedom.

If I were still there in the country, the number of disappeared people would be increased to 15 because I was also among those prominent leaders. If people do not have freedom to protect themselves and their lives from the cruel socialists how is it possible that the jury or the justice system would defend and protect them when the jury and judges must follow the command of the socialist leaders?

In the West, even suspected criminals could refuse to speak to the authorities until their lawyers come and their rights are well protected. In many socialist countries, if the suspected or even the innocent people do not answer, the authorities know well how to make these people to speak according to what the authorities want them to say after series of horrible tortures.

Personally, we believe that President Trump, his Administration and many Americans knew the lies, the deceptions and the nightmares of socialism, which has happened to so many countries of the world, so, therefore, he fought hard to keep socialism from becoming a reality. Yet, many Americans are still so blinded by the well promises of Sen. Bernie Sanders and the socialists that they even opposed him.

President Trump makes sure that as long as he is still the President of the United States, he will not allow socialism to become a reality.

The leftists, the liberals and the socialists cannot bear the fact that their beautiful dream is to be broken because of this strong incumbent President Trump. So, they have been trying to find ways to remove him from Day 1 of his office as the 45th President of the United States.

Remember that President Trump cannot fight for you alone all the time. You need to stand together with him to fight against the corrupted leaders and the disastrous ideology of socialism. His heart is "America First." Yes, he is fighting for the well-being and the security of Americans first while many politicians just want to fight for their ideology and political gains with their unrealistic promises.

It was not long ago, Paul, a Christian lawyer was determined to defend religious freedom in his region as he witnessed Pastors and believers being persecuted and put into prison without justices. He also saw many church buildings demolished. So he took actions to seek justice for the persecuted people. He was given warnings by the government but he thought he would be ok with his many connections.

He kept on defending for the people of faith arguing for religious freedom for the country and quoting religious laws. He went around the country and churches to train leaders and believers on how to quote religious laws and how to answer the policemen or the authorities whenever they confronted the threats of religious persecutions and potential imprisonment.

Things went very well and the prospect seemed to be great and his training was really helpful. Suddenly, he was arrested and he was put into prison without warrant or any trial. He protested. Do you think that will work in socialist nations? People may protest but unfortunately they have no power to protest because the government is so powerful for even lawyers like him to do so.

He may recite all the laws and articles about religious freedom and his rights, yet in a regime, the law is defined by the people with power not by the people without power. He could use all of his logic, knowledge and experiences to argue with the authorities, yet in a regime, the fate of the people is dictated by the authorities not by the powerless people who already gave away their power to the government.

With all of his connections as a lawyer, he could not find a lawyer to defend him. In fact, there was no lawyer who was willing to defend him or on his behalf because that lawyer would also face punishments. After a few months of torture and imprisonment, he was released. Upon his release, he was no longer the same lawyer who was passionate to defend for religious freedom and for the people of faith.

When he was released, many leaders and believers came and visited him. Everyone could see that he was physically tortured and people could clearly see the signs of torture on his arms and face. But he said nothing about that or acknowledged that. His silence alone was already a confirmation that he was beaten and if he was not willing to talk about that then people would not ask anymore.

But they all understood him. They understood that he was forbidden to say anything about that. They understood that if he talked about those things he could receive more severe punishments. They understood that he was now under the watch of the authorities. They understood that they should leave the matter as it is. That was a sensitive issue and people did not want to talk much when the time was not ready.

They understood those things because they also went through many threats, warnings, tortures and persecutions like he did. They understood those things would happen to him because they already told him earlier that the legal system in socialist countries could never allow him or anyone else to fight for freedom or justices especially for political freedom or religious freedom or human rights.

After he was released from prison, he posted many writings to apologize to the government for the wrongs he did and that he misinterpreted the laws. If he did not do that, his "sins" would not be removed by the socialists and he may lose his job and even his title, and, his days would never be easy again or in most of the cases, he would be incarcerated again if he did not "repent" of his wrongdoings.

His short imprisonment was just a kind warning of what he can and cannot do in socialist nations with big government. That imprisonment or torture was enough for him to understand there were always consequences when freedom was not applied properly in socialist countries. Of course, he never dared to conduct any training on religious freedom again ever since he was released from prison.

Sometimes we were invited abroad to speak at a conference or a church and the secretary kept on asking us to give an update on our travelling schedule, biography and ministry in writing. We tried to provide some general information as much as we could, but they needed more information. In our situation, the less we talked about the ministry matter on email or phone, the safer it was for us.

When organizations from abroad support mission works financially, they need detailed financial reports with all the names and information for book keeping purposes, auditing and transparency. They needed many stories, pictures, testimonies and explanations in writing so that they could share to church members making their bulletins and using stories and pictures for fund raisings.

What they require is a must in the free world because church members and donors may not support their ministry if they do not see and feel the missions they are a part of. Yet, in socialist countries, the government may use those pictures and reports to go against and charging people on related crimes. The case becomes more serious whenever there is an involvement of foreigners.

Thus, in most cases, the home churches and the leaders are very reluctant to provide much information, as they prefer to speak in person. It is not because they are not transparent on the financial matter, or that the ministry or mission projects are not doing well. It's just that they are in a very different setting, and they just have different ways of doing things or else they may be in prison for years or for life.

In our ministry for example, we had a financial team and the financial team members met weekly to make report. Each one was in charge of a certain financial aspect and they came together to audit all the financial matters on a monthly basis. After that, they would destroy all the documents of the month because the documents could be used against us if found by unfriendly people.

In the free world, this is not acceptable because our way is different from what people are doing in the free nations where documents must be kept for years and auditing would be done annually. The religious gatherings and offerings in the free world are legal but that is not so in our world. Remember, my co-workers and we were facing persecutions daily in our Christian life and missions.

Yet, there are still many things that the home churches do that are different from the West. They often move the Sunday services from house to house. They save church offerings under personal account. They would not report finances publicly. They would rarely send church activities or plans through email list. They purchased lots to build church building or apartments for church services under personal name.

This is because most of the house churches are not recognized by the government. All of those practices are many more things are not the same and are not even acceptable in the Western world. Yet, if the house churches would operate according to the way of the Western, the world could hardly hear about the significant growth, courage and passions of the house church movements and the members.

With the scale of ministry and the mission mobilization that we did and we have been doing, our coworkers and we were the targets of persecution all the times. We were and are still the major attention of persecutions so we had to be very cautious. Besides, every week we had to go for the regular "tea time." If the documents were found, we would be in bad shape, so we had to destroy them after auditing.

While many partners understand us and have been very supportive of our missions and the system that we have, unfortunately, there were people who were so afraid to do anything, yet, they refused to understand our situation. So we tried to explain a bit on this so that you may know what to do and try to understand the situations if you are helping Gospel-restricted countries with similar cases like ours.

Every time I was arrested or my coworkers and pastors were arrested, the first thing the policemen would get from us was the phones and the personal computer and they also tried to check thoroughly personal computers and the computers of the churches and they also searched the church venues for certain documents. What were they looking for? They looked for contact list and financial documents.

The authorities would not usually charge pastors or believers with illegal religious gatherings, they often charge them with financial issues because they consider church offerings as public fund raising and it is illegal for house churches to do public fund raising. Last year, a senior Pastor was charged with nine years in prison because the authorities said he misused a few thousand US. dollar from his church.

Of course, the Pastor did not misused or got church money, and it was such a ridiculous thing to sentence someone nine years in prison with the false charge but the authorities just used this excuse to incarcerate him because he and his church refused to stop church services and they kept on meeting in small groups. Any jury could help this pastor in this socialist country? Which jury dares to do so?

When I was deported in 2017, the policemen, security officials and immigrant officers took me to different departments and places to process the documents needed for my deportation. I told them that I wanted lawyers, I wanted juries, I wanted... but my voice would not be heard. They told me that was useless as no one could help. That is all I can say now because that is the most of my freedom now.

For the many years, I had to go for the weekly "tea times," should I have asked a lawyer to defend my rights not to go and meet the authorities? When big government with big power is in control, the people would have no choice but to obey, and, even if they call for lawyers, what lawyer would dare to go against the government or what lawyer had the power to change the government's command?

It is a must that people obey the command of the authorities. If not, the people would be charged with more severe crimes because the authorities have that power to do so. So when they came to arrest me without any warrant, I could do nothing else because they used forces and power to do so. This also explains the limited human rights when big government is in control in the next chapter.

O, we forgot to remind you that people have no freedom to obtain jury trials here, but the socialists have all the freedom to put people on trials. They will put you on trials for your disloyalty to the political party. They will put you on trials for your human rights. They will put you on trials for your faith. They will put you on trials for your humiliations, injustices, suffering... Want to try your free trials?

Wikipedia on Human Rights In The Soviet Union reminded everyone that the socialists "regarded law as an arm of politics and courts as agencies of the government. Extensive extra-judiciary powers were given to the Soviet secret police agencies. The regime abolished Western rule of law, civil liberties, protection of law and guarantees of property." So what rights do the people have? Just a little.

So remember to keep your power by maintaining small government, then Americans still have the power to elect their representatives to express the desires of the people. Do not listen to the socialists and the leftwing democrats to vote for the big government in America so that you will still have freedom of trials by jury and human rights as you shall see in the next chapter about human rights.

6th Commandments
"THOU SHALL HAVE NO ADEQUATE RIGHTS"
Human Rights

Wikipedia stated that, "According to Universal Declaration of Human Rights, human rights are the "basic rights and freedoms to which all humans are entitled," including the right to life and liberty, freedom of expression, and equality before the law; and social, cultural and economic rights, including the right to participate in culture, the right to food, the right to work, and the right to education."

Wikipedia also reported that, "Human rights in the Soviet Union were severely limited and for most of its existence the population was mobilized in support of the single State ideology and the policies promoted by the Communist Party... only one political party was permitted in the Union of Soviet Socialist Republics (USSR) and the members of the Communist Party held all key positions, whether in the State itself or in other organizations."

"Freedom of speech was suppressed and dissent was punished. Independent political activities were not tolerated, whether these involved participation in free labour unions, private corporations, independent churches or opposition political parties... According to the Soviet legal theory, it is the government who is the beneficiary of human rights which are to be asserted against the individual."

Do these violations of human rights and freedom only happen in the former USSR? Due to its nature of the big government, the violations of human rights are all obvious and evident in all socialist nations. When the power is not shared by the people and it is only for the exclusive authoritarian groups of people, it is not a surprise to see that the rights of people outside the group will be manipulated.

Lily and her husband wanted to have one more child for many years. Yet she could not conceive even though they tried so many times. They went to medical doctors and sought the doctors' advices. They did and followed everything that various doctors and friends told them to do in their desperation to have another baby. The doctors never tell them the reason why her conception was not possible again.

Later they moved to the U.S. and then she started to feel pain in her abdomen so she went for a check-up but they could not find the reason for her pain. As time went by, the pain increased and was too hard to bear so she went for a CT scan. There the doctors said she must go for an urgent operation to remove something. Only then, she found out why she had that pain and why she wasn't able to conceive.

When she gave birth to her son almost 15 years ago through C-section, the doctor put a sterilized ring in her womb to avoid pregnancy without her consent and she did not even know that this happened to her as the country wanted to limit the number of births. After many years, the ring deteriorated and it caused an infection and, she learned another traumatic lesson about human rights in a socialist country.

You may make excuses for socialism by saying that this is just a rare case. Yes, you are right it is a rare case, because, those stories are not being heard and so many women died without knowing the truth. Millions of mothers were deprived of their rights and they could not do anything except to accept the reality, because, when the order came from the top leaders, who dared to go against the will of the leaders.

Millions of pregnant ladies were forced to abort babies against their will when they were found pregnant. There were many cases that the families tried to hide the authorities about the pregnancy. Yet due to certain sickness, pregnant ladies must go to the hospital for treatments

A.Y Ph.D. and S.Y Ph.D.

and they were brought to the labor room and were forced to abort the babies even in their sixth or seventh month of pregnancy.

Public servants would pay fine and loose jobs if they did not comply with the order. Children who were born without the given permits from the local authorities would not be given identification and they were not allowed to enter public schools for education. Their parents must pay fine or they would bribe the local authorities to get the identification number for their children so their children could have identity.

If Planned Parenthood in the U.S aborted more than 61 million unborn babies, this number was in no way to be compared with the number of unborn babies aborted in certain socialist countries. In the U.S. many democrat leaders and Planned Parenthood encourage pregnant ladies to exercise their human rights and body right to abort unborn babies by using money of taxpayers for abortion expenses.

Many Catholic nuns and lady pastors or lady evangelists were arrested for sharing their faith. It was already sad that their freedoms was lost and it was more painful when their dignity was also lost because the policemen raped some of them in the remote areas. Others were raped by prisoners in prisons or detention centers. A few were raped by mental people as arranged by the authorities.

When Grace refused to deny her faith in God and her ministry. She was locked in a small room with a strong man who had mental issue. The local authorities wanted to destroy her dignity and her faith as they expect the man would rape her to satisfy his sexual needs. Grace was scared to be put together with a stranger who could destroy her virginity, her ministry, her commitment to God and her life.

Grace prayed fervently to God for His protection as she was locked in that room. Then she talked to the man that she was devoted to God and he could not touch her or defy her. Amazingly, this man just listened to her and he never touched her or hurt her even though they were together in the same room and they were sleeping on the same bed for a long time.

After sometimes, the authorities thought that Grace and the man already slept together and Grace was forced to live with that man. For years, Grace pretended to live as a wife in the same house to avoid the persecution and that man never insulted or assaulted her even once. Grace went back to church to serve after more than a decade of humiliation and losses of her freedom and rights.

So many civilians too were also raped, yet their cases were never brought into justices and justices never returned to them. Their voices could not be heard by the cruelties and oppression of the heartless socialists who only cared about their power and evil desires. So many citizens were arrested and beaten as they went on strikes against the many injustices and corruptions of the local authorities.

In recent years, thanking to the widespread of Wi-Fi and social media, there so many recorded videos posted on social media and blogs to show the ruthless oppressions and exploitations of policemen to common people. Policemen brutally beat people because the policemen want to revenge, or they are in bad mood, or they are drunk, or they want people to bribe them.

When people demonstrate peacefully but they were imprisoned and tortured to death in prison and detention centers but their deaths were reported as the causes of sickness. The autopsy showed evidences of severe physical abuses but their cases remained silence. Civic groups were raid, on-line conversations and phone data were strictly monitored, and thousands of lives were arrested.

Sam Meredith reported on CNBC that, "The world witnesses a shocking rollback of human rights last year, according to Amnesty International's latest annual report, with signs of regression across the globe... Leaders have pushed hate, fought against rights, ignored crimes against humanity and blithely let inequality and suffering spin out of control."

Sam Meredith reported the words of Amnesty's State of the World's Human Rights report in 159 countries that, "a broad clampdown on human rights had created a more dangerous world... Venezuelan President Nicolas Maduro has been widely condemned for overseeing one of the worst human rights crises in the country's history" with widespread food shortages, hyperinflation, and unemployment...

The political leaders in socialist countries often say that they are the servants of the people and they always say that everywhere they go, yet the reality is so far from their words. Indeed, the people are the real servants of the political leaders and the slaves of the political ideology. People know that now, but fighting against the government is not possible yet, and it is just like throwing eggs at huge rocks.

Though there were many demonstrations that had taken place to fight for human rights but the rights of the people were already given to the "servants of the socialist countries so the "servants of the country" are so powerful to be defeated when all powers, wealth and the armies are in their hands. The "owners of the country" or the people became the sufferers and victims with the lost of their rights at the end.

As we have discussed so far people in socialist countries have limited freedom and rights to press, speech, religion, traveling, and trials by jury while these rights and freedom are well exercised in the U.S. The serious violations of those rights as discussed earlier showed that the people and their rights in socialist countries are not highly respected as the will of the political party is above the will of people.

The socialist ideology and the will of the political party are more important than anything else and people are expected to sacrifice their rights and even their lives for the existence of the political ideology and party. Yet the political ideology and party can never be sacrificed because without the socialist ideology and party how could the people find equality, happiness and prosperity.

The socialist ideology and party arc the collective rights of the people and are above the individual rights of the people. Thus the individual rights must be sacrificed so that the collective rights could be attained for the good and well-being of the people as the whole. The golden rule is that the collective rights must be protected by all means and at all time and personal rights are just secondary if not the least.

Besides, the socialists do not believe in God and life after death and they perceive human beings are just the animals. Thus human rights are not the major emphasis yet. Importantly, the socialist regimes just like any regime could never allow freedoms to exercise the rights freely or else the socialist ideology could no longer survive because it is far from perfection and it could not deliver its promises.

The people now realize clearly that socialism takes away their freedom to speech, freedom to press, freedom to religion, freedom to travel, freedom to trials by jury, and freedom to human rights. When there is no freedom to exercise those basic rights, then no other rights could be freely enjoyed and exercised in socialist nations. People do not even have their right to change their ideology.

People and their lives are bound to the socialist ideology that is not at their choices now. They are under the control of the socialist ideology that is not at their will now. They are forced to protect the socialist ideology that is not at their willingness. They are commanded to become the slaves of the socialist ideology that is against their conviction now. They have no other option but socialist ideology and its party.

Thus freedom to free exercise of human rights is impossible in socialist countries or regimes. The human rights are still far from them when the people's choices are strongly rejected. The human rights are taken away from them when their wills are cruelly suppressed. The human rights are not available to them when the options of the general public are forbidden.

This leads to serious violations of human rights when freedoms are promised by the inhumane socialist leaders. This leads to the bloodshed of human rights when happiness is ensured to people by the heartless socialist leaders. This leads to the unbearable sufferings of human rights when prosperity is confirmed by the greedy socialist leaders. This leads to injustices, hurts, losses, inequality and more.

After the deportation, I went back the country again hoping that the socialists would allow me to enter the country so I could see my family. Just like any happily marriage couple, I want to be with my wife and I want to be with my children. I want to have family times together. I want to be there when my wife needs me and when she is insecure or not feeling well. I want to hear about her concerns, and so on.

I want to take my children to school with prayers and care, eagerly wait for them, fetch them and give them a big hug of love after classes. I want to see them eat, sleep, wake up, study, laugh, cry, play and grow and all the things that make parents happy; even just to look at the wonderful children. I want to hear their lovely voices, thoughts, laughter, struggles, and I just want to be a good dad to them.

I want to be at home and enjoy my joy, happiness and rights with my family. I want to talk to my friends and enjoy the fellowship with many friends. I want to preach at my churches and I want to minister to my church members. I want to go to places that I like and to my favorite restaurants. But those simple and basic wants or desires are not in my control when violations of human rights are still rampant.

If I could enter the country again, then I would not have to wander to a new country and I would not have to start everything from zero again. I would not have to worry much about many things. I would not have to adapt myself to the new culture, new works, new environment, and many new things. The thoughts of starting everything all over again would be hard and I am sure many of us would feel the same way.

It would be tougher when there is no financial support and no incomes during the long process to apply for an asylum status. It is a real battle between the high call for ministry and the physical call to go to work to help make ends meet. It is so burdensome when the body is in one place and yet the heart and mind are in another place called home or family across the Pacific Ocean.

With the last and full hope, I purchased tickets and took the airplane with all the prayers for a successful journey to go back home. As the airplane landed, my mind was so occupied with the many positive thoughts which earlier the government had given me a warning that, when I was deported out of the country, I must keep quiet about my situations so that they would ok me to come back to the country.

Of course, I was also nervous and worried with the many "ifs." Then, the door of the airplane opened and suddenly many policemen, security and custom officers rushed into the airplane. Everyone, maybe, was thinking about potential terrorists but I was thinking, "Am I such a VIP that the government sent many officials to welcome me?" They came to my designated seat; they already knew all the flight information.

But I was not at that seat then and I could see they were nervous and sweating as they could not find the person they were looking for. It was a big airplane and people were all waiting here and there with their luggage to get off the airplane. So they made announcements for people to exit the airplane one by one. When they saw me, they grabbed my hand and "escorted" me all the way to a special room.

Such was an honor for my human rights because people had to wait for a president to walk out of the airplane to welcome him or her. They came right into the airplane to welcome me and "escorted" me. I had never thought that I was such a VIP that I was given such special treatment. At the same time, what did I do to receive such an "honor of embarrassment" when other passengers kept looking at me.

How would you feel when you are suddenly arrested as a criminal in front of so many people? What were the thoughts, complaints, bad words and curses of the passengers in that situation? It could be worse if they thought that I was a terrorist. By the way, I had no rights to refute or decline their special treatment to "escort" me as such and they did not show or need to show any warrant to do so.

The officers did not allow me to go through the customs because I was no longer welcomed or permitted to enter the country. That was the message that appeared on the computer. Then, I asked for a transit as I already bought a transit ticket to another country for ministry. The officers told me that I was not even allowed to make a transfer here. I was forced to buy a new ticket after 9 hours of "tea time."

I asked the officers again for a transfer as I already had all the documents and tickets needed for that transit, and, I would not have to waste money for new tickets. But that was the order, "You are not even allowed to make transfer here." Since I did not have money available to purchase new tickets, they helped me call my wife to do so. At least my wife felt better to know that I was safe after her long wait for me.

I was "escorted" again to the airplane to fly out of the country. The officers could have stopped me from checking in and boarding the airplane in the other country but they did not. They wanted to meet me in person to tell me once again the clear message, "Your freedom and your human rights in the socialist countries are not possible if you do not follow the direction and order of the political party."

I lost my tickets, I lost my money, I lost my hope, but most of all I lost all the rights to be with my family and to care for my family. I lost my rights to carry out the physical roles of a husband, a father and a child. As the door of the airplane closed, it closed my way to go back home and it also closed my hope. As the door of the airplane closed, it locked up my vulnerable rights in those socialist nations.

As the airplane took off, my hopeful dreams of family reunion and happiness were dashed and so it was with my rights and my freedoms. As the airplane ascended into the air and left the country, I was also left with emptiness and uncertainties. I was also left with many indecisions and insecurities about the future. Where will I go? What will I do? How am I going to live? Where and how should I begin my new life?

At least, I just wished that I could see my home from the bird's eye view in the air, but it was just a wish because the airplane only took me away from home than coming home. It took me to a destination that I did not plan against my will, my desires and my prayer. Even though I knew that God had other plans for me and God was with me but I could not help being sad and confused.

Before I was "invited" out of the country, I told the authorities that I wanted to appeal to the higher court for my case and I wanted my lawyers to defend my case because this was not "proper" for them to just separate my family and I like this. In fact, I already knew my request would never be granted or would work, but, I spoke to them because I wanted to hear what they would tell me.

The policemen just gave me a very clear and strong answer, "You do not need to look for anyone to help you. No one will be able to help you in this situation. This is the order from the central government and no one could change it." Their rights are so powerful that even the law enforcement could not help the victims of injustices like me. Let me tell you this truth before you make your decision again.

The socialists are so deceptive in their promises in that they only speak about the things that people need most and inspire the people to vote for them and to fight to get back the right of equality, the right to health care, the right to free college education, the right for universal basic income, the right for minimal wage, the right to happiness. Unfortunately, these rights are never realized in socialist countries.

What will happen when the socialists are in power? The socialists would tell the people what are their socialist rights, and the people must follow their socialist rights first before the people could have their owns. Unfortunately, their rights are so many, that people only have a few rights left. They have the right to arrest you without any warrants. They have the right to control, to oppress, and to persecute...

Because the socialists never promised the right to free speech, right to free press, right to freedom of religion, right to free trials, right to peaceful gatherings, right to free travel and other rights, then the socialists are still generous enough to allow people to exercise a little bit of these rights. The truth is, people have limited freedoms because they have given all the powers and rights to the socialist.

That was the wrong choice of millions of people in the past and people suffer because of their wrong choice to vote and to fight for regimes and totalitarians and dictators at the promises of wolves under the disguise of harmless sheep. It is not too late for you to make the right decision to exercise your full freedoms or your wrong choice to be controlled by the limited freedoms given by your socialists.

The full human rights are not available yet because the freedom to gather is severely suppressed by the socialist armies and the people do not have enough power and resources to overcome the socialist power and armies, yet. The people have no rights to form their armies or to fight against regimes. Thus their human rights and freedoms are not achieved yet.

Even when I was no longer in the country, and I am now in the U.S, the land of freedom, am I free to exercise my freedom and human rights?

You may say, "Yes and of course because you are in America." That is how you think in the free world. Many victims of socialist nations came to the U.S and openly criticized the socialist regimes where they were persecuted because they thought everything was fine.

But many of them were not allowed to go back to their home countries and their family members were not allowed to go out of the country at their petition. If that happened, it took them a long, long, time before their family members could be reunited. During that time, their children were discriminated against in their home country and they suffered many hardships.

This is also our real struggle. Should we write this book even though the socialist leaders and socialist country are not mentioned, even though the real names of the authors are not mentioned? The English names of the victims are used in this book but it is still a risk to the securities of the authors and their relatives because the socialist leaders do not want to hear or read anything negative about socialism.

Every story in this book is real, but, if you still remember the definition of "truth" and "lies" in the first chapter and the golden rule, the leaders will not be happy even though this book is not to criticize any socialist country or socialist leaders. It is written for Americans and it is to tell Americans that America provides much better equality and prosperity than any socialist nations do.

It was just a few months ago, a family member of mine, David, called me from a socialist country telling me that the leader of the security bureau called him and told him to inform me that I should not keep in contact with a friend of mine and that I should not invite him to my event and I should not go to his event. He was also in prison for many years because of his fight for human rights and religious freedom.

How did the socialist authorities know about our contact and events here in the U.S.? They always monitor our Facebook accounts and social media and they also sent a picture of my friend and I on my Facebook to tell me that that friend of mine is the person that they do not want me to be in contact with. Could any politicians or government leaders in the U.S. stop your right for freedom of friend selection?

Do you know why the authorities talked to David, my family member? The authorities have my Facebook address, my email addresses, and my social media accounts. They know my phone number in the U.S., and even the address where I am living now. Why didn't they just call me or contact me directly? Is it costly to contact me? It costs nothing to contact through social media as you know.

This is what I mean by saying there are risks to our family members. Interesting? Yes, it is interesting for you but it is always a threat and pressure for us and our family members all the time. When I was still in the socialist country, my wife and I basically could not say anything about the ministry and our plans at home or in our car. We just talked about children education and positive things about the country.

You may say, "that is impossible or that is ridiculous." But that is the reality and the truth in socialist nations because the rights of the ideology and the political party are above the human rights of every individual. When my wife and I wanted talk about the churches, missions, plans or my travels for missions, we often went to a river nearby to talk or we just talked as we took a jog.

Even now whenever I called home through phone or social media, we only talked about family and life matters. Sometimes I teased my wife and asked about church situations, country situations or sensitive events happening in the country, she would just switch to different topics. If I kept on talking about those topics she would turn off the phone or the social media. Still like socialism?

I am sure you would not like your freedom and human rights to be interfered with by the authorities or anyone else. Yes you can freely do your things in your homes in America but our phones are being monitored and there is even a bug placed somewhere in our home or car so that they could track us and stop our mission works or gatherings when they needed to.

Just like many socialist victims, I know for sure that the authorities are still watching me closely at my every move abroad as they did to me at home. I do not worry much about their monitoring on my social media here because I already got used to that and because I do not share about the persecutions that my family and I went through, yet. I do not do and will not do anything to go against them on social media.

Regardless of what is happening, I will continue to preach on social media about the love of God and the forgiveness of God, not only to the believers worldwide, but also to the authorities who are still eager to know what I do preach and what I will preach about. I will continue to preach about the salvation of God and His power to change even a murderer like Paul to become His great servant and Apostle.

I will continue to preach about the charitable hearts of God to care for the needy people and people whose freedom and human rights are lost or are being violated. I will continue to preach about the Vision 20% and that there would be an increase of 20% of the population in every village, district, city and nation to come to know the Lord Jesus Christ as Lord and Savior. Will you join us and partner with us to do so?

By the way, do not just think that the authorities only monitor people like me online or on social media alone. The socialist governments already have so many of their spies here in America and they could just be our neighbors next door or they could be inside our churches or they could be our new friends here in the U.S. We could identify many them in many social media groups but many we do not know still.

You may wonder, why do the authorities keep on watching over you or others even though you all are no longer in the country and you do not oppose them? The nature of the socialists is insecurity and suspicious. They want to make sure that they rather persecute an innocent person than to let anything or any movement that is potentially challenging to them to be established.

For young leaders, they want to make achievements so that they could be promoted to higher positions, so, they are eager to watch over people so that they could make reports. The leaders also want to select the new and young leaders for leadership positions. They often select only people who are passionate about persecuting people who are not in agreement with their political ideology and party.

This is also to ensure the protection of the socialist ideology and the political party and it ensures their power and control over the people. As the readers will see in the following chapter that the socialist leaders must monitor quickly and strictly on any small or large gatherings, because, any gathering that doesn't belong to the socialist party may lead to the potential threat of overturning the government.

Whether it is a peaceful gathering to ask for justices to be done or it is a gathering to promote human rights, the socialist leaders would not be happy at those meetings. They would quickly and strictly monitor any small or large gatherings that are not belong to the socialist party and stop those gatherings because these gatherings may lead to the potential threat of overturning the socialist government.

7th Commandment
"THOU SHALL NOT GATHER PEACEFULLY"
Or Freedom of Peaceful Gathering

It was almost three years ago before I was deported out of the country due to religious persecution and before I came to the United States for asylum seeking in 2018, my co-workers and I organized leadership training and other prayer events. The authorities said that we must apply for a permit due to the big scale of the event and the presence of many foreigners to celebrate the 500 years of Protestantism.

We did apply and provided all the documents that they asked for, but, the application was rejected at the last moment. It was not because we were illegal or because we were not qualified that the application was rejected; it was just the insecurity of the socialist countries when it came to any big event and they felt threatened and challenged according to their own judgment and reasoning.

Then we were ready to go to another place in the North for the leadership training. One day before we took the flight, the organizer called us and asked our team to just stay home because the local authorities would arrest us if we went there for the training. Since we had already purchased the tickets, my team and I just flew there to carry out our plan B: 'Missions Through Sightseeing', and it often worked well.

Upon arrival we called the leaders and asked them to meet at a tourist spot the next day. Then we rented a big boat and we started the prayer, worship, preaching and training as the boat sailed off shore. We could pray out loud and could sing as much as we want to in the sea or river. This was one of the ways that we used to carry out leadership trainings before. It is costly yet it is safe and safety is first as we often say.

We also rented a bus so we could meet peacefully. As the driver hit the road, we had our freedom to worship and to pray. People on the streets or other buses looked at us thinking that we were transported to the mental hospital or to places for special treatment because they heard our loud voices, hand clapping and cries probably. They saw people were singing and others were raising their hands or shouting.

We sometimes rented a whole disco house, pub or restaurant, hotels for the revival meetings, outreaches or special trainings. This may sound strange to you yet that is how we could gather peacefully for religious purposes in socialist countries. Amazingly, the disco houses, the boats or the buses were the unusual places where we were being trained, challenged and refreshed in God's supernatural powers.

Though many churches often looked for and rented those unusual places so that there was more freedom to practice our belief, yet, the eyes of the government were still all over the place watching over the churches, the leaders and the religious events through a large number of spies. Many times the events were canceled because the authorities called the owners of those businesses to stop the events.

Probably the majority of American millennials do not know the horrible events that led to the massacres or suppression of many peaceful gatherings by the socialist government. Any big gathering always poses a threat to the government and their leadership. In their analysis, any gathering could potentially become bigger and it could be big enough to challenge their power and to overthrow their reign.

In socialist countries, the government often spends massive amount of money on military and the government always shows the country's military power through military parades or military exercises to send the message to the people and the world, that, the government and the military are very powerful and the military is always ready to extinguish any attempt to overthrow the government.

This is the potential and possible fear of the Republicans and the framers of the U.S. government, we believe. Thus, they did not want to create a legal system with big government but with small government where the leaders should serve the people and not vice versa. To make that to happen, they divided the powers into the three branches of government as it is still operated in the U.S. today.

The forefathers and the leaders knew well that when the government is so powerful and when the citizens have no weapons available to fight against the wicked and powerful government, the people would suffer under their tyranny. The socialists' wanting of big government to have control on gun rights is one of the big steps for the government to gain power and the next step for people to loose their freedoms.

The U.S. Constitution not only indicates the people's right to arms but also their right to form military. These rights are unheard of and totally forbidden in socialist countries. The secure and good government is not afraid when people become wealthy and powerful because its existence is to serve the people. The evil and totalitarian government is insecure and coercive as it cares for power not people.

The U.S. cares more about the people and their rights thus they have freedom to these rights to arms and military so they could liberate themselves in case of suppression and injustices. The socialist country cares more about the political party and ideology, thus, these rights are not accessible to people or else people would have more opportunities to overthrow their powerful but insecure regime.

But now the socialists, communists, leftists, terrorists, liberals, radicals, and the leftwing democrats in the U.S. use these rights for arms and for forming armies to take over the U.S and they try to ban these rights from the Americans so that they could form big government in the U.S. They want to defund the police and they want to remove the police so that they could easily control cities and states.

Recent lootings and violence in the U.S. point to the wisdom of the U.S. framers and founders to make sure that Americans have the rights to arms and military to protect themselves from the attacks of the evil ones when the authorities are not around to help the people in times. The socialist countries take this right from the people to leave people helpless and powerless when injustices happen to people.

Thanking to the right to arms, many families in the U.S. could protect themselves and their homes from the attacks of the radical people, the socialists and members of Antifa who used the cause of Black Lives Matter to rob, to loot, to hurt people, to bring chaos and fears to people and communities. Sadly, many people were killed inside their homes as these mobs broke in their house and killed the owners.

Since May 25, 2020, more than one thousand policemen and policewomen were injured and many of them were killed by members of BLM and Antifa. These members also destroyed communities and businesses. They also hurt and killed many innocent people. If this happened in the socialist countries, these members are already arrested, crushed, imprisoned and even executed by the socialist leaders.

In socialist countries that we lived, the citizens are taught and told and they get used to the thought that people should not own guns or weapons because those people could bring harms to others and cause insecurities to the communities and this is also true somehow. Those who secretly own weapons must be bad people and they have bad intention so they would be arrested and punished if found with weapons.

Yet, the "good" socialist leaders hide weapons to protect themselves and their families but people could not possess weapons to protect themselves and their families when injustices happen to them. The socialist leaders possess guns but they are not arrested but the people will be arrested if found with arms and the people might be severely charged with plans of counter-revolutionary or rebellions.

The socialist leaders know very well that their days and their lives would be over soon if the people ever have the right to own arms and armies because the socialist leaders have done so many injustices to the people. People demonstrated peacefully to ask back their lands and properties that were robbed by the corrupted leaders, yet justices could hardly come back to them.

People demonstrated peacefully to ask the local government to bring the socialist leaders who abused power to justices, and to punish the socialist leaders who corrupt people's prosperities and national wealth according to the laws, and to disciplined the socialist leaders with immoral scandals, yet these corrupted and immoral leaders are still promoted to higher positions.

People demonstrate peacefully to ask the government to protect their living environment damaged by companies and factories in their areas. Yet, the authorities do not often give reasonable answers to the people's legitimate requests, the leaders use arms and armies to suppress and to put innocent people into prisons. The leaders even use gangsters to beat the demonstrators and destroy their homes.

Unfortunately, in socialist countries, the socialist leaders are mostly the people who cause tragedies and injustices to common people. Thanking to the big government, the socialist leaders are so powerful and the people are so powerless. Due to the many evil things that the leaders have been doing, the authorities are very nervous whenever there is a demonstration regardless of the purpose of the meeting.

One day during a regular weekly "tea time," the authorities asked me if I had any upcoming conferences or big meetings. That question was often asked to find out more information. I took the opportunity to ask them, "If you give me the green light, I could organize the international missions and revival conference here in this city or the capital city, if possible. This would be good for the nation and all of you."

They asked what was my plan about. I proposed the meeting was to be organized at a local stadium and I said something like this, "the gathering would show to the world that there is more religious freedom here and local believers do not need to travel overseas where you do not have control over what they are doing there. Christians would be happy to come here to pray for and to support the country."

"Then you will not have to worry about many things when the meeting is inside the country. You have control over the speakers and the content. When the travel is local, a lot of costs are saved. Importantly, many overseas Christian churches, organizations, pastors and speakers would come and you would have more chances to get to know them personally and to partner with them for charity works."

Of course it was a long conversation but they would not take in my great idea with many great advantages I proposed because they knew in their imagination and logical analysis that, if things just went beyond their control when people used this large event to lead the riots against the government, they would not be able to be responsible for it and to bear the unimaginable consequences.

Another time I proposed to them to organize the International Christian Music Festival and my organization would invite international teams, art-performing teams, choirs, world famous singers, actors, world leaders and the state-church would co-organize the event and present the musical awards to certain Christian artists. They felt better with this idea but the answer was still "No."

They reasoned that the impact of this event was too big and would lead to a new movement where Christian artists could widely influence the people and millions of people would also come to know the Lord Jesus Christ through the event and through the Christian artists and actors. The authorities persecuted severely to stop the growth of the Christians and of course they would not say yes to this event.

Jayme Metzgar is accurate in her observation that, "Informal community associations are always a threat to communist governments, which can allow no loyalty higher than the party, and Romania was no different. Spies and informants infiltrated nearly every relationship and every gathering. Those willing to denounce their close friends and family earned special favors."

Even current peaceful gatherings in some socialist nations also tell the same truth, "The socialist government is for the political party not for the people." People are gathering together to seek justices. Yet justices are hardly found. Instead, people who joined the peaceful demonstration were hurt, beaten, and even imprisoned. Peaceful demonstrations turned into violence, wounds and deaths.

The socialist governments know very well about the power of gathering and propaganda that could lead a few people into a powerful movement. They are the experts in this area. The socialists turned over many former governments in so many countries and they did that through small and big gatherings and bloodshed. Thus, they stopped any movement right from the beginning from growing.

In the last two years, there were so many protests and demonstrations; the movement seemed to be getting stronger and stronger and it also caught international attentions. It was not the press of that socialist country that brought the protests and demonstrations to the attention of the international communities, but, it was through people who streamed the events live on social media.

They were there at the peaceful protests and gatherings to demand justices to be done for their properties, lands, environments, communities and people. They wanted the corrupted leaders to be punished for their corruptions and evil deeds. Many people were asking then, "Will the people succeed in getting justice done?" Sadly, they still could not find justices for their quests and their rights.

Instead, injustices were fallen on leaders and people who got involved in the protests and demonstrations. They were shot, arrested, beaten, and imprisoned or disappeared. For months they fought for freedoms but all they found were oppressions, suppressions, tortures, sufferings and even deaths. The socialist leaders would crush them on spot by tanks, weapons and powerful armed forces.

Bloggers were interrogated and threatened by the authorities and many were imprisoned and are still imprisoned and so it is with organizers, leaders, political activists and human rights activists while other leaders run away from home to hide somewhere. Others escaped through the borders to other countries and then sought for asylum from there to countries that are still accepting these activists.

There were times that the socialist leaders seemed to give in to the people and promised people that they would solve the issues and bring back justices for people. Yet when the naïve people dispersed and went back home, their armed forces were already there waiting to capture and imprison them. Readers may go online to find the many suppressions as it is not convenient for us to mention the events here.

The truth is, "the powers are in the hands of the autocrats and the power does not belong to the people" but, the leaders often say everything belongs to the people. When the leaders have all the economic, political, military powers in their hands, they would use their powers to oppress those who want to rise against them. They would crush those who fight for economic and political freedom and human rights.

When the leaders are so obsessed with power, they don't want people to challenge them. If people do, the leaders tend to use the power to oppress or suppress people so they can control people and protect their wealth. As mentioned earlier, socialism is believed to be the best form of government and economy, and there is no better form. So the people are expected to support it and to protect it.

Public gathering or opposition then is always a threat, a real threat to the existence of their political party and power and wealth, of course. The socialist leaders are very afraid that their regimes will be overthrown. They are afraid that their power and wealth will be destroyed. They are afraid that their lives would be executed. They would sacrifice people but not their power of control over what they have.

A few years ago, we were preparing for a leadership summit for key leaders from our mission networks, and it happened to take place at the same time with an international leadership summit organized by the county. For some reason, our meeting was posted on social media and it gave my co-workers and I a really hard time with the policemen and the national security leaders.

One day I received a call from a policeman who often called me for the meeting saying he was "coming soon to pick me up." This was not the regular day of our weekly "tea time" so I guessed something was very serious. Upon arrival, they took me into the office with a few new officials and they looked very serious. After their introductions, I was shocked and I really prayed hard to prepare for new situations.

They asked if I organized a big leadership summit next month and I did not answer right away, but asked, "what's happening?" They told me that they received information from Internet police that our group contacted leaders and invited them to attend the leadership summit. They ordered me to stop immediately because our meeting was a direct opposition to the international event organized by the country.

For them, this was just like a competition against the government. The socialists always think of the worse scenario due to their chronic insecurity and they always think that people plan to oppose them even though people like us did not have that intention. I realized that they misunderstood us again but they were correct that someone sent out the information of the meeting with the title, "leadership summit."

I did not expect that they would think that way and that the case was so serious. So, I told them that we did not plan any big meeting and we just had a small meeting with some friends for fellowship. They did not believe because they had already read the information. They told me that this was a very serious issue and that was why they brought me here so I should not lie to them but tell them the truth.

They even told me the location where we planned to organize the event. Remember what I said earlier that spies were everywhere and they were quick to find out information. All I could say was we did not have a big meeting and I assured them of that. Whenever I assured them and that I would be responsible for what I said, then the situation always got better. At least they still trusted the words of pastors.

The top leaders seriously told me again about the serious consequences if I did not listen to them. They told me the security was extremely tight these days to prepare for the event and for the welcoming and the securities of top leaders of the nations who came for the summit.

At least they appreciated my cooperation and reminded me again to cancel the meeting as we said goodbye and some of them took me home.

But there were also miracles in our many peaceful gatherings in the socialist soil. Our peaceful gatherings were not for political purposes or human rights of this world. Our peaceful gathering was to introduce the love, the forgiveness, the salvation, and peace of God into the lives of people who are longing for the peace of their minds, the peace of their hearts, and the peace of soul for eternity.

The peaceful gathering of ours is to bring God's hope to the hopeless, God's power to the powerless, and God's salvation to the suffering. Our peaceful gatherings or evangelistic meetings are to reach out to the lost souls with the Word and Power of God. Our prayer for you is that you and your family members may find God, His love, His salvation and His protection during the coronavirus pandemic.

On an average, our ministry organized more than 200 evangelistic events annually whether the meeting was large or small across nations, provinces, cities or towns. In the socialist country we could organize the event from 50 people to 2000 people depending on the location. Internationally, our crusades may have 10,000 to 40,000 attendants or more. You and your organizations are welcome to partner with us.

We would share the Gospels and pray for people on the streets or market places. The events would be at the residential areas, plazas, restaurants, parks or factories. Many times we were called to stop by the local authorities during the events and they just told us to leave the place. Many times our teams were brought to the police stations for interrogations. There was a time that God surprised us.

One day, when we were organizing an evangelistic meeting in a basketball court, the party secretary of the county and the policemen came as they heard the sound and the complaints of people. They came with shouting and asking who allowed us to organize the event and telling us this was illegal. The party secretary ordered people to remove the sound system and the equipment. Suddenly, something happened.

He kept on asking his people and the policemen to remove things but his people did not make any move so he shouted even louder but the same thing happened. As he looked around, he saw many young people had formed a circle around him and his people. When he took a closer look at these young people, his attitude just changed. Suddenly, he said, "quickly remove things and do not stay here for too long."

Then he just walked away with his people including the policemen following him. The event went on with songs, testimonies, dance team, drama team, preaching, and altar call until late at night, but, the party secretary and his people did not come back. Why? Who were those young people? They were the famous gang group in that area and the policemen all knew them. That was the reason why they left.

The gang leader was just newly converted and I had just baptized him a few days earlier. On that evangelistic night, he called many of his subordinates to come help us set up the place for the event and then listen to the Gospel. God sent them to protect us. Sometimes, God uses the audiences to speak to the policemen to leave because they like our dramas, songs and dance.

One of the most challenging evangelistic meetings was for the college students. The socialist leaders strictly controlled education and the intellectuals because they knew so well that many revolutions came from the intellectuals. They always kept a close watch over the content of education, educational settings, and student meetings, thus the outreaches to college students were not easy.

There were even cameras and recording systems in certain classes to monitor the content taught by the teachers. We organized different events to invite the students to come and join us so we could share the Gospel to them. One of the activities that attracted them the most was music or sport event in those days. We organized those events regularly and we got more students and young people to come.

One time, our ministry decided to organize a big event at a wedding hall called Heavenly Garden. It took many months for the team to prepare for the event and the event was so successful plus the number of attendants was overwhelming beyond our imagination and the police's estimation. The authorities thought we might only have about 100 attendants as it were in our other events.

The place was packed with more than 1,500 college students and young people and, this was the first largest Christian meeting organized for young people in a public meeting place since the socialists took over the country. This event was historic in those days because the persecution was so severe and the authorities could not even imagine where did so many students and young people come from?

Suddenly, many police cars rushed to the place where the event was organized. Of course they did not come to give security for the meeting as people often see the security members around big gatherings in the U.S. They came because the authorities were immediately alarmed by the sudden large gathering especially as to the many young people attending the event.

They sent so many policemen with arms to surround the entire place and to prepare for any worse thing to happen. Even though they knew that it was a religious event, they could not hide their nervousness and worries. Of course there was always a big price to pay for organizing evangelistic events in a socialist country and the price came with many forms of persecutions.

Even today, it is still very difficult to organize a big religious event but miracles do happen and doors could be opened at any time. Thus, it is worth to keep trying. Thank God hundreds of churches were planted through the many evangelistic efforts. You are most welcome to partner with GMV to plant 2000 churches and then 10,000 churches when it is still possible in these socialist countries.

Of course, the socialist leaders are afraid that the political activists or human right activists would mobilize young people in masses to go against them and the political party. They know very well the youth power because they were the ones who called and manipulated the young people to become the red guards to carry out the socialist utopia for equality, distribution of wealth and prosperity and freedom.

They witnessed and knew very well the disasters, the sufferings, and death sentences that the young red guards had brought upon the lives of millions of innocent people. They took advantages of hundred thousands of the young people to carry out their political agenda and yet they were terrified at the cruelties and brutalities that these young people did to the people.

The leftist leaders, the democrats and the socialists in the U.S are also using the same method to bring about a political revolution that they have long wanted for or at least they could take down President Trump, their so strong rival in this 2020 presidential election. If President Trump still wins and he would we believe, these power-thirsty leaders would mobilize the innocent millennials for more riots.

The leaders have been employed "Black Lives Matter" platform to carry out many demonstrations and riots in many states to call for changes that they want. They demand the government to comply with their demands or they would burn down the U.S system. They demand for reparations. They demand for no bail. They demand to release all prostitutes from prison. They demand for no death penalty.

They demand for free education. They demand for free health care. They demand to defund the police. They demand to cut the military budget. They demand for the redistribution of wealth and they demand for publicly-financed campaigns. Please take note of these demands and Americans would realize that the socialist nightmare is not over when Sen. Bernie Sanders stopped the 2020 presidential race.

These demands are not different from the agenda of Sen. Bernie Sanders and the Democratic Socialists of America for America and Americans. In other words, the leaders, the rioters and the socialist members demand for socialism to take over the United States or they would take over this country by force. The threats of socialism and terrorism are now at the feet of Americans and on the land of America.

Just like the young red guards did in the socialist nations, violent members of Black Lives Matters, the Left extreme members of Antifa, and anarchists are now dominating the streets and communities. They looted homes and businesses. They destroyed and burnt houses, businesses, churches and communities. They raped, wounded, tortured and killed innocent people including children and seniors.

Yet the red guards in the socialist countries did not just stop there. They went from house to house to arrest people who were against the socialist ideology. They put millions of innocent people and intellectuals in jails and labor camps. They sent the family members of the victims to countryside and remote areas so that they could take over their houses, properties and lands and lives.

They took over businesses and factories. They took over the lands and the wealth of wealthy people. They abolished private land and they applied big government or government control over the mode of productions and the means of distribution. They took over industries and they abolished free enterprises. They executed the capitalists and wealthy people who were the enemies of the socialists.

They accused one another as disloyal people, betrayals or counter-revolutionaries in order to destroy their opponents and to take over the leadership. They even accused their own family members, relatives and even their parents to prove their loyalty to the socialist party and leaders. They even humiliated, denied and tortured their own parents because their parents were the enemies of the social class.

The socialist leaders allowed these young red guards to do anything they wanted to do so that they could take down and destroyed all of the enemies, rivals and opponent leaders until their enemies were gone. This is also happening now when the democratic leaders allow the members of Antifa, BLM and radicals to do anything they want in order to take over places and the U.S.

The American socialists and the democrats are now waiting for the U.S. to become a socialist state if the mobs, the radicals and the rioters were to be successful to take over the U.S. Joseph Alcott aka Jose Martin already wanted to see that happened in 2018. He wanted "a world that is without capitalism, without private property... that is socialist and communist" reported CFT Team on Christians for Truth.

Attorney General William Barr considered Antifa as the violent far-left extremist group. According to him, these "antigovernment extremists engaged in indefensible acts of violence designed to undermine public order. Among other lawless conduct, these extremists have violently attacked police officers and other government officials, destroyed public and private property, and threated innocent people" reported Jay Greenberg on NeonNettle.

Jose Martin "is a radical communist and Antifa leader operating in the U.S. He advocates for the violent overthrow of the government and for the murder of the rich and claims to have international involvement in left-wing movements." He said, "Police lives don't matter. They can all burn in Hell." "I have this country. It isn't half bad. It's all bad" reported Political Editors on The Patriot Post.

Should American wait for that next step? Of course Americans would not wait for those horrible days to come as it had happened to so many former socialist nations. We are sure that President Trump and the patriots of the U.S. would not let the mobs, the communists, the socialists and the anarchists and the leftists to make the socialist or the communist dream to happen in this beautiful land of freedom.

As President John Adams once said, "Government is instituted for the common good: for the protection, safety, prosperity and happiness of the people; and not for the profit, honor, or private interest of any one man, family, or class of men." Neither the socialists nor the terrorists, BLM members, Antifa or the anarchists would focus on the common good but they are for power at the sufferings of the people.

Do not let the same painful socialist history to be repeated in

America. America and Americans cannot be lost into the hands of the brutal socialists, terrorists and anarchists. It is time for Americans to stand side by side with President Trump and the patriots to take back the victory, to put America First, to Make America Great Again, and to protect Americans and the Republic.

If the majority of Americans just keep quiet and do not protect the U.S., their rights and their freedoms, America and Americans are just steps away from the painful losses of their freedoms and serious violations of human rights. They would face horrible experiences of injustices and inescapable moments of sufferings, as well as many religious persecutions, imprisonments and executions.

Global Missions Vision is calling millions of American and global believers and churches to gather together at October 9-12 Global Revival Conference, and the October 30-November 2nd Prayer and Prophetic Conference through Zoom to pray for God's protections over the U.S., Americans, and to pray for President Trump and Vice President Mike Pence, and the 2020 Presidential Election. Will you join us?

For now, let us move on to the 8th Commandment of socialism: Freedom For Due Compensation. The readers would find out that one of the main principles of socialism is against the privatization of land ownership and this principle is very tricky in socialist nations, because, the socialists claim that all the land and the properties belong to the government not the people.

8th Commandment
"THOU SHALL NOT BE PAID DULY"
Freedom For Due Compensation

In America, the government cannot just go and take away private properties without making a due compensation to the owner. Freedom for due compensation is written in the Amendment and well protected by laws. Americans may agree or disagree with the government to use their own lands or properties. It takes negotiations and understanding, not forces to come to a mutual agreement.

In the U.S., even the government must respect the ownership of intellectual properties or the copyrights of the authors and the government must pay for the services that the government received from the contractors based on agreement or auction. It is a common thing that businesses make generous donations or contributions but businesses do not do that because they are coerced to do so.

The U.S. authorities cannot just inform people to leave their lands or properties as the country needs the land for city developments or highways. Of course, the citizens would not block the government to do so for the common good of the people and the nation. But the point is, Americans are the real owners of their properties and they can make their own decisions to sell, donate or not to do so.

The situation is very different in socialist countries where the land belongs to the government and the citizens are only temporary users of the lands. Even though the government says that the land belongs to the people but those are just the kind words to fool people and to make people happy to support the socialists at the beginning. The reality is the land and the properties belong to the government.

Even though a family and their forefathers already purchased and lived in the same piece of lands for many generations but the land still does not belong to them. They are just the caregivers of the land and the private of land ownership does not belong to them. The socialist government can ask them to leave the land whenever the government needs the land or whenever the government wants it.

The **first** sad thing is that the people never received duly compensations for their lands and their natural properties. They used to own huge lands with gardens and farms since the population of the country was a lot smaller before and the people were mostly farmers. Now they were given a small piece of land as big as a standard apartment. The value of their properties was big but they received little.

The **second** sad thing is that the people not only lost their lands but they also lost their jobs, or, they had to find new jobs but, they could hardly do anything because they were farmers all of their lives. They lost their hobbies and the leisure of farmers and they had to adjust to new life, new situations, new environments and new jobs that were not very easy for them but they did not have much choice.

The **third** sad thing is that the people were all forced to leave their lands and properties, not at their wills, and, they had to leave many cultural traditions. Hundred of thousands of people were relocated to the new places at the command of the government, leaving their ancestral lands, ancestral homes and the relics of the forefathers, plus great memories of their childhood. They did not want to, but...

The **real** sad thing is that the people suffered great losses but the corrupted socialist leaders got wealth from peoples' lands and properties. If the people could be duly compensated, they would become rich because their lands were often big enough for a business complex but, the corrupted leaders just gave compensations according to the farmland prices instead of the prices of industrial or business land.

The **last** real sad thing is that many people lived on a fortune but they did not know that. When the researchers discovered that there were rich natural resources or gold mines, the government would not tell the people first. The government would relocate the people first, then the socialist leaders corrupted the wealth linking it to social ownership, and, the people were fooled by them.

Even if the owners of the land discovered the treasures or the natural resources in their lands, the treasures or the natural resources do not belong to the owners or the users of the lands. The treasures and the natural resources belong to the public or social ownership. Yet in most cases, the local people benefit nothing from the social ownership, but the local socialist leaders do through their corruptions.

Before the socialists took over the former government, the socialists promised the poor peasants that when the people supported the socialists to take over the country, the socialists would take away the wealth, properties and lands of the landlords and the rich people and share the properties and the lands equally to all people. They would make the landlords and the rich to become equal to everyone.

Social ownership of the land by the people was thus one of the ways to eliminate the wealth and the poor gap among the people and eliminate the social classes and the inequalities in the society. Social ownership of the mode of production and means of distribution was also the great promise to stop the rich from any opportunity to exploit the poor and to make the equal sharing of wealth available to everyone.

And social ownership was obviously the best way that the socialists could get the overwhelming supports of the poor people and poor peasants because millions of the poor peasants did not have much lands while the landlords and the rich had many lands and properties. The poor also had to work for the landlords and the wealthy people and they had to depend on the rich for the living.

It was the great promises of the socialists to distribute wealth and the lands to the common people that the socialists and socialism were able to gain their power. The socialists were able to create the hatred among the poor toward the wealth and the prosperity of the wealthy and the rich people that the socialists and socialism were able to gain the popularity and great supports from the common people.

There could be nothing greater than the promises of the socialists. The poor people and the innocent peasants were very happy at the concept and at the thought that one day in the near future they would own their own land, possess their own property, live their own lives and they would be their own bosses. They happily followed and strongly supported the socialist revolution, and, they made it at last.

The socialists took over the country and they took all the businesses, lands and properties of the landlords and wealthy people, and millions of landlords and the wealthy people were either executed or sent to the labor camps to work as farmers so that everyone could be equal. That was how the socialists repaid the wealthy people when they received so much financial supports from these wealthy people.

Millions of Americans today are also being attracted to the socialist concept of social ownership. On the theory, the concept is great and this was the reason why people of the nations were attracted to it. In reality, common people could not enjoy much the benefits of social ownership but they loose more economic opportunities and their rights through social benefits.

By the way, American billionaires, millionaires and wealthy people should also be ready for this when socialism takes over America. This is not just a reminder but also a real warning because socialism is gaining popularity now in the U.S. and the DSA really want to make social ownership of land, properties, businesses or anything so that they could take down all the corporations and their exploiters.

The socialists really distributed the lands to the people so that everyone would have land to cultivate and to make their own living, but of course, they did not share the wealth that they took from the landlords and wealthy people because, just like everyone else, they also wanted to be wealthy and had been longing for the wealth for so long. Now it was their time to become wealthy at the losses of others.

The people were so happy at the beginning because they thought that they were the real owner of the lands, their lives and their future, but, they soon found out the painful truth. The truth was, the land was given to the people so that the people would cultivate the land and then they would bring the produces of the land to the government and then the government would equally share the produces to all.

Factory workers also received the same payment as farmers or office workers regardless how hard or little they worked. People also wanted to be rich but this could never happen because they are all the workers of the government and they must be equal to one another. They must receive the same salary, the same benefits, thus people were equally poor and equally suffered while leaders enjoy wealth.

That was equality. They wanted to be rich and they wanted more but they could not because everything was determined and ordered by the socialists. In the previous free market, they could at least negotiate and they still had their rights to make decision if they would want to make a deal or not but in the socialist regime, they did not have any right to do so but to obey, accept and to follow the socialist orders.

Another big issue was that the leaders were good politicians but they were not great business people. They could fight very well but they did not know how to manage the country. They spoke great promises but they did not know how to make their promises a reality. The socialist theory was great to hear but it did not work well in practice and it went against the principles of economy.

The reality was the socialist leaders did not know how to carry out the principles of socialist economy but the theories. They did not know that there was no country before or after that could bring about real equality to all people. They sought help from the international socialist community to send the international experts into the country, but the experts just rewound the wheels of failures.

The socialist leaders and the people could only learn later that the socialist countries that sent the experts and that they once worshiped and revered as the great successes of socialism and equality were also trying out their socialist theory in their own lands. Those countries also struggled hard to carry out the unreal promises and then their countries were also collapsed.

As the result, the country and the people were soon faced with an economic crisis because most of the people were not really working but they spent more time speaking about the ideology and persecuting, criticizing, torturing and killing those who were not in agreement with the socialist ideology and party. If they worked hard, they just received the same as others so they relaxed and talked as others did.

Then the famine took place in the country just when many people had nothing left. This led to the deaths of at least 50 million to 100 million people by starving or famine alone in many socialist countries. People ate grass, leaves and barks of the trees if possible or anything that they could catch from fish to bird, from snakes to grasshoppers, crickets or anything to eat in order to survive.

Just like millions of people who owned big lots of land in the former government and then had their precious lands and properties taken over by the new socialist regime; my grandfather was also a landlord and he had to run for his life leaving behind all of his property, wealth, his business, his vast lands and his comfortable life to a new province after the unsuccessful assassination of the socialists.

My grandfather was very wealthy, a powerful businessman and a respected landlord, but now he lost everything to the socialists in his hometown. He started over his new life in a remote, poor and new area by the sea. The whole family came to live in this new land after having lived there for more than 20 years. Gardening was their new way of living and keeping themselves protected as poor farmers.

In this new place, my grandfather, eldest uncle and aunties cultivated a big land which was only 10 minutes walking to a beautiful beach. We often played in the big garden where we could run around as much as we could. There were so many trees with so many fruits. We often walked to the beach and went swimming in the sea early in the morning before we went to school or after school in the afternoon.

Suddenly one day, the local authorities came and asked the whole family to move out from the land and they only provided a small piece of land around 90-meter square in the back corner of the same land without any other compensation. The reason was very simple, because, all the lands were the properties of the government in socialist countries and the government could take it back at any time.

Due to the background and the situation of my grandfather, the family just obeyed to avoid any worse thing that may happen. "Through relationship," my uncle got a better slot in a better position of the land instead of the back of the land. Recent compensation is better; yet, the people are still victims because the authorities would get many fortunes from city development where lands are diamonds.

At the needs of urbanization, strategic lands are needed where new communities are being built. Local and foreign investors also need lands for factories, real estate development. The rich people would claim any lands they liked and of course they gave large sums of money to the authorities. In the early days like in the case of my grandfather, the authorities simply gave the order and people just obeyed.

At the increasing oppression and unfair claims of the land and property, the people went on strikes and the government began to give better compensations. The compensations for the relocation of their lands and properties kept increasing every time the people went against the government and the local authorities. People who lost the lands earlier repealed their cases but justices never came to them.

If justices were to be done for them, the government had to trace back everything to the former corrupted leaders who were in-charge then and the ill-gotten wealth that was transferred to them. Justices could not be done to these victims because these former corrupted leaders are now promoted to higher positions and they became the powerful leaders in the central government so who dares to touch them?

The people knew very well that the lower-ranking officials would not fight for them, because these officials need the help of the higher-ranking officials to be promoted to higher positions. The land fight is still going on up to this time and the land issues are still the very hot issues of human rights at the fast pace of modernization, economic development and urbanization where golden lands are badly needed.

In July 2020, a group of local people decided to make a big event to catch the attention of the top leaders of the country and hoping that the country leaders would bring justices to them because their lands were taken away by the local government without proper compensations and they were oppressed by the local leaders whenever the local people appealed to the courts and the media.

They fought for years and they also gathered with peaceful demonstration for years but they were still at loss. So they made the announcement that they would burn themselves alive on a certain day if the local government did not respond to their request. Instead of solving the conflicts and bringing due compensations to the local people, the local leaders still tried to cover the event with their powers.

On that day, the local government sent many policemen to surround these local people and they also sent fire trucks and firefighters to extinguish the fire. But there was no local media came to cover the event and there was no news released by the local authorities or local media. The news was spread on the social media by local people who live-streamed the event.

The local people and users of social media helped share the video in hoping that they may catch the attention of the top leaders. But there was no sign if the country leaders already got the news or the country leaders would bring justices to the local people. It is also unlikely that the country leaders would pay attention to such situations because they are also too busy to protect their powers and positions.

Every time, the local people set themselves on fire, the firefighters would immediately extinguish the fire while the local people shouted and asked the top leaders to solve the issues. Many people also came and took a look at the injustices and the tragedies but they also knew that they could not do anything to help when the powers are in the hands of the socialist elites not in their hands.

Besides the land issues, innocent people are not compensated for the injustices they received. In the U.S, when newly found evidence proved that a prisoner was innocent, the government would pay a lot of money to the person to make up for the losses and the wrongs that were done to him. This does not happen to people who were wrongly charged or sentenced for years and life imprisonment in the socialist prisons.

This could not just be done because the government does not have enough money to pay for the compensations of countless innocent people who suffered the injustices. How much could the government pay to the millions of people who were forced into labor camps and developing-economic zones? How about the payments to the hundred thousands of freedom fighters, human rights and religious workers?

People in the West often make remarks that the copyrights of their products or their intellectual properties are often imitated or taken by people in socialist countries and other countries in the world. This could be because of the unethical acts of the business people or because the law enforcements are not so strict to reinforce the laws on copyrights, patents or intellectual property rights.

This could also be the application of social ownership in socialism. The ideas, inventions, arts, properties... that are made known to the public are owned by the community or the people. They are made for and sold to the people thus the people could use it the way they want. Just like the lands are not owned by the users, people are not the owners of the invention or products but the communicators of the ideas.

If all the wealth, resources, and the natural properties are owned and shared by the people, there is no need to speak about the individual rights or the intellectual rights or the compensations for those rights. Just like how Sen. Bernie Sanders wants to make almost everything free to the people, then there is no need to ask about the prices or the cost of those freebies.

Unfortunately, only the greedy socialists have the power to share the wealth and the resources but not the common people. They make use of the social ownership to accumulate their own wealth, position and power. They use their power and position to get the shares from businesses or projects or they even abuse the power to force others to give the wealth to them.

The people who are promised with equality are indeed the victims of the socialists' exploitations and inequalities. By the way, if their physical properties could not be compensated duly, how is it possible that their abstract properties would be well protected? If the people do not even have the freedom to freely exercise their human rights, they will not care much about intellectual rights or copyrights.

Every year, I sent evangelistic teams to various provinces to reach out to the local people. There were places that we partnered with the state churches as it is safer to organize evangelistic events inside the church buildings. But, these opportunities with the state churches were rare due to the strict control of the local government where every move of the church would be reported by the church guards or spies

So, we usually partnered with the house churches or Christian business people, if we could, to organize the evangelistic events in their home churches, factories, restaurants, movie houses, or companies. Many times we organized the events in public places under charity events or concert outreach in the parks, public plaza, or markets depending on the availability and accessibility of each place we went.

The policemen would find out soon enough and they would arrest the whole team and confiscate all of our simple sound system, light system, musical instruments and other equipment. Sometimes we would get something back, but most of the times, things were never returned to us because they like to collect many things and everything for their personal gains at very great reasons. Want the compensations?

Rev. David was put into prison many times and was under strict control for more than 10 years. He was not given identification and he could not go anywhere except to his hometown whenever he was out the prison. He and his family suffered because he was fighting for the rights of the minorities especially the Montagnards whose lands were taken away by the socialist leaders.

Due to the natural beauties of mountainous areas, certain lands were taken by the government to develop those places as tourist zones. Other lands were taken to expand the city and many lands were taken for mining the natural resources. In any of these cases, the local people were forced to relocate to new areas. The new areas were not suitable for their gardening, farming or raising of livestock.

In the U.S., if the oil or the mines or the natural resources or treasures were found on people's land, the owners of the land would become very rich and they could enjoy the wealth from the lands because they are the real owners of the land and the properties on the land. They could make contract with private companies or the local government to develop the lands or do the mining as their own.

This is not so in socialist nations because the land and its natural properties such as natural resources or any precious thing in the land where people live do not really belong to the people. People are just the temporary users or the caregivers of the land. People would be removed first from their homes and their lands and they have no share from the natural resources. It sounds unfair but it is the painful truth.

The mountainous people went on strike and they were suppressed by the local authorities. As the pastor of many mountainous people, Pastor John also raised his concerns of the unfair treatments of the socialist leaders to these people and he asked the international communities to help their cases. Thus he was seen as a dangerous human right activist who went against the will of the government.

The disobediences of the tribal peoples and Pastor John were considered as against the government and counter-revolutionary crimes. Thus many people including Pastor John were put into prisons for many years and many were killed in the riots. The socialist leaders had better legal reason to confiscate or to take over their lands. Thousands of them ran away from the country to save their lives.

These people become the refugees or wanderers in foreign lands. Some countries do not recognize them as asylum seekers or victims of wars or political persecutions or human rights. Thus, they have no identity in the foreign countries and their children are not allowed to go to the public schools. They are considered low class and are discriminated by the people of the countries where they are living.

Their lands, their homes, their properties, their jobs, their families and every material and cultural things and almost their lives were taken away from them by the greedy and cruel socialist leaders. They escaped the socialist country in hopes of a better life and freedom but now they are being discriminated by people and the governments of foreign lands and many are even imprisoned.

I met many of them before coming to the U.S., and listened to their stories, their cries, their hopes, their wishes and their desires. They hope that their miseries and their pains would end soon. They long for the day that their family members, their spouses, their children could be reunited and it is not possible now. They are longing for the opportunities to go to free countries to start their lives again.

When will their dream come true? I don't know as well and if I could make the decision to help I will be more than happy to do so. I really do understand their pain because I am also in their shoes. I just pray and propose that the U.S. and the free world of the West would give these pitiful victims another opportunity so that these 3,000 to 5,000 victims can soon be relocated to the U.S., Canada or somewhere.

These victims appreciate the opportunities for life and freedom and they would not ask any financial assistance from the countries that are willing to receive them. They are still young and they are still strong to work for a living and they just need the love and mercy of the free countries to give them an opportunity for new life. That opportunity would be greater than any compensation that the socialists could give.

If you are in a position to help these victims for the opportunity to be relocated in the U.S., Canada or somewhere in the free world, please help and please contact us for more information. Your open hands to these victims is another evidence to the modern world that justices, equality, happiness and freedoms are not possible in socialist nations as millions of former refugees experienced before.

American friends and friends of the world, socialist ideology may sound good and great but please remember that the socialists are not going to give you free stuff for nothing. Their nature is to rob from you as much as possible. As socialists, they have nothing from the beginning so they have to get from you first. Surely they would give you, not what they promised, but sufferings, oppressions, inequality...

9th Commandment
"THOU SHALL NOT NEED TO VOTE"
Freedom to Vote

I have lived for half a century now and never once have I voted for any country leader because my vote was never really needed in the socialist country. Of course, I am not the lone person in the socialist country who did so. You may think that this is the same in the U.S. as Americans could choose to vote or not to vote. There are many differences between voting in socialist countries and democratic countries.

Firstly, in the socialist countries, voting is just a matter of formality and the people know very well that the higher leaders have already decided who they need to put into the positions. So voting is better to be seen as the way the government uses to announce to the public the leaders that the government selected. This happens from village level to the central government level.

Oh I need to tell you that I studied at a National Law University in a socialist country for almost 5 years and I was supposed to become a lawyer. At least I know enough about voting to tell you that people have so much freedom in socialist countries that they do not need to vote but yet leaders are still appointed. The socialists believe that their voting system is the most democratic one in the world.

Yes, the list of names is already determined by the higher authorities and the people just check their names for fun. Where do the votes go and who could verify the transparency of the voting process? The people do not know. If the vote is changed, the people do not know. People demonstrate to go against really corrupted leaders, they still are elected for the offices. So what is the use of voting?

Secondly, voting is to consolidate the power of the party instead of the will of the people. Leaders who do not follow the will of the political party and leaders would be eliminated. This must done in accordance to the guidance of the higher political leaders to make sure that, the selected leaders would carry out the commands of the party leaders and the party. People, power and freedom are not real here.

Socialist leaders often talked as if they are doing everything for the people and because of the people. In reality, the power and the will of the political party and political leaders are the top priority so that the leaders could control and monitor people at every level, and, to make sure that usurpation would not be possible, but only total loyalty and submission to the regime.

To make sure that there is total loyalty and submission to the regime and to consolidate their power, the socialist leaders help one another to vote for their children and their relatives into the positions. It is not legal for a leader to recommend his or her family members or relatives, but it is legal if other leaders recommend or vote for family members of other leaders.

Thirdly, voting is to bribe the higher leaders for favors. People just voted to make the leaders happy so that the leaders could give them more favors or make things easier for them when they need help from the leaders. People voted first for the children and relatives of the leaders and then the children and relatives of the leaders would return favor by appointing relevant people for lower positions.

Please take note that the popular votes are basically for show, and, in most cases, the common people do not even know much about the list of candidates whom they vote for. Voting then is not for the purposes of making the voices and the desires of the people to be heard. It is not for the defenses and justices of the people but for political purposes and control of power.

In America, the voter turnout was always less than the number of eligible people for voting because the process may be complicated to some people or people may tend to forget the day of their voting. There might be other urgent things coming up and they did not go to vote.

Others may not feel the need to vote as they also think that their votes do not change their lives so they do not cast their votes.

But the votes in America are really counted and every vote is important. Eventhough in the U.S. there is a chance of voting corruption taking place, as there are always corrupted leaders everywhere, at least the overall process is quite transparent and the votes are really checked. The appointment of the candidates does reflect the peoples' choice of candidates.

How about the candidates? There is no independent candidate to be selected for the leadership in socialist countries. A candidate must first of all be a loyal and active member of the socialist party. A candidate must live, show and prove that he or she follows the leadership of the party. Secondly, the new leaders are appointed by the higher leaders, not people, thus election or voting is just a show and a political game.

Is it possible to have a socialist member to run for a presidential campaign in socialist countries? The mayors or presidents in socialist countries are not elected by the people so there is no place for presidential campaign or whatever the campaign as people often see in the free world. No socialist members would do that because they know well that it is the higher leaders who select them not the people.

Because the higher leaders are the people who appoint new leaders, the lower ranking leaders would try their best to please the higher-ranking leaders for their chances to be promoted to higher position. This leads to so many corruptions, internal conflicts, abuses of powers and unfair competitions as leaders just use money and relationships to get the positions. People are still their pitiful victims.

Just imagine that you were the wealthy billionaire Michael Bloomberg and you wanted to run for mayor or presidency in a socialist country. You would hire your staff to run the operations and to advertise your presidential campaign in all the provinces of the country. Unfortunately, this only works in America and democratic countries. You would be put into prison for life in a socialist country by doing that.

Why? Because the people have no freedom to vote for a president. That freedom and power belongs to the Politburo Standing Committee and you would be challenging the leadership and ideology of the socialist leaders. Your freedom for free speech, free press, and free thoughts are not welcomed here in socialist countries. What you are doing is considered counter-revolutionary and dangerous.

Oh, the appointments for many political positions could happen at any time. Why don't you send a short resume to apply for an office? Make sure you send your resume early so that it is received in a timely manner by the leaders. You must have the following qualifications listed on your resume:

1. A Standing Socialist Member Certificate.

2. A Statement of Your Socialist Faith.

3. A Short Declaration of Your Commitment to and only to Socialism.

4. A Summary of Your Achievements In Criticizing or Persecuting People Who Want Free Press, Free Speech, Freedom of Religion, Free Travel, Free Trials by Jury, Freedom of Peaceful Gathering, Free Human Rights, Freedom for Duly Compensation...

5. A Strong List of Recommendation Letters from Political Leaders.

Oh, I forgot to remind you that if you are not a standing socialist party member, don't waste your time writing your resume. If you are not a standing member and you still insist to send your resume for a chance, I still do not think that you will have any chance. Just like in the voting process, the ballots have no meaning to the socialist leaders and so it is with you resume.

Oh, maybe this piece of advice may be of help and importance to you standing a better chance of acceptance especially if you do not have a strong socialist background to support you. Please make sure to state clearly and soundly that the socialist ideology is the only ideology that you believe in, that you support and that you would die for. You may have a good chance as I did.

If you do so, you may have a good chance as I did in the following story and in the discussion of 10th Commandment, "Thou Shall Have No Other Ideology." The socialist ideology is everything for the socialists because it is the guide and the shining star for the people to find equality, happiness and prosperity. Thus there is no other ideology allowed but only socialism.

10ᵗʰ Commandment
"THOU SHALL HAVE NO OTHER IDEOLOGY"
Or Freedom of Thought

When I took the entrance exam for a Law University years ago, I did not worry much about the exams of other courses but literature and especially written compositions. In fact, I liked literature but in socialist countries, all literatures from poems to novels were mostly about praising socialism. Students especially praised or listened to the greatness of socialism and the socialist leaders to the sky every day in school.

People and students must compose their speeches, songs or essays to praise though many of them no longer believed that. I heard and saw many sufferings of my family members, relatives and neighbors so I at least knew some real truth about the "greatness and glory" of socialism. Thus I did not want to lie or just simply praise the ideology in order to get higher grades for the many essays as many students did.

Thus, for as long as I could remember, I never got any good grades for my essays in the first 12 years of education and of course the teachers dared not give me a good grade or an excellent mark when praises and "lies" are not present in the writings. On that day when I took the entrance exam, one of the major questions was to analyze a famous poem that compared the socialist ideology as the sun and light.

This major question got the most points and if I did not do well I could not enter the law university. After analyzing the historical background, the metaphors and the language structure, I must then write an essay about the relationship between the figurative languages and their meanings in comparison to socialism. At last I made the decision that I must write something beyond the reality.

With my family background, it was hard for me to enter a law university in those days because it was mainly the place for students with political backgrounds or students who pursued and supported socialist ideology. I was not interested in the ideology but only in my dream to become a lawyer. If I could not get a good grade then the chance would be very slim, if not impossible to enter into a law university.

That question on the entrance exam alone was already a test and a guarantee pass to the students really supporting the ideology and how idealistic they were about the ideology and the party. So I tried my best to praise the gladness, the greatness, the glory, and the great prospect of the socialist ideology, the party and the leaders to the skies and moon. I used all the great words and affection I knew for the essay.

Yes, as you could guess, I got the highest grade for my writing composition for the first time ever in my life and especially in this critical entrance exam. The great and funny thing was that I got the high marks to write something unreal and something that I did not really believe in. I got the high marks for the "lies" I wrote about socialism. That is exactly the thing that the party and the leaders want to hear.

Because their ears are not in tune to negative responses toward socialism, their hands are not used to receive bad reports about the political party. Their eyes are not happy to read the news of the socialist failure. Their speech was not encouraged to mention about the worse of the socialist leaders. Their hearts are not trained to take in criticism. Their feelings about socialism are stereotyped.

But the reports about the failures of their rivals are acceptable and criticism on other ideologies is highly encouraged. The news about the disciplines or punishments of people who are against the socialist direction, leadership, ideology and the political party are widespread because those news are used as a way to remind the people that they behave and they should not go against the authorities.

In socialist countries, the praise of the opposite ideology then is not acceptable. In the past, no one even dared to talk publicly any good things about any capitalistic countries except socialist countries because socialists can only take praises about themselves but not others. Just like millions of children in schools today, I was taught to praise the political leaders and the political parties.

Millions of today's children in socialist countries are still praising the leaders and the party daily. They are taught to write, sing and recite great things about the leaders and the party. Teachers or professors who happen to say negative things about the country, leaders and party would be disciplined or removed from their teaching positions. In fact, teachings are strictly monitored in schools.

When I was teaching at a university, I applied various teaching approaches to include students in the learning process. One time, I gave the topic, "Do Disasters Come From God or Man?" for students to debate. Then, I was called to the office the next day and I was questioned about why did I give students such a topic to debate. Just a simple topic for debate, you may think and what is wrong with that topic?

But in the mindset of the socialists, they would think that I intended to lead the students to talk bad about the government because there were many disasters in the lands. If disasters came from people, then the government and the leaders did not do a good job to prevent or protect people from the disasters. They did not want people to know that many disasters were the consequences of their corruptions.

Besides, the common cultural thought of the people is that when the leaders of the nations are bad, the nature will reveal that through strange signs and disasters. The worse of this cultural thought to the socialists is that when disasters happen often, that is the sign of heaven to bring about changes in the leadership. So the debate may lead to the overthrow of the socialist regime at the signs of disaster.

You may laugh but that is the truth about socialists. Yes, they are so insecure and vulnerable that they may think all of the worse situations. They would stop any potential harm to the government and ideology right at the beginning. No ideology is allowed to challenge the perfect socialism because socialism is the best form of government and the best way of governance.

Yes, it is the best form of government for oppressions, exploitations, brutalities and suppression. Socialism and socialists are great for revolution and overthrowing other governments because of their great promises, lies, centralized power and brutal killings. This form of government is best for violent places or warfare areas that need the military type of the government to fight against one another.

Socialism is not good then for the exercises of freedoms and rights because the government would lose the power to make these freedoms and rights of press, speech, travel, arms, militaries available to people. Unfortunately, when these freedoms are available to people, the socialists know their rule would never last due to their many misuse of power, lies, corruption, oppressions of people...

The story of Mrs. Faith was a very painful one. She was charged with the crime of counter-revolutionary because she spoke against the cultural revolution. She was put into the male prison and she was raped by many prisoners. Any prisoner who raped her would be allowed to cut short their days in prison or have their sentences reduced. Her family was not allowed to visit her during her imprisonment.

Who could ever feel the pains and the shames that Mrs. Faith must go through in prison when she was daily humiliated by so many strangers? Who could understand her fear and loneliness when she was surrounded by many people who just wanted to devour her and torture her? Who could give back to her the dignity and relieve her from the many nightmares in her sleep?

Because any prisoner who raped her would be allowed to cut short their imprisonment or their sentences, so many prisoners were just like in a riot to humiliate and to press and violate her fragile body of Mrs. Faith one after another. She was insulted so many times. She survived all the humiliations for months. Her family was not allowed to visit her during her imprisonment.

At last she was put to death by execution. To prevent her from speaking during the execution, they cut her throat and put a metal tube in her throat. She was humiliated and was stripped of all of her rights and dignity until her death. That was the consequences of freedom of full speech. She spoke the truth about the revolution, but the socialists did not want to hear that kind of truth.

Mr. Power was a very good man and a good neighbor of my grandfather. He was just a tailor who was diligent to work to provide support to his family members. One morning, the whole city was shocked at his horrible death. His throat was cut and they threw his body on the hillside. Someone wrote on the wall of his house, "Fight Against The Socialists." Yes, anyone who went against the socialists would die.

Do not think that the socialists would not do that to their people again in this modern time. As long as the socialists are still in control, injustices, imprisonments and murders will continue to happen. They would not allow anyone to block their way. Their motto was, "it is better to kill wrongly rather than to let any suspect run away alive." Just think thrice about that motto when you want to oppose them.

In America and in the free worlds, the citizens can freely express their different views and they can freely support the political parties that they like. The liberals, the democrats, the republicans, the socialists, the humanists, the leftists, the communists or whatever the "...ists," may fight for their rights and they can still live happily together for ever when socialists and the leftists are still the minority.

But if the socialists and leftists were to take control of America, none of the other parties and their leaders could survive in this horrible land of America then. Before that happens, my family and I would be among the first people to run again to another free world. Yes I had been on the run for so many years and I am praying that I don't have to run again ever. This is still depending on your decision then.

The socialists do not only control people's lives and actions, but also people's thoughts because the new thought could damage their ideology and power. The thought could lead to revolution and the overturn of the regime. This was the reason why hundreds of thousands of intellectual people were arrested and suffered. Do Americans want the socialist government and leaders control their thoughts?

The scary thing is that the socialists are the experts of propaganda. They are so good at attracting people to their ideology through their great promises. Their talks are very inspiring. They are excellent in indoctrinating people to the great concepts of equality, prosperity and happiness. They are now winning the hearts of millions of Americans. Yet many Americans still do not know that real freedom is in the U.S.

In America and the free world, the citizens may support and promote any ideology they want. They can freely write their opinions about that ideology. They could write books about any ideology. They can even find grants from the government to promote their ideology. They can organize the parades and marches for their ideology. They can publicize and recruit people for their ideology.

This is not possible in socialist countries. When freedom of speech and freedom of press are not available, it is not possible for freedom of thought or ideology. Any writings and any thoughts that are against or that are incompatible with the ideology of socialism and its policies are not allowed. Anyone who expressed their thought differently would first be reminded and severely punished.

When the socialist government took over the country, they ordered that any literatures and arts that were not in accordance with the ideology of socialism would be burned. Then tons of materials including precious literatures of the past were destroyed by fire including the Bible. The authorities would go from house to house to search if people still kept the materials that the government disliked.

The Bible was forbidden many years ago and, as the result, piles of Bibles and Christian literatures were also burnt. Christians around the world tried to smuggle the Bible into the socialist countries so that the leaders could have new copies of the Bible if their Bibles were confiscated and burnt. The border and custom officers also worked hard to find smuggled Bibles and burnt tons of Bibles.

The authorities even dug the floors of people's houses if they suspected that the people hid the "dangerous" materials somewhere. So many Christians and pastors especially were put into prison because they hid Bibles as Bibles were considered dangerous materials that indoctrinated people with unscientific thoughts and superstitions. Words or actions against socialism have consequences.

Information and materials from abroad through printed or electronic copies are being filtered. Internets and links are being monitored and many links and websites could not be opened in the socialist nations because the government and the political leaders do not want their people to be indoctrinated by any other ideology or philosophy but the socialist ideology alone.

It was not too long ago; the country was hot with a new rising star. He sang very well and he was very gifted at composing great pop songs about love and romance. He had many big shows and he was very popular then. One day, all the shows of this famous singer and song composer were suddenly canceled and brokers of different companies canceled the contracts with him and his brokers.

They declined all of his requests to arrange the new shows because they did not want that. He suddenly became jobless overnight. It was not because of any crimes or immorality that he did but because of his only one "wrong" answer. When the reporters asked him about the backgrounds of the many famous songs that he composed, he was incredibly happy to describe the backgrounds of those songs.

He innocently and happily answered that when he was in prison, he was so desperate and unhappy and that pain and loneliness in prison was the backgrounds and the motivation for him to write those songs. He was speaking the truth, but that was not truth that the socialist leaders wanted to hear. His answer was honest but it embarrassed the country leaders and the political party.

If he could have just avoided using the word "prison," or, it would have been better if he could have praised the socialist country and the leaders for giving him the motivation and the passion to write these famous songs, then, his situation would have been very different and he could have enjoyed his glory and great life. If he just changed his tone, he would still maintain a popular star but that came with lies.

Unfortunately, he forgot who were the ones who put him into prison in the first place. Unfortunately, he forgot that he should not talk anything about the pains and the sufferings that the socialist ideology and socialist leaders caused to him and his family. Unfortunately, he was so straightforward in a socialist country that did not and still does not accept anyone speaking against socialism.

That was the end of his career but at least he was still lucky to make his songs popular. Many song composers were given the warnings to stop composing songs about freedom. If the thoughts and emotions are forbidden, then what is left for the artists to compose, to write, or to draw? Others lost their jobs and were even put into prison as they shared their "dangerous thoughts" in writing, songs or media.

There are many writings and movies talking about the end of the world and the end of America and the country leaders still laughed and even liked the concepts or the ideas presented in the movies or writings. All of those things are not acceptable and welcomed by the socialist leaders. The movies and the writings or arts can only speak about the growth and the glory of socialism not the destructions or the problems.

You may say, "That is ridiculous." Yes, that may not happen often in the U.S. where freedom of thought and many freedoms and rights are truly respected and appreciated. Writers, movie producers, artists, song writers, poets and all the people are encouraged to make their debuts of their original ideas and thoughts. In the worse sense, they could even mock and criticize the government heavily.

Yet, the freedom to express different ideologies may not be that free in the U.S. as it was many years ago especially in the mainstream media and public schools. Public schools are critical of Christian thoughts and practices but they are open to thoughts that lead students to further left-wing ideologies. The mainstream media also promote leftwing ideologies and their contents are partisan and not even accurate.

Ariana Pekary, the "MSNBC Producer Quits Because It's Liberal Fake News: We are a Cancer and There is No Cure." "This cancer stokes national division, even in the middle of a civil rights crisis. The model blocks diversity of thought and content because the networks have incentive amplify fringe voices and events, at the expense of others... all because it pumps up the ratings reported Tim Graham.

"This cancer risks human lives, even in the middle of a pandemic. The primary focus quickly became what Donald Trump was doing (poorly) to address the crisis, rather the science itself... This cancer risks our democracy, even in the middle of a presidential election. Any discussion about the election usually focuses on Donald Trump, not Joe Biden, a repeat offense from 2016" reported Tim Graham.

"On leaving the New York Times, Bari Weiss described a hostile work environment in which her colleagues would much rather 'cancel' her than allow her to express a different opinion... Andrew Sullivan, formerly of New York Magazine, had a similar lament. He spoke of his endless frustration at the lack of diversity of thought" reported RT on Infowars.com

Just a few years ago, millions of Chinese loved to watch a talent show by Mr. Bill on a Central TV Channel. The program was very popular and Mr. Bill was favored and loved by millions of viewers at home and abroad and the government leaders. His talent show developed many famous talents for the country and he also invited many famous people to be special guests on his show.

One day, during a dinner -time with his friends, they happened to listen to an old song and they sang together. The song also reminded them about past and the hard-old days and the former leaders. He suddenly made a bad comment about the leaders and continued speaking about the sufferings and hard life that he and the people went through those days. He did not notice that someone recorded those moments.

Then, millions of viewers were shocked because he did not appear on his regular talent show the following week and then the many following weeks. The talent show was still going on but others took over the show and Mr. Bill was never seen on any shows nor was invited to many great events of the country as he was before. Literally he just disappeared from the public and no one has heard from him since.

If he was still alive or anything happened to him after his sudden disappearance from the public, the millions of viewers still did not know. But people in socialist countries know for sure that there is no happy ending to those who spoke or went against the socialist ideology and the socialist leaders even though they talked the true incidents that had happened many years ago.

The other "Half truth" or anything that is negative about socialism and the leaders is not welcomed in the socialist regimes but absolute submission to the authority of the socialist party and the leaders is required and praised. Obeying the leadership of the socialist party and the leaders is the top condition for promotion. Following the will of the socialist party and the leaders ensures the safety of one's life.

The regime always needs the total services, surrender, and submission of the people to the socialist ideology. If the people are not willing to do so, then death could be the only solution of freedom to those people. Sadly, these people could not even choose how to die because their deaths and their ways of deaths are even determined by the strong hands of the bloodthirsty socialist leaders. How does that happen?

11th Commandment
"THOU SHALL NOT LIVE WELL"
Freedom of Death

Serious warnings, threatening, punishments, tortures, incarcerations, and executions are rampant in socialist countries as those things often happened in ruthless regimes. It was accounted that more than 250 million people died due to famines, hard labors, tortures and wars caused by the socialist movements and reigns. And hundred of millions of people suffered inhumanely by the socialists.

My families saw "numberless" of deaths under socialist regimes. There were millions of deaths that were caused by famines and hunger and numerous deaths that were caused by the unavoidable wars and civil wars. Unknown number of deaths happened in prisons, labor camps and detention centers. They saw horrible deaths when the angry socialists murdered the people of the former government.

They saw the deaths of innocent people by merciless hearts when socialist soldiers just shot down any civilian they saw as they entered villages and towns. People screamed and fled yet their bullets were faster and stronger than the deteriorating bodies of people who had been suffering from war, famines and poverty for too long. Skinny and pitiful children were not spared from death.

They saw the deaths of thousands of people in prisons, detention centers and labor camps. They saw the deaths of the people who were given the crimes of betrayals of the country and the crimes of counterrevolutionary. They saw the deaths of people who stood up, demonstrated and fought for the injustices. They saw the deaths of many people who were beaten and tortured to death for human rights and freedom.

Dr. Jack Graham again said, "The 20th century was the bloodiest century in the history of the world, primarily because of socialist dictators. Three million people were slaughtered under Lenin's dictatorship in Soviet Russia. Twenty-five million died in World War I. Joseph Stalin murdered close to 60 million peasants, along with his opponents during his socialist reign.

During the Nazi dictatorship of Adolf Hitler, more than 50 million people died around the world, including 6 million Jews, Gypsies, and Polish people. Forty-five million Chinese people were butchered under Mao Zedong's communist dictatorship. Many of them were of the Christian faith. This is the record of brutal socialist dictators in the past 100 years.

America has blood on its hands too. More than 60 million babies in the U.S. have been murdered by abortionists. Planned Parenthood and the entire abortion movement were inspired by the racist and socialist Margaret Sanger. She taught that babies were expendable. If helpless babies can be eliminated at will, what does that mean for people of all ages? It cheapens human life. This is where a godless system of government leads-to misery, poverty, disease, and death."

The real number of deaths caused by socialist regimes or by some dictators mentioned by Dr. Jack Graham was just the tip of the iceberg. How about the total number of deaths in other socialist countries? All we could say is that at the rise of socialism, innocent blood was shed everywhere the socialists went. If they could kill their own parents and their siblings, would they spare others?

The motto of the socialists was "it is better to kill the innocent that they suspected rather than to let the suspected people escape." This was the scary truth and the cruel commandment of socialism. That devilish and satanic indoctrination blinded the minds and hearts of the young and passionate socialists and led them to the acts of persecutions and murdering their relatives and even their parents.

At the call of the socialist leaders for cultural reform and for creating an egalitarian society, millions of young people responded to the call. They gave up their studies and they went around the cities, towns, countryside and every corner of the country. They would purge the rightists and those who showed dissatisfaction or discontent with the socialist leadership and ideology.

They would torture and beat the people that they suspected. They would kill on spot the people that were against them. They forced and sent millions of people to labor camps. They were the nightmares of the people and even to their own families because many of them even persecuted their own relatives for the socialist ideology and they even accused their parents for their promotions.

That was the most painful moment in the history of morality and ethics. That was the saddest moment in the history of humanity and love. That was the darkest moment in the history of the political ideology. That was the speechless moment in the history of human development. Ruthless killing was the undeniable evidence of an evil regime where suppressions, injustices and deaths are inevitable.

My grandfather was one of the rare survivors of the socialists' thirst for blood of innocent people. The socialists disliked the capitalists because they were considered the root causes of inequality, exploitations and oppressions according to socialism. This is just like how Sen. Bernie Sanders and the American socialists consider the wealthy American millionaires and billionaires are the cause of people's sufferings.

In the early days, the socialists needed the financial support from the wealthy capitalists like my grandfather so that they could have the resources to raise and train the armies and to build up their power because the poor has nothing to give them. My grandfather and many capitalists faithfully provided what the socialists needed to maintain the socialist operations.

But when the socialists were strong enough in their finances and powerful in their armies, they did not need the "delicious chickens" to lay daily golden eggs for them anymore. They wanted to kill the "fatty chicken" and to share the "meats" to the poor and the hungry people so that the poor would be well fed and prosperous by their distribution as the socialists promised the poor earlier.

Though the socialists were not taking over the whole country as it is today, yet, they had already taken over many provinces and cities and they gained more power. So they began to kill many landlords and rich people to take over their wealth and distributed the lands to the poor peasants except wealth. The landlords and the wealthy families tried to run away and many were killed on the way.

One night, the socialist soldiers came to break the door of my grandfather's house. The family members were shocked but they already knew this would happen one day as this happened to many people in their city and other places. My grandfather could not run away immediately so he hid inside the huge fishing net. They asked my grandmother and my uncle for my grandfather.

My grandmother quickly replied, "He is not at home yet." Of course they did not believe her word because they had been watching the house and they knew that he was inside the house. So the socialist soldiers searched every room and everywhere in the garden but they could not find him. They looked inside the huge fishing net but they could not see anything.

To make sure that he was not hiding inside, they used the rake and the long bamboo with sharp head to spear into the piles of fishing nets from all corners, yet, they did not hit my grandfather and that was a miracle. The soldiers were so disappointed that they left. My grandfather stayed inside the fishing net until early in the morning and he ran for his life. He was really a rare survivor of the brutal killings.

If you were in that situation like my grandmother, my uncles, my aunties and my mother, how would you have felt? Would you be terrified? What if the soldiers had found my grandfather? What if he was killed in front of our eyes as they often did to other capitalists and their families? Have you ever witnessed your loved one tortured or beaten to death? Those cases are not uncommon in socialist countries.

Recent riots, violence, lootings, shooting, and murders that have been happening in the U.S. since May 25, 2020 is just a very small capture of the political revolution happened in many former socialist countries. Yet, the small scale of the violence happened in the U.S. would be enough to remind Americans about the great destruction when the political and cultural revolutions are to take place in the U.S.

Unfortunately, the mainstream media are siding with the rioters to carry out their political agenda and political revolution to make the U.S a socialist state, thus the mainstream media do not cover the news on the many destructions that the rioters, the radicals, the racists, the terrorists, the Soviet-type socialists and the members of BLM and Antifa have brought to America and Americans so far.

More than a thousand polices were injured, about 40 people were beaten to death, shot to death or murdered by the rioters across the U.S. and hundreds of people were hurts. The rioters destroyed people cars, police cars, businesses, houses, churches, and monuments. They set fire on police vehicles, churches, and communities. They caused damages to people and businesses in billions of dollar.

Americans would see a lot of bloodshed from their communities and even their homes when the socialist revolution to take place. Americans would feel the pains of their neighbors or their family members when they are to be tortured and beaten. Americans would face the fears when mobs are to move toward them and their homes. They would experience the sleepless nights and nightmares in their sleep.

Then the rich and wealthy people or the capitalists would run away for their lives because if they are to remain in the country, the socialist millennials would come to torture the wealthy people and their family members and to take away their wealth and their properties just as many members of Antifa and BLM demanded recently. They would kill the rich and send them into prison because they hate the capitalists.

Another truth that you should know about the socialists is that they are the experts who know how to use and exploit people when they need. When people are no longer beneficial to them, they just simply desert people without any regret or strings attached. They can be super-nice to people in a moment and then destroy lives seconds later. That is their ethics for power and they are doing well at this.

Do you really know why the socialists want to destroy the capitalists? **First of all**, this is a good reason to attract the attention and the support of the people, because, people tend to hate wealthy people and they also want the shares of that wealth so that their lives could be better. Thus, the socialists' promises always touch the basic needs and desires of the common people who are manipulated by the socialists.

Maybe many Americans also want to share the wealth of many billionaires like Jeff Bezos, Bill Gates, Warren Buffett, Bernard Arnault, Mark Zuckerberg, Amancio Ortega... The wealth of these billionaires and millionaires are the main targets of the American socialists and the distributions of those wealth are the good hooks and baits for many million Americans now.

Sen. Bernie Sanders asked millions of Americans to vote for him so that he could share the wealth and provide many freebies to people. He failed and he was out of the 2020 presidential race now, but there will be new socialist leaders to run the presidential race in the coming years until the day they could knock the doors of Bill Gate, Michael Bloomberg, Donald J. Trump... at the socialist reign in the U.S.

Secondly, it is the great way to destroy all potential threats to them. The wealthy people are immensely powerful and they have enough power, wealth and connections to go against the oppressors. Through people's power, the socialists could accomplish this purpose to get rid of the wealthy people easily. When these wealthy people lose everything, the socialists could easily rule over all the people.

The common people are their greatest supporters at the beginning. It usually takes a long time for the people to realize the true ugly face of socialism, as the socialists are exceptionally good at their promises, brainwashing and indoctrination. When the common people want to go against them, the socialists are already powerful enough to suppress the common people who could hardly gather power to go against them.

The reality is, the socialists do not want the wealthy capitalists, they only want the wealthy socialists. They want to destroy the wealthy capitalists in order for the wealthy socialists to emerge and to be in power. The wealthy capitalists may not listen to their command but the wealthy socialists do. The wealthy capitalists may go against the socialist rule but the wealthy socialists would protect them.

So the painful truth that people of the world and Americans should realize as soon as possible is that, the socialist promises to eliminate the wealth gap and inequality would never be realized because their purpose is to build up a new group of wealthy socialists. This group of wealthy socialists is powerful, greedy, wicked and ruthless. Their existence is to serve the purposes of the political party not the people.

What we just said is not a hypothesis or something untested. This is the truth that is concluded from tons of tears, pains, sufferings and the blood of millions of victims in socialist countries. This truth is not just the conclusion of the past but it is still truth to any modern socialist countries of the world today. American socialists are using the same tricks here in America at the ignorance of many Americans.

How many tons of deaths were there in the prisons, labor camps, concentration camps, and detention centers? How many mountains of deaths were there as the result of hunger due to the failures of socialist policies? How many millions of deaths were there as the result of selling human organs, injustices, hard labors, suppressions...? Only the socialists know and they still keep those secrets.

When asked about the number of the death toll, the socialist leaders and their subordinates just keep quiet. Of course they do not let the people know the truth, or else, how can they continue to rule their people. Of course they do not want Americans to know the truth, because, they want the young and passionate generations of America to regret later after they decide to follow socialism.

The socialists rewrote their history and they put the blames of all the destructions, poverty and deaths to the previous government and the capitalists. Their history is filled with their sacrifices and their victories. If they could even rewrite the history to suite their purpose and ideology against the historical facts? What else wouldn't they do to make people to believe in the "perfectness" of their ideology?

Oh, wait a minute. Yes, the socialists are correct that people will have the freedom of death in many cases, but this means people do not have the freedom to die their way, but, people are free to die the socialists' ways. People were forced to die, they were tortured to death, they were beaten to death, they were raped to death, they were robbed to death, they were buried to death and they were persecuted to death.

What else? People were incarcerated and hung to death. They were forced to work and exhausted to death. They were beaten and electrified to death. They were injected and shot to death. They became sick and died of hunger. They were interrogated and cut open to death. Do you prefer any kind of death mentioned above? The socialists for sure can satisfy you.

Mr. Power was a very good man and a good neighbor of my grandfather. He was just a tailor who was diligent to work to provide supports to his family members. He was gentle and kind and he was not the one that someone would pick for a fight. Yet, one morning, the whole city was shocked at his horrible death. His throat was cut open and his body was thrown by a hillside near the town.

Was he a secret agent or spy for a capitalist country? Was he shouted and mocked at the socialist ideology and leaders? There was no sign that he was a spy or he did something wrong to the government. But, someone wrote on the wall of his house, "Fight Against The Socialism."

Then he became a victim of the ruthless regime. Yes, anyone who went against the socialists and socialism would die.

Do not think that the socialists would not do that to their people again in this modern time. As long as the socialists are still in control, injustices, imprisonments and murders will continue to happen. The socialists would not let anyone to block their way. Their motto was "it is better to kill wrongly rather than to let any suspect to run away alive." Just think thrice that motto when you want to oppose them.

By the way, death is still your real freedom, because, if you don't die you will suffer the horrible consequences of socialism because of your freedom to choose socialism today. Death is your solution from injustices. Death is your choice from the abuse of their power. Death is... Anyway, death is really your freedom when you are no longer under the injustices, inequalities, and inhumanness of socialism.

Unfortunately, people do not even have freedom to choose how to die, the socialist leaders would make the decision on how to press you to death. Scott Manning gave an incomplete list of death count in socialist countries and the number is already 150 million deaths. This number was only a mid-estimate of citizens who were killed and starved to death excluding the number of deaths by wars.

If I was still in a socialist nation, my life might be over then. The 14 coworkers in our networks were suddenly disappeared one day and no one knew about their situation so far. I could be among the 15 people who would be disappeared as well. Yet God still has a great plan for my life so he allowed me to be deported out of the country to save my life. How about the families of those 14 people disappeared?

Americans, You may be the next ones to be added onto the long list of death count if you were to let socialism become a reality here in America. But why do you have to choose your death end with socialism when you already have better freedom and better lives here in the U.S. than what the tricky socialists could ever offer. What they are offering to you are just promises and the ending would never be happy.

If you really want to know more deadly stories and the unhappy endings of the millions of victims of socialist nations, you will find more in our book, "The Boat of Destiny." Let us now close this section with the final commandment of socialism which is the signature promise of every socialist and socialist nations: equality. Will the socialist's promises of equality and happiness be realized to people?

12ᵗʰ Commandment
"THOU SHALL NOT BE EQUAL"
Freedom of Inequality

The important signature of the socialist promise is equality just as Sen. Bernie Sanders said, "At its core is a deep and abiding faith in the American people to peacefully and democratically enact the transformative change that will create shared prosperity, social equality and true freedom for all" reported Tara Golshan on Vox. The socialist idea is always great but it never happens in socialist countries.

The many economic reforms by socialist nations failed and leading to the deaths of more than 50 million people due to starvation alone according to Soviet historian J. Arch Getty. How many millions of people in these socialist countries suffered poverty and economic hardships? And millions of people risked running for their lives to nations of the world that provide freedom and human rights.

These facts are more than enough to say loud and clear: prosperity, happiness, and economic freedom is not what socialism could bring to people and those things would never be realized in more than 100 years of socialist history. Some modern socialist countries today are running their economic system based on the capitalistic economic system or free market enterprises with socialist form of government.

The economic situation may be better yet equality is forever a great promise of the socialists that could never be realized. It is an unattainable goal and it is skillfully used by the socialist leaders continuously and repeatedly to challenge and encourage people to strive forward to equality. Unfortunately, socialism creates so many gaps that are totally opposite to what they promised.

Socialism creates the wider gap between the rich and the poor. In its pure sense, if socialism works it may only provide some basic needs of the people to survive. Its economic system always failed because it is largely dependent on some leaders. It killed the creativity, ability to respond to current situations, and motivation. Thus there is no such thing of wealth distribution or sharing of wealth in socialist nations.

While the common people are still struggling for their daily needs, the socialist leaders become richer and are spending extravagantly at high-class resorts and luxurious places. The wealth of so many socialist leaders if not all are basically accumulated not by their hard works, salaries or achievements, but by corruption, exploitations of the people and their abuses of power, position and people.

Socialism creates an unfair gap between the lawmakers and the observants of the laws because the lawmakers or the leaders are really above the laws and the people are suppressed under the laws. The leaders could twist the laws according to their will and the people suffer at the dictates of the lawmakers. People know that the socialist leaders' wealth are not clean but no law could touch them.

Socialism then creates the incredible gap between justices and injustices due to the misuses of powers by the socialist leaders. When the justice system is determined by who we know but not the fairness of the laws, then black could become white and vice versa depending on who the judges will be. The winning of a legal case could be decided by the fact of which leaders the people know.

Socialism, **first** of all, could never create equality due to the political hierarchy it creates. In theory, it always stresses equality through social ownership and wealth distribution. In practices, the leadership positions are clearly defined with the political background of the leaders. The political background is more important than the educational background, talents, or other achievements.

The socialist leaders would do a three-generation search of the political background of new members for government positions. The check on the political is to ensure that the new members and leaders really support the political party, leadership and the socialist ideology. It is a very clear that candidates without the political background would not be chosen to be in the leadership of even local government.

Secondly, the centralized structure of socialism would never make equality a reality. The unbalance power between the leaders and the people would never make people to be equal with the leaders. The top-down leadership would only give the order of command, thus people would not have their voices or opinions in the matters. Changes and policies are mainly decided by the leaders.

Since socialism needs strong power to maintain order in socialist countries, then socialist countries must run the countries in a military style. This military style can never produce equality but only submission at every level. To maintain order, coercion and punishment must be used and this always leads to the abuse of power. Thus, socialism cannot guarantee equality but only limited freedom and Inequality.

Thirdly, socialism could never create equality because only limited freedom and rights are allowed to be exercised. Equality is not possible when people are imprisoned for speaking what is true and when people are forbidden to pursue various ideologies. Equality is not possible when different political parties are not allowed to compete on equal footing.

Equality is not possible when the wrongdoings, abuses of power, and corruptions of the leaders are not properly punished and when the justice system is not transparent to the public. When freedoms and rights are to be freely exercised, then, socialism could hardly to survive. The socialist leaders do not want this to happen or else they would lose their power, position, wealth and even their lives.

Fourthly, socialism could never create equality because of its materialistic orientation. The socialist leaders talk much about prosperity and wealth distribution to people but this never happens. They talk about social ownership where people would share the social wealth and people would have their voices in social owned corporations and businesses but this never be realized.

When materialism is the goal of life, the socialist leaders and members just exploit every opportunity to get wealth to themselves. Without wealth, the socialists could not consolidate their positions and powers. Most of them do not have time to care for the common people and their needs but they spend more time to build political connection and to please their superiors so that they could be promoted.

Fifthly, socialism could never create equality because its structure breeds corruption and injustices. When law and order are not in place, bribery easily find its way to thrive with the approval of corrupted leaders. When the situations could be changed from black to white and vice versa by the decisions of power leaders, then corruption becomes rampant in the society at every level.

When the legal system and justice system are not upholding justices at the influences of powerful leaders, then justice could not be guaranteed and injustices happen. Common people are always the victims at the power game and corruption of the leaders. If people are not even equal before the laws and justices, what else that they could be equal?

Sixthly, equality is not possible in socialist countries because the socialists place the political ideology above humanity. The political ideology must be protected even at the mass massacres of the people. Human beings are just the instruments used by the ruthless and heartless socialist leaders for their political purposes. Then people will only experience suppression but not equality.

The ideology is supposedly to enrich people's minds, encourage people in their pursuit of happiness, excel their direction of life and enhance their quality of life if possible. Socialist ideology is to control people's thoughts, emotions and beliefs so that people will not be free. Socialism does not allow equal footing and co-existence of other ideologies. Socialism is the regime where equality is absent.

Last but not the least, socialism could never create equality due to the lack of good morality. Good government is always guided by good morality. The socialist government is guided by materialism, political hierarchy, corruption, power and greed then people could hardly receive benevolence, care and love. At the lack of good morality, evil, immorality, injustices would dominates at people's sufferings.

How equality is possible when the socialist leaders sit in small and luxurious cars while the massive groups of poor people sit in the big public buses? How is it possible for equality when what the socialist leaders spend on one meal is what the common people must work months to collect such an amount of money? How is it possible for equality when some leaders are "kings" and the people are slaves?

How equality is possible when the socialist leaders became corrupt to be wealthy and powerful while the common people were laboring day and night to be poor and to become exploited? How is it possible for equality when the socialist leaders commit crimes and are above the laws while the innocent people are incarcerated? I could list more but that is enough to say, equality is impossible in socialist countries.

How is it possible for equality when innocent people are subjected to injustices and imprisonments while the corrupt leaders are above the laws and free from their illegal deals? If equality is possible then the socialist leaders would deliver equal sufferings when they promise happiness. They would deliver equal miseries, equal injustices, equal oppressions, and equal poverty.

People will never have equal power with the socialist leaders. People will never have equal economic status with the socialist leaders. People will never have equal opportunities with the socialist leaders. People will never have equal rights with the socialist leaders. People will never have equal freedoms with the socialist leaders. People will never have equal worth with the socialist leaders.

It is also important to note that people will never have equal corruptions with the socialist leaders. People will never have equal lavish spending with the socialist leaders. People will never have equal abuses of power with the socialist leaders. People will never have equal corrupted wealth with the socialist leaders. People will never have equal cruelties with the socialist leaders

If the people do not follow the socialist ways, then they must be thrown out and then people will have equal unemployment and ill treatments. People will then have equal zero benefits and loss of promotions. People will have equal sufferings and injustices. People will have equal nightmares and tears. People will have equal oppression and suppression. People will have equal poverty and struggles of life.

Today Western world are filled with many children and relatives of the socialist leaders. Where do they get the money to buy villas and luxurious houses? Where does the money come from for them to buy business complex and blocks of houses? How is it possible for them to purchase wealthy companies, diary farms, acres of farmlands and corporations?

Yet millions of poor people in many socialist nations are struggling to survive their daily needs. That is equality in the many socialist nations.

A RELEVANT EXAMPLE

Victor Davis Hanson accurately stated, "Russia and China are still struggling with the legacy of genocidal communism. Eastern Europe still suffers after decades of Soviet imposed socialist chaos. Cuba, Nicaragua, North Korea and Venezuela are unfree, poor and failed states. Baathism—a synonym for pan-Arabic socialism – ruined the postwar Middle East. The soft-socialist European Union countries are stagnant and mostly dependent on the U.S. military for their protection."

Let us take a look at Venezuela as a good reminder. Sen. Bernie Sanders was once very proud of Venezuela for making the wise decision to embrace democratic socialism. Many people may still remember that Venezuela used to be a wealthy country and now their wealth is just a memory of the past. It used to be a wealthy and democratic country but now it is under extreme poverty and red line.

Venezuela is a great but sad example of the application of democratic socialism. The economy thrived for a short period. Today, Venezuela is no longer ranked the richest country in South America as it used to be according to PRI's The World. Venezuela is no longer ranked one of the world's leading exporters of oil. Venezuela is no longer ranked as a stable democracy and economic powerhouse.

Sen. Bernie Sanders once praised Venezuela for pursuing her democratic socialist dream, but he no longer talks about that socialist dream or admit that prosperous socialist Venezuela because the country that he once praised for the realization of the democratic socialist dream is now in bad shape as the result of democratic socialism. Yet Sen. Bernie Sanders still promotes that downfall for America.

Today, Venezuela still ranks among the top nations of the world. It's the number 1 country with the highest homicide rate in the world. "The land is also well-known for pertaining criminal pursuits on its land and in its society. Drug trafficking, homicide/murder, corruption and human trafficking are among the routine matters of state. Every 21 minutes a victim falls to murder according to WhichCountry.Co

- It ranks one of the top countries with poverty rate and economic crises
- It ranks one of the top countries with totalitarian and the worse political crises
- It ranks one of the top countries with issues of human rights and corruption
- It ranks one of the top countries with hyperinflation and unemployment
- It ranks one of the top countries with food shortages and deaths

According to BBC.com on Venezuela Crisis, more than four million Venezuelans fled from their country. The annual inflation rate reached 1.3 million percent by 2018. The IMF forecasts that the inflation may reach 10 million percent by 2019. On average, prices became double in every 19 days. Food, fuel, power, medicine shortages hit the country amid crisis.

Venezuela ranked the worse number 1 in stock market and number 3 in the top list of countries with the highest murder rates in the world. "Only 19% of local residents felt safe when walking alone at night... every year, more than 50 people out of 100,000 are killed in Venezuela and the number has been constantly growing over the last decades" according to List25.com by Peter H.

Sen. Bernie Sanders, and many democrat leaders also know that this would happen to the United States when democratic socialism is applied. Yet they still work hard to promote democratic socialism for their political indulgence and dreams. For others who are craving for political power and control, this move to democratic socialism would soon realize their dreams at the suffering of millions of people.

Venezuela is now in the midst of social turmoil, economic crisis, inflation, and political struggles. Someone wrote this short timeline of Venezuela on Facebook and the country's application of the democratic socialism and we find the information is also helpful to remind the Americans about the destructive consequences of democratic socialism. This is Venezuela's timeline:

- 1992 Became 3rd richest country in Hemisphere
- 1993 Became 2nd largest purchaser of F-150
- 2001 Voted for Socialist president for "Income Inequality"

- 2004 Private healthcare is completely socialized
- 2007 All higher education becomes "free"
- 2009 Socialist banned private ownership of guns
- 2012 Bernie Sanders praises their "American Dream"
- 2014 Opposition Leaders are imprisoned
- 2016 Food/healthcare shortages become wide spread
- 2017 Constitution and elections are suspended
- 2019 Unarmed citizens massacred by own government

It did not take much time but only one generation of progressive leadership to plunge this country into civil war, poverty, and tragedies. The living are also suffering and so are the dead. Families cannot even afford to purchase a coffin, casket or a piece of land to bury their dead. They have to rent caskets or turn wooden furniture into coffins for their dead.

Today, "Death has become an overwhelming financial burden for many of Venezuela's poorest, who already struggle to find dignity in life. They scrape together food and shelter needed to get through each day. So a relative's death can become the breaking point." The cost of a funeral is about hundreds of dollars while the minimum wage of people is roughly $3 a month explained Scott Smith.

The word of Dr. Jack Graham may conclude well the possibility of America to become another good and great example of the destruction of socialism when America put into practice what Venezuela did, "Just look at the example of modern Venezuela. It was beautiful and magnificent country just a few years ago. It had one of the largest reserves of oil in the world."

"But under the hobnailed boot of socialist government, the Venezuelan people have been deprived, murdered, and allowed to starve. That is what happens when ordinary people are seen as nothing more than advanced animals. They have no legal protections and no guaranteed liberties. They are expendable and will live or die at the pleasure of the state." Is this what Americans are looking for? Good Luck.

Venezuela has high tax on the rich so much that the rich are now getting richer and more powerful, and the middle class is disappearing and the poor are now eating grass to survive the hunger and poverty. According to Nicole Acevedo, Venezuela faces the world's worst refugee crisis in 2020 after Syria with 6.5 million Venezuelans left the country and they are struggling in the 17 host nations.

Venezuela has a high level control of the government so high level that they can kill anyone when they are against the socialist leaders and the socialist ideology. Venezuela has total control over the mode of production, the national economy and the distribution of goods by the government so much that the free enterprises and the free markets have been paralyzed leading to the dying economy and inflations.

Venezuela bravely calls itself a socialist country and Venezuela government bravely applies socialist economic system. So why did a hard-core socialist and socialist leader Bernie Sanders cowardly reject the great example of Venezuela? Why does he, a socialist leader reject and refuse to learn from the socialist country that he once praised for their great move and bold step of Venezuela to socialism?

If Sen. Bernie Sanders and socialists already admitted the failure of socialism in Venezuela, why do they still propose socialism to America? Venezuela is a great reminder of failure of socialism and socialist regime of the modern time. The truth is that whenever socialism is applied, the same tyranny, abuse of power, limits of freedoms would take place, why do the socialists still want a socialist America?

The answer is obvious because the socialists are always thirsty for their powers, their positions and their prosperities at the high stakes of the poor, the powerless and the pockets of all people. Their purposes would be achieved easily through their socialist political agenda. To do this quickly the socialists need to convince people to vote for their ideology and agenda with great benefits that people want.

When people approve a new leadership with high level of government control on the mode of production, the means of distributions, and the military. Then they would return people's favor and supports with their abuse of power, corruption, evil, oppressions and injustices. If they do not do so they cannot achieve their wealth and power and making the poor as socialists. Sorry, we may be so straightforward.

Sen. Bernie Sanders praised Venezuela for their socialist dream before as Venezuela adopted socialism when it was a prosperous country and growing economically. This nation is now facing extreme poverty, inflation, hardship, violence against the unarmed protesters, and abuse of power, death, and suppression of dissent. Now Sen. Bernie Sanders now condemned this socialist regime as he said,

"The Maduro government in Venezuela has been waging a violent crackdown on Venezuelan civil society, violated the constitution by dissolving the National Assembly as was re-elected last year in an election that many observers said was fraudulent. Further, the economy is a disaster and millions are migrating." He knows this would happen to America but he still proposing socialism for America.

He still wants to make America a socialist state. He still wants America and Americans to face the horrible things that Venezuela and nations experienced and are experiencing now. Only you have the power and your vote to stop socialism. Now, you still have your power to make your decision but when socialism took over you would have no more power because you voted to give them the power.

At that time, when you went for protests or demonstrations and you may shout and cry all you wanted but freedom and justices would no longer belonging to you because the socialists would use violence and armies to suppressed you. They would incarcerate you and murder you if needed. They would wage violent crackdown on you to take away your freedom and your properties.

Yes, socialist leaders would wage violent crackdowns on people when they are in power as Sen. Bernie Sanders noted about that in Venezuela. He also knows this does not only happen in Venezuela but in all socialist countries. Personally we know more and better probably because we lived in socialist countries and for decades we had survived a lot more horrible things than what he described.

Yes, these things would happen for sure in the U.S when socialism took over. Even, socialism has not taken over this free world of America yet; Sen. Bernie Sanders and socialists have already planted widespread seeds of socialism through their appealing socialist agenda. When their seeds grow, you would reap your consequences as explained in our other book, "**Be Free Or Not Be Free.**"

President Trump said firmly that, "We renew our resolve that America will never be a socialist country." Yes, President Trump and his Administration tried their best to stop socialism, the chance to bring about tragedies to America and Americans. He needs your votes to make sure that America is great and it is not great by the principles of socialism, but, In God We Trust.

UNNECESSARY REMINDERS

By theory, socialism is the belief of equal wealth distribution and government control of the economy as well as land. Democratic socialism is the political ideology that combines political democracy and "social ownership of the means of production." It is believed to be a transition from a capitalist economy to socialist economy. "The socialists seek to extend democracy to the economic sphere."

"Now, we must take the next step forward and guarantee every man, woman and child in our country basic economic rights-the right to quality health care, the right to as much education as one needs to succeed in our society, the right to a good job that pays a living wage, the right to affordable housing, the right to a secure retirement, and the right to live in a clean environment" spoke Sen. Bernie Sanders.

Sen. Bernie Sanders proposed a 21st Century Economic Bill of Rights reported Tim Hains on Real Clear Politics. "A Bill of Rights that established once and for all that every American, regardless of his or her income is entitled to:

- The right to a decent job that pays a living wage
- The right to a quality health care
- The right to a complete education
- The right to affordable housing
- The right to a clean environment
- The right to a secure retirement

Over the course of this election, my campaign has been releasing-and will continue to release-detailed proposals addressing each of these yet to be realized economic "rights." We would say 1000 Yeses to all of those rights but people cannot trust socialists to make these rights and freedom become a reality because no socialist nations could make those rights available though they already tried for one century.

Though the new name of socialism as democratic socialism sounds great with the concept of democracy, freedom and human rights will never ever became a reality in socialist countries. At the root of socialism is the rule of socialist leaders as dictators. Thus, democracy is far from the dreams of the people as the 12 Commandments of socialist countries have become evident and rampant in socialist countries.

Powers belong to the State and the socialist elites rather than to people though everything said is for people and on behalf of people. The government owns, regulates industries or mode of productions in the economy and directing the mean of distribution. In reality, most of the modern socialist countries, are applying a capitalistic economic system to save their countries from miserable collapses.

Freedoms and equality are the luxurious terms for common people. People can hardly enjoy the promised freedoms because their freedoms are often seriously violated. Yet freedoms and equality are the always the best motto of the socialists and their ideology. Deceptions, lies and suppressions are still rampant in socialist countries today, yet Sen. Bernie Sanders and the socialists still advocate such socialist freedoms.

Socialists often attacked capitalists commenting that the powers and wealth are in the hands of elites and common people suffer. Yet when the socialists are in power, people are in the hands of the tyrannies and Americans could not escape from that. Yet they use very well the mark of freedom, equal wealth distribution and equality, free health care, free education and the likes to cover up their ultimate plans.

Our advice is, "Do Not Just Listen To What The Socialists Say, Look At What They Did And Are Doing". Many socialist countries collapsed and they had to change to a capitalist economy or free-market economy in order to survive, but, they do not want to change the form of the socialist government and, they still want to control the mode of production just because they want to control power and their wealth.

You may say, "America is very different and even though America embraced democratic socialism, America cannot face that kind of suffering like Venezuela or other nations." Yes, that was the common thought of people of the nations and they were just happy to make it an experiment. Their experiment and experience of socialism always led to their many sufferings at the hands of the wicked regime.

Many of the drugs addicts today still do not believe that they became addicted and devastated at the result of drug addictions. Many of the prostitutes today still do not believe that they have to do this for living. They were just curious for high moments and new experiences, and their curiosity led them to the tormented thoughts, sufferings, bondages and nightmares. The curiosity of socialism would kill the cats.

Dr. Jack Graham warned Americans "against the leftists corrupting America through the sinister ideology... What we are facing here is a culture war that is driven by those who hate Christianity and the Church of Jesus Christ. If the far left is successful in capturing the hearts and minds of Americans, the entire world will descend into a spiritual darkness unlike anything that has ever been seen. Please make that a matter of fervent prayer during these next 14 months, and do pass this letter on to your friends and pastors" reported News Division.

Ralph Benko reminded American millennials, "But as the Victims of Communism Foundation demurely points out, 'despite Millennials' enthusiasm for socialism and communism, they do not, in fact, know what those terms mean. Memo to the Millennials: Communism and socialism suffered repeated Epic Fails at creating a Socialist Workers Paradise."

When Joseph was put into prison. His wife, the family, did not even know where he was and he did not have any chance to hear any news from his family members. While he was mistreated in prison, his family suffered greatly due to discrimination and poverty. The country also went into a great famine and the situation was made worse for his family members.

There was nothing left to feed her children, the children became so hungry that they had to eat snow to satisfy their hunger. Could their hunger be satisfied that way? But that could satisfy the hatred and the discrimination of the socialists and their followers toward his wife and children. His wife immediately sent the children away to relatives and even gave a daughter to a stranger.

Though it was hard for a loving mother to do so, she had no other choice as it was better for the children to be alive than to die in hunger. She still had one daughter left but no one wanted to adopt the daughter. As days passed, the daughter was getting very weaker due to the hunger, and so was she. She got up and went from door to door to beg for food but every door was closed.

Her daughter was dying and she garnered her little strength left to carry her daughter in her arms and they went to every door again. She event knelt down and asked the leaders and the people to have pity and mercy on the innocent dying child. It was not that people did not really want to help or they were not willing to help, but, they were too afraid of the socialist leaders and the socialist ideology to help.

If they helped the criminals of counter-revolutionary, the socialist leaders would punish them as well. They could have pity and compassion on the child and the mother but the socialist leaders would have no pity and compassion on their children and family. People wanted to help, but, if they went against the socialist leaders' will when they could not even help themselves, how could they help others.

Yes, the brokenness of a mother at the tragedy of her child could not break the cruel hearts of the socialist leaders. The desperation of a mother at the death of her child could not remove the coldness from the merciless hearts of the socialist leaders. The hunger-dying child could not even touch the little humanity left in the emotionless soul of the bloodthirsty socialist leaders

She could cry as loud as she could in her freedom of speech but her voice would be gone with the wind. She could show all the misery of her child and her life in the public, but the free press would picture her story as the consequences of going against the will of the political ideology. She could barely travel from house to house in hopes of changes but the life of her loving child ended in the socialist regime.

She could freely call the lawyers, the judges, trials by jury but the case of her daughter was already closed and sealed with non-repealing words, "Death Penalty." She may claim all the rights for her daughter to live, to pursue education and happiness, to be equal, to be prosperous... Unfortunately, there were no such rights then for her to claim. If there were, they were just promises.

She may call for the gathering of righteous people, kind people, benevolent people, brave people, human rights activists, political activists so that they could help her vote for her daughter's rights to live and to be happy, yet none of them came. They could not even vote for themselves because they also faced their life sentences and death sentences in prisons and labor camps.

Who is she to us? Who is her husband? Unfortunately, we still cannot tell you the truth now because that freedom to reveal the truth of their identities and others would bring more tragedies to our love ones. If one wants to live peacefully in socialist nations, don't ever violate The 12 Commandments of Socialism as our family and our relatives did.

The socialists makes it clear that when people violate their commandments: "Thou Shall Have No Other Ideology and Thou Shall Have No Freedom of Religion," then the consequences that these people would receive is: "Thou Shall Not Be Equal and Thou Shall Not Live." The bad news is that our "violation" of those commandments is just a small part of the million of stories of socialist victims.

If socialism was already forgotten and abandoned in the past, just let it be as many former socialist nations did. The grave mistake of many Americans today is to revive socialism out of ignorance and at the deceptions of the mainstream media and the socialist leaders. When socialism is alive, it always causes sufferings and death no matter how great the promises may sound. Kill it or it will kill you.

Now that many readers know about the reality of freedoms in the socialist countries, the readers may help the socialist victims in any way. Please make sure to keep your freedom first and keep your country away from the socialists and socialism first. If you have no freedom, how would it be possible for you to help people without freedom?

You would help more people by sharing these books, "The 12 Commandments of Socialism," "Be Free Or Not Be Free," "The Boat of Destiny," and other books of ours to people surrounding you through hard copies or electronic copies so that more Americans and people around the world would better appreciate the republic that provides them with precious freedom, human rights and prosperity.

You may help more socialist victims by supporting many church planters and missionaries to go to the socialist nations and share the Gospel to the people so that they could be encouraged by God's love and strength to face their situations and they could be free from their pains by God's power. You may also help to bless the poor and the needy people through charity works that we have been doing.

Importantly, each of you could help connect Global Missions Vision to a church, an organization or a donor that is willing to support 1 church planter with $50 or $100 a month. If each of you could help this way, then Global Missions Vision could sponsor thousands of church planters to share the Gospel to millions of the lost souls who could only find true freedom in Christ Jesus.

If each of you is willing to help Global Missions Vision this way, then in the next two decades many of the socialist countries would have at least 20% of their population to come to know the Lord Jesus Christ as their Lord and Savior. You may also help greatly to sponsor a church planter, to do charity works with us, to bless financially in any way or to serve according to your talents and calling.

Let us close with the freedom call for those who are still suffering and persecuted at the 12 Commandments of Socialism in the socialist nations. This Freedom Speech is revised and modified based on the main speech delivered at the U.S Congress on September 2018 at the Religious Freedom Conference.

THE FREEDOM SPEECH

Freedom! It is just a simple word yet it means so much to billions of people around the world and it means everything to those who are in incarceration and long for Freedom to become a reality. They long for Freedom at the absence of oppression, imprisonment, and suppression. They thirst for Freedom at the state of being inhumanly controlled, brutally restrained and unthinkable enslaved.

Freedom reveals one's philosophy with the freedom to think and to be transparent with what is thought. It reveals one's rhetoric with the freedom to speak and to reveal the truth. It reveals one's will or determination with the freedom to act and to fight for justices. It reveals one's choice with the freedom to believe and to live up to their belief. It reveals one's moral with the freedom to act from their consciences.

True freedom is the desperation cry of millions of people for liberation and deliverance from oppressions in socialist countries and nations where tyranny reigns. Oppression is a short word yet it reveals abuses, cruelties, inhumanities, despotism, ill treatments, brutalities, injustices, pains, sufferings, suppressions, persecutions, tyrannies, imprisonment and murders and many more.

The freedoms of press, of speech, of religions, of pursuing one's happiness and life are very limited in many socialist countries. Those Freedom may just be the memories of the long past. Those freedoms could not even be bought with mountains of gold for everyone in socialist countries. But those freedoms could be available to the people again when the leaders make the decision to do so.

The Bloody Prices For Freedom

Dear Beloved Delegates and Leaders of The Nations,

My father was put in prison for almost two years just because he wanted a better FUTURE for his children and family. Is this the "abnormal" desire of a father? Yet the INJUSTICES deprived him of his grand desire for family and children. Then, children were separated from father and mother, husband was taken away from wife and the siblings were separated. That was just a small cost for Freedom.

My teacher and mentor, Rev. Dr. Paul, was in jail for all kinds of suffering and humiliation for more than 10 years just because he wanted to see the Hopeless to see Hope and the Sinners to become the Saints in the salvation of the Lord Jesus Christ. Is this not a noble desire to bring HOPE to the Hopeless? Yet the cruelty kept him incarcerated and millions of people remained in hopeless situations

My dear Joseph was imprisoned and in a labor camp for 20 years at two counts just because he was a rightist and a servant of the Almighty God. Is this how we want to spend our prime time? Joseph had no FREEDOM to pursue his dream but was forced to suffer the worse treatment conditions and to suffer the separation, the loss of his dear daughter and the scattering of his own children to different families.

My friend and co-leader, Rev. David, was sentenced and was behind the heartless bars for more than 10 years just because he wanted to see PEACE and PROSPERITY for his own family and the families of millions. He wanted to see Justices restored for the Montanards. Instead of PEACE, JUSTICE and PROSPERITY, he and his family suffered PAIN, OPPRESSION and POVERTY.

My youth was spent in fugitive for exactly 20 years now at the threats of incarceration and the risk of my own safety in one socialist country.

Then, I was persecuted, threatened, interrogated and later deported and separated from my family by another socialist country. I wanted to see Bondage people be Set Free, the Victims to become Victors, and the Oppressed to be the Overcomers.

Today is also the precious birthday of my dear wife and yet, due to the inhumanity of the authorities, I have not been able to celebrate this happy day with my wife and children for two times now. How many more times or years do I have to be separated from my loved ones and how long should I celebrate the birthdays of my wife and my two children just by looking at this emotionless phones?

Today many of us are being deported to live in other countries that are far away from family members, relatives and dear friends. Why? INJUSTICES and CRUELTIES are still rampant in our homeland.

Today many of us are forced to live in new places that we did not really plan to live, adapt and adopt to new cultures, learn new languages that we are still struggling to comprehend. Why? FREEDOMS are still not available in our homeland.

Today, many of us have opted to run for our lives to other nations in search of brighter futures, equal opportunities and better living conditions Why? PROSPERITIES and EQUALITIES are only applicable to certain groups of people.

Today, many of us are not even allowed to go back to the places of our childhood, homes of our own, countries of our birth, spend time with our loved ones, or enjoy the foods we love. WHY? You know well the many answers to these WHYs of mine.

Who or what can repay the absence, care and love of a father, mother or loved ones that a family is supposed to have but is derived of? Nothing could repay the lost care, love, and protection except the presence and the reunion of the loved ones.

Who could compensate for the humiliation and sufferings that our families encountered during those long and terrible periods? Nothing can do except at least having the PEACE of mind that our sacrifices may bring better changes for the new generations.

Who could replace the loss of a father, the loss of a mother or the loss of children that we love dearly? Nothing could replace that loss but JUSTICE and the Reunion of families who are now facing the similar situations that we faced before.

Who could return our lost youth, our lost dreams, and our lost opportunities for better lives? Nothing could return those but the FREEDOM of those who are under suppression and of the generations to pursue their dreams, opportunities and futures.

I am not here today to condemn any leader, any regime, or any nation for the inhumane Treatments and terrible Sufferings. I am here to ask you to return PEACE to our homes, our communities and our nation.

I am not here today to seek revenge on any leader, any regime, or any nation for the great Inequalities and the horrible Deaths of people in the millions. I am here to ask you for Equal Opportunities for everyone and not just a special group of people.

I am not here today to seek the overthrow of any leader, any regime or any country for the terrible Oppressions and unacceptable Injustices. I am here to ask you to give FREEDOM to our families, individuals, and common people.

I am not here today to blame any leader, any regime or any country for the unbearable Injustices and unbearable Humiliations. I am here to call you to carry out JUSTICES to our loved ones and everyone.

I am also here to ask, do you really want to be separated from your family just like what you did to us and the pains we did go through and are still going through? If your answer is NO, and I am sure that you do not want that to happen to you and your loved ones, please, let those who have been separated for so long be united and let PEACE now be brought back to them.

I am also here to ask, do you really want injustices to happen to you and your family like what you did to us and sufferings we went through and are still going through? If your answer is NO, and I am sure that you do not want that to happen to you and your loved ones, please bring back JUSTICES to those who have been suffering with injustices.

I am also here to ask, do you want terrible incarceration to accompany you like what you did to us and the humiliations we did go through and are still going through? If your answer is NO, and I am sure that you do not want that to happen to you and your loved ones, please give back FREEDOM and EQUAL OPPORTUNITIES to those who are wrongly incarcerated.

Let us together bring PEACE, JUSTICE, FREEDOM, PROSPERITY and EQUALITY back to every home, village, city, province and nation. We can do that with the help of God the Almighty and "let justice roll down like waters and righteousness like an ever-flowing stream. May God bless America! May God bless socialist nations and May God bless nations of the World! Thank You

The Loss of Freedom

That was our speech and it still remains an empty and meaningless speech if the socialist governments and leaders did not take quick actions to now release thousands of the victims who were wrongly accused and are still in incarceration like Bishop John did. He was a highly respected leader not only for his dedication to God and his life of integrity but also for his commitment to God and sacrifice for God.

Bishop John was serving God and he was the vice president of a seminary. Out of the blue, the policemen came one day. They were not there to tell him how free he was or what freedoms he had but they handcuffed him and took him away. He thought he would have been fine and would be released soon. Yet his loss of freedom took him to an unknown and unsure future. He was incarcerated for 30 years.

Nobody knew that how long that he would be incarcerated but he himself knew very well that he was there to die. He received "special treatment" as the member of water prison. During the day he worked hard in the labor camp and he went through the night by standing inside the water. It was still a mystery that how could he survive that horrible water prison for a long time.

Indeed, it must be a miracle from God that his legs were not swollen by the long period in the water. The water was dirty and the bacteria could enter his body through the scratches or the open wounds on his legs. The bacteria could eat up his flesh and could cause the unbearable pains and sufferings. How could he survive the cold wintertime in that icy water? He was the only lone survivor of the water prison.

Yes, his freedom was 30 long years in loneliness, hard labor, pains, maltreatment, hunger, tortures, freezing, humiliation, desperation, frustration, and sickness and so many more. His **Freedom of Speech** was completely silenced in those long years of being re-educated by socialists. Every wrong word he made was recorded and used against him to add more years for his re-education and hard labors.

His **Freedom of Press** was far from him in the prison cell and all he could experience was their Freedom to Press him to pieces. Who dared publicize his pitiful stories anyway? Does anyone dare in socialist countries? His **Freedom for Information** was totally cut off. He wanted to know the whereabouts of his parents or his loved ones but prayer was his only way to connect to his loved ones in spirit.

His **Freedom of Travel** was confined to the four cold and motionless prison walls with freezing water where he stood and slept from nights to weeks and from weeks to years. How many times in those years did he wished and wished thousands of times that he could be Freed from those emotionless walls though these walls were his only faithful supporters and listeners during his anguishes.

His **Freedom for Pursuing Happiness** was dying every day and every time the prison doors closed, closing down his happiness with his family members and friends. Closing down his happiness to love and to be loved, closing down his happiness to search for truth and to pursue his dream. Even his simple happiness to just walk around and to smell the flowers was also closed down as an impossible wish.

His **Freedom of Religion** was only available in his long, travail and endless nights and that Freedom was available and silent in his thought only. His **Freedom of Expression** was completely lost and he was forced to recite the socialist ideology that says Freedom but he was not Free at all. His **Freedom of having a Fair Trial** was not fair at all or else he would not have faced the loss of his Freedom for years.

His **Freedom for further Education** was inaccessible and could never be realized except the constant repeats and re-education of the mind by the socialists to force him to reject what he truly believed and to accept the socialist ideology that destroyed him. His **Freedom for Equality** in this socialist country and ideology for Equality was indeed the horrible inequality. He was equally treated like animals.

- Was he a Murderer that he had to face 30 years of punishment? Nope.
- Was he a Terrorist that he had to face 30 years of tortures? Nope.
- Was he a Freedom Fighter that he had to face 30 years of bondages? Nope.
- Was he a Betrayer of the country that he had to face 30 years of humiliation?
- Was he a Spy that he had to face 30 years of being checked?

It was none of those reasons. He was God's servant and he had no real Freedom of Religion in his socialist country as the socialists say. While he was behind the bars and the real world, he worked hard during the days in the labor fields. He was re-educated at night and he stood and slept in water in the prison late at nights. The bacteria in the water could invade his open wounds and torture him to death.

Yet he miraculously survived through prayers and by faith in God throughout those 30 horrible, long and merciless years. If it had not been for his faith in God, he could have died frustrated like many prisoners did. If it had not been for his trust in God, he could have died depressed like many prisoners did. If it had not been for his hope in God, he could have died by many suicidal attempts like many prisoners did.

Does he receive any **due compensation** for those 30 years of imprisonment? If he was wrongly charged and imprisoned like that in the U.S., he could receive millions of U.S. dollars to at least compensate for his loss of freedom, the physical exploitations of the labor camp, the wasting years of his life, the violations of his rights, and the emotional struggles. All he got was to be released from prison.

The Cries for Freedom

This is the true face of socialism and the injustices are still happening right now as you read this book for the many freedom fighters, human right activists, religious workers and so many innocent people. Now that you are already informed about the true face of socialism, you will understand that the freedoms and rights you have in America are very precious. Please do not take them for granted.

We risk many lives including our own and out family members to tell you the truth that you would hardly hear and see from mainstream media. We risk the freedoms of many loved ones to let you know truth from deception so that millions of you will not be trapped in the concentration camp or the labor camps of the socialist governments so that you may enjoy your Freedom and be blessings to nations.

You don't need to take that risk in your free world and you don't need to take that risk in the future. All you need to do is to take your Rights, your Freedoms, your Faith, your patriotism and your votes to make sure that godly leaders will be in charge of the U.S. or your nations so that justice would flow. All you need is to take your Freedom to vote for your Freedom, and for the Freedom that we, the socialist victims already lost.

Americans are so blessed and they already have great freedom and rights. Do not fall into the trap and nice words of socialism and you would loose your great freedom and practice limited freedom as described and discussed in the 12 commandments of socialism. More than ever before, this is the time that Americans must be united together to protect America and Americans from socialism.

America and Americans are now facing the critical time when the American communists, the socialists, the anarchists, the terrorists, the betrayals of the U.S., the leftwing democrats, the liberals, the leftists, the radicals and the mobs are all working together to destroy Americans and American communities, American cultures and American values, American freedom and American rights.

They have been causing disorders and lawlessness. They have been vandalizing streets and attacking people. They have been setting homes and communities on fire. They have been dividing the peoples, races and America. They have been destroying businesses and the economy. They have been planning for the radicals and the socialists to take over the United States.

They are increasing child abuse and elder abuse. They are promoting gang violence and lootings. They are encouraging sex trafficking and human trafficking. They are promoting sexual assault and raping. They are approving vices and murders. They are opening to drug dealings and drug addictions. They are welcoming all the ungodliness and abominations.

American patriots and believers could not just sit and watch the U.S. to be divided and destroyed, and Americans hurt and murdered. It is time for Americans to protect their nation, their faith, their rights and their freedom. Your decision today to support President Trump, Vice President Mike Pence, the Republican candidates and the conservative leaders would save America and Americans from:

- The Deception of the Ungodly People
- The Moral Decline of America
- The Destruction of the Left
- The Oppression of the Socialists
- The Tyrannies of the Radicals
- The Reign of the Regimes
- The Violence of the Extreme Racists
- The Loss of Precious Freedom
- The Violations of Human Rights

- The Incarceration of the Innocent People
- The Persecutions of Religious People
- The Sufferings of the Civil War
- The Wicked Ways
- The Rampant Lawlessness
- The Ungodly Immoralities
- The Horrible Destructions
- The Unnecessary Deaths and Pains

This is the time that American patriots and Americans believers must take a stand for their faith to protect their religious freedom. This is the high time for Americans to take actions against the violent mobs and the extreme rioters. This is the significant time for Americans to put back laws and orders. This is the historic time for Americans to save this prosperous nation from destructions.

Wherever the United States of America faced the crisis, wars or turbulences, the people always prayed and called on the name of the Lord Jesus Christ. When the people come together to call on the name of the Lord Jesus Christ, the deliverance from God would come and peace would reign. It is the critical time for Americans and people of the nations to call upon God for His protection and blessings.

God is always faithful to His promises and God never fails His people. "For everyone who calls on the name of the Lord will be saved" (Romans 3:13). Millions of American believers need to stand together to pray for the salvation and protection of America and million Americans from the rise and the destructions of the ungodly people, the atheists and the socialists.

The unity of American believers and churches to protect their faith, their nations and their lives during this critical time would also spring forth a great movement of a powerful spiritual revival and awakening in the U.S. Do not miss the powerful touch of God upon the U.S. and Americans when the Body of Christ is coming together in Unity, Missions and Revival in His name.

MILLIONS OF AMERICANS MUST COME TOGETHER FOR THIS

One Vision, One Mission and One Heart For Missions
Uniting Hearts, Hands and Minds To Bring The Gospel Back To Jerusalem

Global Worship and Revival Conference 2020

SEPTEMBER 4th, 7AM - SEPTEMBER 7TH, 10PM, PST (NORTH AMERICA)
SEPTEMBER 4th, 9PM - SEPTEMBER 7TH, 12 NOON (VIETNAM TIME)

60 Anointed Speakers 60 Powerful Worship 60 Prayer Teams 60 Nonstop Hours

Zoom Meeting ID: 875 5799 6233   Password: Jesus

Livestream on Facebook, Youtube
www.globalmissionsvision.com | www.agapevisiontv.com

"One Vision, One Mission and One Heart For Missions"
Uniting Hearts, Hands and Minds To Bring The Gospel

Global Prayer and Prophetic Conference

October 30 - November 2nd PST. (North America Time)
October 31 - November 3nd . (Vietnam Time)

An Interdenominational Gathering of 200 Nations and 10 Million
Believers To Pray for Global Revival and President Trump

Zoom Meeting ID: 857 3488 7   Password: Jesus

YouTube f LIVE

www.globalmissionsvision.com | www.agapevisiontv.com

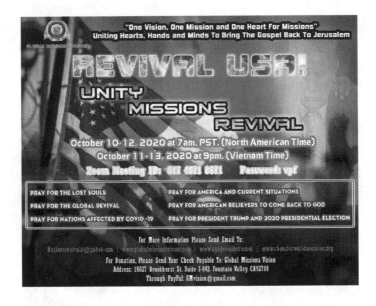

W e Are Called For Such A Time As This,
Connecting 1 Million Believers To Pray For the Global Unity, Missions, Revival, Vision 20% and President Trump and Vice President Mike Pence, America and The 2020 Presidential Election

Three-Month-Challenge: For Global Believers To Pray, To Serve and To Be On Fire For God. Will You Take The Challenge

Global Missions Vision Is Called To Bring The Global Body Of Christ To Come Together In Prayer, Repentance, Unity, Missions and Revival To Prepare for the Global Revival and Mission Movement. September Global Worship and Revival Conference and October-November Global Prayer and Prophetic Conference aims at connecting 1 million believers to pray together for global revival, to pray for nations that have been affected by coronavirus, and for President Trump, Vice President Mike Pence, America and the 2020 Presidential Election.

America and American believers are just a step away from the losses of the religious freedom, precious rights, great morals, and godly values if the left and the radicals were to take over the U.S. Their radical and dangerous ideologies would soon turn America to another Venezuela if the left and the radicals were to take over the U.S. Then, millions of people would run for lives to seek asylum in other countries just as millions of victims have been running away from their socialist countries and tyrannies to make the U.S. a new home and a new county.

It is the critical time that American believers need to realize the coming destruction and to come together to support President Trump and to protect America from the wicked plans of the ungodly leaders.

The Global Body of Christ would accomplish this goal when each of us is willing to give a hand to connect believers across the nations and American believers to come together. Will you partner and serve together with Global Missions Vision in connecting believers, family members, friends and organizing the Global Worship and Revival Conference, Global Prayer and Prophetic Conference through Zoom Conference by forming one of the following supporting teams? The time is short and we need prompt actions.

100 Mission Supporting Teams: Any leader or believer is called to form a supporting group on the social media and invite 30-300 friends for the group to pray. Will you be willing to open 1 supporting group?

Supporting Team 1:	30- 300 Gideon
Supporting Team 2:	30-300 Gideon
Supporting Team 3-100:	30-300 Gideon

100 Prayer Teams: Any believer, prayer warrior or leader may form a prayer group on the social media and invite 30-300 friends and believers to the group. GMV will have Zoom accounts available for prayer warriors who are willing to form a prayer team and arranging team members to take turn to intercede for the global revival and America on Zoom.

Prayer Team 1:	30-300 Gideon
Prayer Team 2:	30-300 Gideon
Prayer Team 3-100:	30-300 Gideon

100 Church Supporting Teams: Any pastor or leader or small group leader may form a church supporting team by inviting his or church members into this group on the social media, and pray for the global revival, missions and the local church.

Church Supporting Team 1:	30-300 Gideon
Church Supporting Team 2:	30-300 Gideon
Church Supporting Team 3-100:	30-300 Gideon

100 Supporting Nations: Any pastor or leader from countries of the world may form a group of pastors, leaders, ministry team leaders and believers for their nations and encourage leaders and believers to pray for the global revival. Praying that every American church would mobilize their church members to pray for America in this critical time.

National Team 1:	30-300 Gideon
National Team 2:	30-300 Gideon
National Team 3-100:	30-300 Gideon

Kindly let us know if you are willing to start a supporting team, a prayer team, a national team or a church supporting team so we can be connected and pray together. Basically, supporting teams and members would do the intercessory, they also encourage group members to send out flyers, videos, information of the events to friends. Supporting members also invite friends to attend their churches or ministries. Group leaders may also challenge group members to participate in church's missions or ministries. That is how we can mobilize the whole church around the world to pray and to take actions for missions.

It is only about 100 days away from the 2020 Presidential Election in the U.S. It is impossible for 1 person or 1 church to mobilize 1 million believers to be connected and pray together. But with the great supports of the global Body of Christ, we can make it together and it is you and your networks could make the number of 100 groups to 1000 groups and more when we are trusting God and standing together for such a time as this.

Please contact GMV, if you are willing to start a supporting group: nationsrevivals@yahoo.com

Please Make Sure That You Would Post This Message On Your Social Media, Share The Message and Send The Message To Every Friends and Believers. Your Brave Actions Today Would First Save America and Million Americans and Would Bring About A Great Revival That We Had Never Seen That Before. Type Amen if You Are Called To Pray Together With Global Missions Vision and To Trust God To Make This Vision To Come To Pass. Amen

The 3-Month-Challenge Begins Now. Will You Take The Challenge Now?

One Vision, One Mission and One Heart For Missions
Uniting Hearts, Hands and Minds To Bring The Gospel Back To Jerusalem

The Promise: if my people, who are called by my name, will humble themselves and pray and seek my face and turn from their wicked ways, then I will hear from heaven, and I will forgive their sin and will heal their land (II Chronicles 7:14)

Theme:	**Revive Us, Lord!**
What:	**Global Revival Conference**
Time:	**October 9-12, 2020 (70 Nonstop Hours)**
	(Friday @10am till 10 am of Monday, PST)
Through:	**Zoom Meeting ID:** 875 5799 6233 **(Password: Jesus)**
Theme:	**We Are Your People**
What:	**Global Prayer and Prophetic Conference**
Time:	**Oct. 30, 31, Nov. 1-2, 2020 (70 Nonstop Hours)**
	(Friday @10am till 10am of Monday, PST)
Through:	**Zoom Meeting ID:** 857 3488 7696 **(Password: Jesus)**

The Vision of Global Missions Vision is to connect churches around the world for the global revival and to mobilize the Body of Christ for world missions. This needs not only the global Body of Christ to come together for Unity but also for Missions and Revival. Global Missions Vision partners with national churches to carry out crusades, evangelistic events and mission mobilization.

Global Missions Vision also partners with nations and regions of the world to carry out Vision 20% with the local churches in the region so that there will be an increase of 20% of the population in their villages, cities, counties, provinces, states and nations to come to know the Lord Jesus Christ as their Lord and Savior. That is the long term plan.

For 2020, millions of believers around the world need to come together to pray for nations and millions of families that have been affected by coronavirus, the economic crisis, unemployment, disasters, violence... We pray that God would bring healing and restoration. At the same time let the global Body of Christ also prays that millions of people would open their hearts to receive the Lord Jesus Christ as their Lord and Savior through this trouble time.

Importantly, millions of believers also need to come together to pray for America from the destructions of the leftist and liberal, radical, atheist and ungodly leaders, so that God continuities to bless this nations to even send more missionaries to nations to accomplish the Great Commission in partnership with nations of the world. This is also the call for American believers to come back to God and confirm their faith in God.

So the October 9-12 Global Revival Conference and November Global Prayer (September 4-6, 2020) and Prophetic Conference (Oct. 30-Nov.2, 2020) aims at connecting a million believers to pray for President Trump, Vice President Mike Pence and of course America and Americans and that there would be a great revival in America when American believers are coming together in Unity, Missions and Revival.

These events present 60-70 nonstop hours of God's word, praise and worship, prayers, repentance and calling out to the Lord for His mercy and touch at His promise, "if my people, who are called by my name, will humble themselves and pray and seek my face and turn from their wicked ways, then I will hear from heaven, and I will forgive their sin and will heal their land." (II Chronicles 7:14)

These events will be interpreted and operated in 10-15 major languages or more of the world depending on the availability of interpreters. Each language needs 30-50 interpreters, will you serve to make your languages available to your people. Each even presents more than 300 powerful speakers in many languages, 100 praise and worship teams, 100 prayer teams, 100 dance teams from 100 nations.

GMV needs 3000 supporting members to pray for the event, connect GMV to pastors, worship teams, prayer teams, dance teams, media teams... Members of the supporting teams also send information, flyers, videos, interviews of these events to millions of people and inviting them to pray together for the global revival and America 2020. Will you form a supporting team with 30 members through a social media to do this?

In order to mobilize 195 nations of believers to pray together for Unity, Missions and Revival of the nations, GMV also needs coordinators of each country. The coordinators would volunteer themselves to invite pastors, leaders, prayer warriors and believers in a group so that we can mobilize more people to pray together to break down the misunderstanding and division walls between denominations, churches and believers. Will you be willing to serve as one of the national or regional coordinators?

Will you, your churches and your ministry teams be willing to connect, partner, serve and pray together for the said purposes. You may encourage your church to pray for these events. You may send information, flyers and videos of the events to your members. You may form supporting groups so the members would help share information of the event to their friends and social media.

You may invite your church members to join the event and pray together with millions of believers around the world for the global revival and especially America this year. You may help GMV to invite World Revivalists, Generals of Faith and Mega-Church Pastors to be our Speakers. You may be GMV coordinators to organize the events. You and your teams may serve to lead worship, prayer. We need hundreds of interpreters for 10-15 languages and we really need you

You may also make financial contribution so that GMV would have sufficient fund to make preparation to organize these world changing events by God's Grace and Blessings. Kindly let us know your involvement by sending the areas of ministries that you or your church, your team, your organizations are going to serve to this email: Nationsrevivals@yahoo.com

www.agapevisiontv.com
www.globalmissionsvision.com
www.chinaforworldmissions.org

Email: nationsrevivals@yahoo.com

For Generous Support and Partnership, Please Send Your Check Payable To

China For World Missions
Address: 16027 Brookhurst St. Suite I-642. Fountain Valley. CA92708

Global Missions Vision:
Address: 16027 Brookhurst St. Suite I-642. Fountain Valley. CA92708

Through PayPal: GMvision@gmail.com

For Wiring to Global Missions Vision:
WELLS FARGO BANK
-Routing number: 122000247
-Account number: 3301902296

A.Y Ph.D. and S.Y Ph.D.

JESUS, THE NAME THAT SAVES

"For Everyone Who Calls On The Name
Of The Lord Will Be Saved."

It is such a big shift from the 12 Commandments of Socialism to this topic, "Jesus, The Name That Saves". It seems there is no logical connection but indeed there is a powerful connection. While the 12 commandments of socialism brought about the temporary material promises of this world, the 12 disciples of the Lord Jesus Christ brought about the everlasting heavenly promises.

While the 12 commandments of socialism became the bad news for millions of people, the 12 disciples of the Lord Jesus Christ provided the good news to billions of people. While the former led people to hopelessness, the latter led people to the living hope. While the former made people sad, depressed and dead, the latter turned people to joy, celebration and life.

Today, there are great Christian revivals that have been taking place in socialist countries and millions of people have come to know the Lord Jesus Christ, The Name That Saves. That name of Jesus saves them from depression, pain, hopelessness and suicides. That name of Jesus gives billions of people a new look on life and new meaning to life. They did not come to Jesus because they were frustrated or fearful.

They did come to the Lord Jesus Christ because in their many experiences of life and death, they discovered that all philosophies or religions led them to "death" in this life and the life after that, but, the Lord Jesus led them to "life" both in this life and the life after leaving this world. Many of you have been in search of truth and freedom and you find none or you think that you have found the truth and freedom.

Will you be willing to take a few more minutes to find out the truth that has been liberating and giving meaning to the lives of billions? That same truth that works for billions of people, it could also do that for you as well. There are some areas of life that you really need liberations and breakthroughs and you may not even know or you may have taken it for granted.

One day, after preaching, we began to pray and give time for the believers to respond to the Word of God and to make a reflection in prayer. I noticed that an aunty was praying and crying as she said, "I cannot do that, I cannot do that." Next week, the same thing happened to her. So I asked her what was happening and how could I pray or do something to help her. She shared her secret and her story.

For almost 20 years, she never wanted to meet or talk to her father. She did not say what was the cause of that broken relationship but things happened and they quarreled. In his anger, her father said, "If you dare to come back to this house, I will beat you to death." She also replied in her fury, "You are not qualified to be my father and I will never come here again" and she walked away from him.

They still lived in the same village. Whenever she saw her father from a distance, she would turn another way to avoid him and maybe her father also did the same thing. If her father came to an event, she would not be there. Why was she crying now? She just became a new Christian and she heard preaching about love and forgiveness. Every time she prayed, God spoke to her to forgive her father.

But she did not know how to forgive him and she was not willing

A.Y Ph.D. and S.Y Ph.D.

to do so as well. That was why she said, "I cannot do that." Forgiving someone who hurt her deeply was a difficult thing to do and it is even impossible for many people like her to do. But God did not want her to be bound in her unforgiveness, hatred, guilt and shame. She knew for years that hating her own father was not right.

The same hatred and unforgiveness are now dividing the United States of America. That hatred and unforgiveness are now the cause of many violence and destructions. That hatred and unforgiveness lead to many riots and protests. That hatred and unforgiveness bring about lootings and fighting. That hatred and unforgiveness create disorders and death. It is time to forgive and forget.

Her friends talked to her about that and her husband and relatives talked to her about reconciling with her father for years but she just could not do it. She did not care any longer about how people talked about her and her behaviors. Now God spoke to her every moment on forgiveness and she struggled about that. So all the church members prayed together with her for the courage to do so.

So she obeyed God, she prayed and she tried. A few times, she walked close to her father's home and then just withdrew, as she did not know what to do or what to say to her father. The demons did not want her and her father to be freed from those bondages, so, they planted in her mind many doubts and negative thoughts that her father would not welcome her, accept her, forgive her, or be kind to her.

When I visited her home and prayed for her, I found out that her house is just next to her father's house. It was only three meters away to be exact. Yet, they never talked or met in person for 20 years. Hatred and unforgiveness could put millions of people in bondages for that long and even until death. It makes people unhappy, have sleepless nights, pains, sicknesses, murders, and imprisonment.

She prayed and made another try. When she came to the door, she saw her father sitting there and she did not really know what to do and she wanted to run again. God gave her strength to walk close to him and suddenly she said, "Dad, I am sorry. Please forgive me." That was not a philosophical or sophisticated long sentence, yet it brought the healing power, freedom and restoration that no medicine could do.

Her father hugged her and both of them were crying like babies. That heartfelt cry destroyed all the pain, shame, anger and negative thoughts that kept them in bondages for 20 years. That cry brought back the joy, happiness, restoration, and the complete healing of the broken relationship and agonizing days. That is also the freedom and deliverances of body, soul and spirit that God wants for you and me.

Christians are blessed to worship and to serve the living and all-powerful God. This God is not impersonal and far away but He is close to us, He hears us and He answers our prayers. Romans 10:13 says, "For everyone who calls on the name of the Lord will be saved." This promise of God is available to everyone who believes and receives this powerful promise of His.

This Scripture may be short but its promises will miraculously change your life for eternity. The truth of this Scripture will lead you to have many great experiences that you have never ever seen before. You will understand and experience the supernatural power of the Name of the Lord Jesus Christ and His Name will set you free from all your fears of the devil and the power of darkness.

God's Love Is For All

First of all, God's love has no favoritism and no boundaries. God gives this promise to everyone because God loves us and God sent His only begotten son, the Lord Jesus Christ to come to this world to die on the cross as the ransom for every individual. Regardless of our nationalities, cultures, ethnicities, colors or religions, God loves us all and He loves every single one in the same manner and He wants to save us all.

Do you know why God want us to be saved?

- We are so precious because we are made in His image.
- We are so unique because we are made beautifully by Him.
- We are so dear to Him because He created you and I.
- We are so valuable to Him because He is our wonderful Father.
- We are so priceless to Him because we are His lovely children.
- He died to redeem us and forgive our sins at the cross.
- He still loves us while we are still sinners.
- He does not leave us abandoned and hopeless.
- He wants to give us life and life in abundance.
- He wants to rescue us from eternal punishment and eternal death.

Whether we are Americans or Africans, God does not love us less. Whether we are from the city or the countryside, God does not love us less. Whether we are employers or employees, God does not love us less. Whether we are tall or short, God does not love you less. Whether we are educated or not educated, God does not love us less. Whether we are married or single, God does not love us less.

The Bible says, "For God so loved the world that he gave his one and only Son, that whoever believes in him shall not perish but have eternal life" (John 3:16). God came in the flesh to this world through the Lord Jesus Christ to seek and save what was lost as the result of the fall and the sin of Adam and Eve. The Lord Jesus came to show us the way, the truth and the life because He is the Way, the Truth and the Life.

The Lord Jesus Christ came to restore our lost relationship with him, restore the lost image of Him in us and save us from our sinful ways. He came to this world because he did not want us to die in sins and to die in the eternity loss of our souls in the eternal punishment of our souls in hell. He came to give opportunities to all people regardless of their cultural and religious backgrounds.

The Name You Should Call

Secondly, all we need is to call on His Name to be saved. We don't have to bribe Him to ask for His forgiveness of our sins and our shames. We don't have to walk 1000 stairs to the mountain to ask for His answers to heal our sicknesses and sadness. We don't have to be rich to ask for His protections and presence. We don't have to be perfect to ask Him to restore us from our wrongdoings and our wrong pasts.

God just wants you and I to call upon Him in our current situations. The Bible tells us the story of blind Bartimaeus in Mark 10:46-52 who was blind from birth and he was in that blindness for 40 years. When he heard that it was Jesus of Nazareth coming to his town, he immediately went and looked for the Lord Jesus Christ. He knew his life would never be the same and his sight would be restored by His power.

He heard so many miracles that the Lord Jesus performed to heal the sick, to multiply the breads, to cast out demons, to restore life, to calm the storm, to walk on the water, and to raise up the dead. He knew that he could not let this golden opportunity pass him by and he would be left in his darkness and pitiful life forever. So he began to shout out loud, "Jesus, Son of David, have mercy on me."

He wanted to grasp the opportunity while Jesus was still in town. He wanted to call on Jesus while Jesus was still available. Will you call on the Lord Jesus as Bartimaeus did? You don't need to be a wise man to call upon him. All you need is to grasp your golden opportunity and to call on His name. You don't have to be someone to call upon him. All you need is to grab your precious chance to call on His name, now.

You don't have to wait until you are righteous to call on Him to be saved. All you need is to call on Him. **Will you call on His name now?** You don't have to offer a lot of money to be saved. You don't need to do all the hard works to be saved. You don't need to pretend to be pitiful to be saved. All you need is to call on Him to save you. The Bible says, "All have sinned and have fallen short of the glory of God" (Romans 3:26).

- If you want to be saved from your brokenness, just call upon His name.
- If you want to become children of God, just call upon His name.
- If you need Jesus to do something for you and your family, just call on Him.
- If you need Jesus to relieve your heavy burdens and break the grip of unforgiveness, just call on Him now. He is here for you.

You may said, "I am a good man, I don't do any wrong to anyone. I don't need to call on anyone. I am fine, I can save myself." Thank God that you are a good man and you are doing good things. Yet being a good man does not mean that you are not sinful or free from sin. The Bible says that if anyone says he has no sin, he is deceiving himself and the truth is not in him. All have sinned and we are no exception.

Even many people are considered as good and great people, but they still cannot avoid and commit the following sins. The Bible says that even anger or lying is a sin, looking at someone lustfully is a sin, indulging yourselves in game, drug, alcohol, sex is also a sin, knowing what is good and not doing it is a sin before God, and knowing that someone's corrupted and do nothing about it is a sin before the Lord.

The Bible says that knowing someone is in need and doing nothing about it is a sin before the Lord, abortion of unborn babies is a sin, premarital sex is a sin, homosexual is a sin, raping is a sin, masturbation is a sin, unnatural sex is a sin, unfaithfulness to your spouse is a sin, thinking yourself as having no sin is already a sin before God, and rejecting God as your Creator and Savior is also a sin...

- I don't think that you can save yourself from sickness & death.
- I don't think that you can save yourself from being hurt and wounded.
- I don't think that you can save yourself from the curses of witchdoctors.
- I don't think that you can save yourself from the spells of witchdoctors.
- I don't think that you can save yourself from the devil's hand.
- I don't think that you can save yourself from the terrible nightmares.
- I don't think that you can save yourself from the wrath of God.
- I don't think that you can save yourself from the eternal punishment.
- I don't think that you can save yourself from the lake of hell.
- You can only be saved by faith in the Lord Jesus when you call upon His name.

Some of you may say, "Mr. Writer, what you write is good and persuasive, but my religion, my culture and my atheist teachers teach me that I am not a sinner. I may make mistakes but that is not a sin. I may do something wrong but that is not a sin." Thank you for your insightful thought. Many people try hard to explain away their sins so that they may not live in guilt and shame, but, they cannot escape from it.

- Do you think that stealing, robbing and destroying others are just mistakes?
- Do you think that lying, hurting and deceiving others are just mistakes?
- Do you think that adultery, unfaithfulness, and deception are just mistakes?
- Do you think that fornication, incest, and sexual maniac are just mistakes?
- Do you think that enmities, strife, and jealousy are just mistakes?
- Do you think that murdering and killing people are just mistakes?

- Do you think forcing and hurting others for personal gains are just mistakes?
- Do you think that drug smuggling and money laundering are just mistakes?
- Do you think that human massacre and chemical weapons are just mistakes?
- Do you think abortion and violence are just mistakes?

I believe that now you will not think those things are just mistakes but human intentions. They are sins and they are committed by willful and evil thoughts and desires. I believe that now you agree with me every one has sinned and fallen short of the glory of God. I believe that now you will recognize that you have also committed many of those sins in your life.

The Bible teaches us that, "The acts of the flesh are obvious: sexual immorality, impurity and debauchery; idolatry and witchcraft; hatred, discord, jealousy, fits of rage, selfish ambition, dissensions, factions and envy; drunkenness, orgies, and the like. I warn you, as I did before, that those who live like this will not inherit the kingdom of God" (Galatians 5:19-21).

"But the fruit of the Spirit is love, joy, peace, forbearance, kindness, goodness, faithfulness, gentleness and self-control. Against such things there is no law. Those who belong to Christ Jesus have crucified the flesh with its passions and desires. Since we live by the Spirit, let us keep in step with the Spirit. Let us not become conceited, provoking and envying each other" (Galatians 5:22-26).

Those who follow the works of the flesh will not receive eternal life in heaven but eternal punishment in hell. The Bible also teaches that the true seriousness of sin can only begin to be understood when it is seen in terms of a rebellious relationship against God and a rejecting attitude to God himself. People do not want their sins to be reckoned and they oppose God who condemns those sins.

Sin is a revolt and rebellion against God. It is man asserting his will against God's will. They say there is no need for God. Man is God himself. Sin is to deny the true God and to accept the worship of the man-made god and idols and objects of creation. They say the sun, the moon, and the stars are their gods. They even blaspheme to say that man came from monkeys and is a by-product of evolution.

Sin means defying God, fighting against God, rejecting God and refusing to live for the glory of God. The rebellious people curse God and they choose to live in lust, greed, and corruption. They choose to reject God's call to forgive one another, to love one another, to edify one another, to help one another, and to protect one another. Do you think those are mistakes? They are done by our will.

Many years ago, my cousin brought my family including my parents, brothers, sisters, and many relatives to visit his python farms. My cousin said the pythons are harmless, they are well trained, well behaved and we can play and take pictures with the pythons. He even put the big pythons around our necks and taught us how to embrace them. Everything was just fine and the pythons were really harmless.

Everyone was very happy and they really played with the pythons and took many pictures. Another cousin put a big python on the head and neck of my sister and for some reason, the python made a strong bite on my sister's face. Her face was bleeding and she screamed as the python squeezed her. My cousin quickly removed the python from her, and the laughter and fun turned into unhappiness.

As the result of our excitement and our ego, many of us today are the victims of many things we were crazy about such as drugs, alcohol, and smoking. As the result of our self-centeredness and wrong desires, many of us are still today the victims of many things we were curious about such as gambling, sex, power game, money, black magic... Many regretted but there is no medicine for regrets.

At first those desires seemed to be harmless and fun. At first those games seemed to be harmless and great. At first, those fights seemed to be harmless and helpful. At first, those addictions seemed to be harmless and high. Then one day they bit us and squeezed our lives leaving us suffering, paralyzed and even dead. If we are still alive, we still realize the painful truths and face the many consequences.

- As the result, many people are now HIV victims.
- As the result, many people are now the victims of broken families.
- As the result, many people are now the victims of drugs.
- As the result, many people are now the victims of violence.
- As the result, many people are now the victims of witchcraft.
- As the result, many are now the victims of incurable sicknesses and diseases.

- As the result, many are now in sufferings and incarcerated.
- As the result, many are now regretting what they did.
- As the result, many are now on dying bed and wishing for another chance.
- As the result, many are now sinners under God's wrath and punishment.

The Bible says that the wages of sin is death, the eternal death and the consequences of sin are sufferings. Please be reminded of a very important truth: no one can escape the eternal death. I want you to know a very important fact: your religion cannot help you escape the eternal punishment. There is good news for you because, in His name, your sins are forgiven. Your sins are washed away in His blood.

The Power of His Name

Thirdly, only His Name can save us from sins and eternal death. No name of the religious leader or political leaders could save us from sin and eternal death. No name of the scientists or witchdoctors could save us. Make sure that you call on the right name. Do you know His name? There is only one name that can save and his name is **Jesus.** Only his name is powerful to save us. Why can the Name of Jesus save us from?

- There is power and breakthroughs in His Incredible Name.
- There is salvation and restoration in His Irresistible Name.
- There is transformation and renewal in His Beautiful Name.
- There is security and peace in His Unchanging Name.
- There is healing and comfort in His Glorious Name.
- There is blessing and providence in His Sweetest Name.
- There is regeneration and revelation in His Amazing Name.
- There is hope and happiness in His Magnificent Name.
- There is deliverance and protection in His Powerful Name.
- There is forgiveness and cleansing of your sins in His Holy Name.

Wait, Mr. Speaker, "My religion says, Jesus is only a good man. He is only a prophet. He is not God. How can he save me?" You are right that Jesus is a good man and a Prophet. But He is not just any good man and not just any Prophet. The Lord Jesus is called the Wonderful Counselor, Mighty God, Everlasting Father, and Prince of Peace (Isaiah 9:6). He is called the Emmanuel God, the God who is with us.

- Can any prophet have power to forgive people's sins?
- Can any prophet be born without sin?
- Can any prophet dare say, "I am the Way, the Truth, and the Life."
- Can any prophet have the power to cast out demons in their name?
- Can any prophet have power to resurrect from the dead? Only God can do so.
- Can any prophet be allowed to have people of all nations bow down and worship him?
- Can any prophet die on the cross for our sins?
- Can any prophet save man from the death of sins?
- Can any prophet save man from the punishment of eternal death?
- Can any prophet save man from the lake of hell? Only God can do that.

One day a girl attempted to commit suicide as she jumped down into a river from a high bridge. Yet, death was not the end or death was so scary to her that, at that last moment, she struggled in the deep water trying to get out as she was now scared of drowning. So she called for help. Many people stopped by the bridge just looking at her struggles.

Some asked around if anyone could swim and could jump into the river from the very high bridge to rescue the poor girl but there was no response from the people. The bridge was too high and it was even scary to look down into the river, so nobody took action. People also knew well that before they could save the girl they would drown first by her squeezing and movements in fears.

Suddenly people saw a young man jump into the river to rescue the girl. A big applause was given to this courageous man young man. Everybody was nervous to see if the young man would be able to rescue the girl or if he would drown together with her. The young man tried hard and at last he made it and brought the girl to the riverbank and the girl was safe. They were both exhausted.

The journalists immediately took the opportunity to interview the man, praising him for his courage, and asking him what moved him to perform such a heroic act. The young man did not say any word as he rushed to the bridge. The journalists and everybody were so surprised at that. They ask him, "why did you want to come back to the bridge?" The man raises his voice and asks, "Who pushed me into the river?"

Do you think people of this world want to save you? They cannot even help themselves. How can they help you! They do something for you based on their hidden agendas. They do something for you and they expect something from you. Whether you are jumping into sin by yourself or being pushed into sin and you cannot get out. They are not willing to rescue you unless it is for their own benefit.

There is a good news for you. No name can save you and I from the attacks of the enemies but the name of Jesus, who is the God of creation. No name of the prophets can save you from sins. **Do you know what name can save you?** His name is Jesus, and he is the God who saves. No name of religious leaders can save you from eternal punishments but only the name of Jesus, the Almighty God who heals.

No name of the scientists can save you from the eternal death. **Do you know what name can save you?** Jesus, the God who delivers you and I from eternal death. No names of Doctors can save you and I from death. **Do you know what name can save you?** Jesus, His name can move mountains and His name is mighty to save us. He will give us salvation because He already conquered the grave and death.

The Bible says: There is only one name under heaven whereby man can be saved. That name is Jesus. Because "God exalted Him to the highest place and gave Him the name that is above every name, that at the name of Jesus every knee should bow, in heaven and on earth and under the earth, and every tongue shall confess that Jesus Christ is Lord to the glory of God the Father" according to Philippians 2:9-11.

We Will Be Saved

Lastly, we will be saved. Psalm 91:3-11 says, "Surely he will save you from the fowler's snare and from the deadly pestilence. He will cover you with his feathers, and under his wings you will find refuge; his faithfulness will be your shield and rampart. You will not fear the terror of night, nor the arrow that flies by day, nor the pestilence that stalks in the darkness, nor the plague that destroys at midday.

A thousand may fall at your side, ten thousand at your right hand, but it will not come near you. You will only observe with your eyes and see the punishment of the wicked. If you say, "The Lord is my refuge," and you make the Most High your dwelling, no harm will overtake you, no disaster will come near your tent. For he will command his angels concerning you to guard you in all your ways."

God will save our body, soul and spirit. We will be saved from our broken relationships. We will be saved from our hurtful emotions. We will be saved from our sinful minds. We will be saved from the terrible nightmares and the generational curses. We will be saved from the spells of the witchdoctors and the attacks from the power of darkness. We will be saved from eternal death.

When we call on His name, salvation is at our doorstep. Salvation is a promise and an assurance from God for you and I. Salvation is a free offer and a precious gift from God for you and I. It is mercy and grace from God to you and I. His promise is "If we confess our sins, He is faithful and just and will forgive us our sins and purify us from all unrighteousness" (I John 1:9). He will save us:

- From our terrible sins and evil deceptions.
- From eternal punishments and death in hell.
- From every curse and incurable sickness.
- From terrible violence and abuses.
- From every bondage and addictions.
- **Can your religion and your knowledge save you from those things? No. Only the Name of Jesus does.**

- From the horrible oppression and attacks of the devil.
- From generation curses and spells of witchdoctors.
- From your emotional depression and unforgiveness.
- From terrible nightmares and fears.
- From the wrath and eternal punishment of God.
- **Can your political party and your wisdom save you from those things? No. Only the Name of Jesus does.**

The sad news for you and I is that no one, except, the Lord Jesus Christ, is willing to die on the cross on behalf of your sins and mine's. No friend except the Lord Jesus Christ lived a sinless life to save you and

I from our sins. No one except the Lord Jesus Christ would take your sins and mine's upon him. No philosophy or ideology except the Lord Jesus Christ washed away our sins.

No religion except the Lord Jesus Christ redeemed you and I from the punishment of eternal death. No political or religious leader except Jesus purchased our lives from the control of the devil. No technology except the Lord Jesus Christ can offer you and I eternal life. Only His name can save us and that is the beautiful name, the powerful name, and the glorious name of Jesus Christ.

The Lord Jesus is here to bring transformations to your communities and your lives. He is here to bless you, your family and your country. When Jesus is present, miracles will take place. When Jesus is present, your lives will be transformed. When Jesus is present, there is a releasing of His unlimited power to save and to heal and deliver. When Jesus is present your lives will never be the same.

One day I was going from door to door to evangelize. After sharing the Gospel to one family and was about to go to another home, I saw a family of five who were standing in front of the house. They smiled happily when they saw me as I greeted them. They ran towards me and invited me into their house. I was surprised but was so happy to enter their house so I would share the Gospel to them.

They said, "we have been waiting for you here since the morning." I was more surprised because we never knew each other and I never told them that I would be at this place today. The father told me that last night he saw me in a dream. In that dream he saw he was falling down into a dark and deep pit. He was so scared as he kept falling deeper and darker. So he started to shout, "Help, Help."

At that moment, he saw a man in white that was reaching out his hand to take him by the hand and get him out of the pit. In the dream he was also told that tomorrow morning, the one in a white, long sleeve shirt would come and visit him. So his whole family dressed up and they had been waiting for that person until they saw me who was in white long sleeve shirt. God had his amazing plan to save this family.

What were their problems? The father said that his children were under nourished and they were not healthy and skinny to the bones. Their heads were big and their whole bodies were so tiny with just skin and bones. Four children were in the same condition. They ate a lot but they were not growing. They went to doctors for check- ups but the doctors could not explain the reason why they were so skinny.

I felt that they were under curses and satanic oppressions. I first shared the Gospel to them telling them that, the man in white in the dream was the Lord Jesus Christ and the Lord Jesus wanted to save them and set them free by sending me to this place. They were so happy to receive Jesus as their Lord and Savior. We then prayed for each of them and broke the curses and sicknesses in Jesus' name.

In just a few months' time, the four children started growing normally and they were no longer looking like children who were dying of starvation when the yokes of curses and sicknesses were broken. The family was under curses, sickness, depression, hopelessness and oppressions for so many years. They are now free because they called on the name of Jesus Christ of Nazareth.

Whether you are a doctor or a patient, a teacher or a student, a driver or a passenger, an employee or employer, a scientist or researcher or whoever you are, there is still great hope and deliverance for you when you call on the name of Jesus, the King of kings and the Lord of lords, the God of heaven. He is faithful and His promise still stands, "ask and it will be given to you."

Just like the four children and the man who fell into the pit, only Jesus could get them out of that pit. Many of us are falling into pits of hell without any hope of surviving. Many of us are drowning in the sea of sins and many of us are in waves of addictions and desperation. Many of us are in the grips of sufferings and many of us are in the last opportunities of life and death with no way out.

Do not wait any longer. As the Bible says, "Today if you hear His voice, do not harden your hearts as you did in the rebellion" (Hebrews 3:15). Just obey and open your mouth and call upon His Name. What is keeping you from praying and calling on His name now? Do not hesitate any longer, your freedom is just a step away and your deliverance is just at hand at your call.

- He will pull you out of the drowning sea of drunkenness and losses.
- He will pull you out of the nightmare storms in pits of hell and home violence.
- He will pull you out of the tsunami of drug addictions and terrible abuses.

- He will pull you out of the evil waves of party life and corruptions.
- He will pull you out of the painful storms in broken relationship and homes.
- He will pull you out of the sinking sands of marriages and brokenness.
- He will pull you out of the dark clouds of despairs and disappointments.
- He will pull you out of the raging waters of agonizing soul and spirit.
- He will pull you out of the flaming fires of sexual desires and lusts.
- He will pull you out of the electric shocks of unfaithfulness and betrayals.
- He will deliver you from oppressions or any forms of tortures.
- He will grant you the desires of your hearts and your dreams.
- He will heal your wounds and your hurts.
- He will heal your sickness and your diseases tonight.
- He will set us free today because His Truth will set us free.

There is hope for you and Americans. This nation and nations have become so lost in abortions and organ selling that they don't even feel the guilt of doing that anymore. They have become so lost in drug addictions and highs that they don't even know why they are in that addiction. They have become so lost in sexual orientations and genders that they cannot even distinguish between male and female.

They have become so lost in unnatural sex and incest that they cannot even recognize what is disgusting and what is acceptable. They have become so lost in sexual desires and sex drives that they don't even consider the value of virginity any more. They have become so lost in lies and deceptions that they can hardly discern what is right and wrong. They are lost in immorality, corruptions, violence and sins.

But God does not forget you, Americans and people of the nations.
But God does not abandon you, Americans and people of the nations.
But God does not reject you, Americans and the people of the nations.
But God does not despise you, Americans and the people of the nations.
But God does not turn away from you, Americans and the people of the nations.

God will save America and the nations from hatred and unforgiveness
God will save America and the nations from angers and revolts
God will save America and the nations from chaos and violence
God will save America and the nations from losses and destructions
God will save America and the nations from riots and burnings
God will save America and the nations from the virus and the pandemic

God will save America and the nations from the crisis and worries
God will save America and the nations from fighting and hurting
God will save America and the nations from immoralities and evils
God will save America and the nations from nightmares and fears
For God never fails. Amen

Prayer of Dedication and Confession

The Bible says, "If we confess our sins, he is faithful and just and will forgive us our sins and purify us from all unrighteousness" (I John 1:9). "If you declare with your mouth, "Jesus is Lord," and believe in your heart that God raised him from the dead, you will be saved" (Romans 10:9). Yes, you will be saved by calling on His name, confessing your sins and receiving him into your life as your Lord and Savior.

If you are willing to re-dedicate your life to Him or if you are willing to accept Him as your Lord and Savior, kindly pray this prayer of confession and declaration. This prayer is only a basic prayer.

Dear Lord Jesus Christ,

I thank you for your love and your promises of salvation. I understand now that you were born of the Virgin Mary into the world to seek and save lost ones like me. I know that you died on the cross as a ransom for my sins and my life. You were buried and you rose again from death to life to give me the power to live and overcome sins and her temptations. You ascended to heaven to prepare a place of eternity for me.

You will come back again to reign and to bring the final judgment to the world and I will reign with you as your child. I recognize that I am a sinner and I need your forgiveness of my sins and my past. I am willing to follow you and learn more about you from your words. I am willing to open my heart and accept you as my Lord and my Savior for the rest of my life. Please transform my life according to your words.

In the Name of Jesus, I ask that the blood of Jesus cover me and cleanse me from all of my sins and the original sins. In the Name of Jesus, I break every curse from my life and my family. In the Name of Jesus, I break every sicknesses and diseases from my body and my home. In the Name of Jesus, I ask for your protection and blessings over my life and my family.

Thank you Lord Jesus for dying on the cross to redeem my life. Thank you Lord Jesus for your resurrection power. Thank you Lord Jesus for everlasting life. I dedicate my life and my family into your hand. May your grace and goodness follow me all the days of my life. May your will and your plan be done in my life. May your protection and abundant blessings be upon me and my family.

Thank you Lord. I pray this in the Name of Jesus. Amen.

Please Keep In Touch With Global Missions Vision

After this prayer of Confession and Declaration, please take your time to visit any Evangelical Churches or Pentecostal Churches nearby in your area. If you have any questions about the churches or you need guidance to find a church in your area, kindly contact us and we will love to assist you in any way possible.

Please send us a note about your decision to recommit or dedicate your life to the Lord Jesus Christ so we can rejoice with you and pray with you and for you and your family. Welcome to the Kingdom of God and welcome to your new life in the Lord Jesus Christ. We rejoice with you and "In the same way, I tell you, there is rejoicing in the presence of the angels of God over one sinner who repents" (Luke 15:10).

Congratulations on our new life in Christ. "Therefore if anyone is in Christ, he is a new creation. The old has passed away. Behold, the new has come" (II Corinthians 5:17). Thank you very much for your response to the message and thank you for contacting us at: Email: nationsrevivals@yahoo.com

Coming Books

Thanks a lot for your generous and continuous support for the books. If these books have really helped you in anyway, please help make these books available to your family members, friends, neighbors, colleagues, business partners and others.

The 12 Commandments of Socialism: Socialist Promises
The Boat of Destiny: Socialist Victims
Unbeatable: The Great Record Achievements
of President Donald J. Trump
Be Free Or Not To Be Free: Socialist Freedom
Trump or Biden

Thanks a lot for your blessings and partnership. Global Missions Vision and China For World Missions are blessed to partner with you and your organizations.

For More Information, Please Contact Us at
Email: Nationsrevivals@yahoo.com
www.agapevisiontv.com
www.globalmissionsvision.com
www.chinaforworldmissions.org

APPENDIX: GLOBAL MISSIONS VISION AND VISION 20%

Global Missions Vision and Missions To Gospel-Restricted Nations

Global Charity and Missions Festival

Global Expo

Global Missions Vision (GMV) is an inter-denomination mission organization and faith-based ministry and GMV is blessed to partner with you and your church or organizations to bring the Gospels to the nations. For two decades, our ministry has been reaching out to Gospel-restricted nations through the following ministries:

- Bible Schools and Seminaries
- Charity Works: Livelihood project, Clean Water (Well), Food and Gift Distributions, and Wheel Chair Outreach...
- Christian Literature Distributions and Church Planting Training
- Evangelistic Crusades and Financial Support to Church Planters
- Leadership Training and Mission Conference
- Missionary Training and Missionary Sending
- Pastoral Training and Revival Conference
- Short-Term Mission Trips and TV Ministry
- Vocational Training: English, Music, Media Training, Handicrafts...

Each of us has different callings and giftings. GMV is pleased and blessed to have you come to conduct different trainings and seminars, partner for charity projects, and organize events as you are called to do. You are most welcome to partner with GMV by providing financial support or joining GMV fund raising teams.

For Ministry Involvement and Partnership, Please Contact Joshua
Email: nationsrevivals@yahoo.com

For Joining Fund Raising Team, Please Contact Tiffany
Email: nationsrevivals@yahoo.com

For Joining Our Media Team, Please Contact Christine
Email: nationsrevivals@yahoo.com

For Sending Your Financial Support, Please Contact Henry
Please Make Your Check Payable to: Global Missions Vision
Address: 16027 Brookhurst St, Suite I-642, Fountain Valley, CA 92708
Paypal: gmvision7@gmail.com
For Wiring to Global Missions Vision: WELLS FARGO BANK
-Routing number: 122000247
-Account number: 3301902296

For More Information Please See Our Websites

www.agapevisiontv.com   www.globalmissionsvision.com
www.chinaforworldmissions.org   Email: nationsrevivals@yahoo.com

MISSIONS PARTNERSHIP AND FINANCIAL SUPPORT

Global Missions Vision and China For World Missions are also looking for mission partners and generous donors to stand with us and to accomplish Vision 20%.

I was brought for a "tea time" when they caught me at a new church. The persecutions had been intense and widespread in the land. My co-workers and I also faced tough times with the local authorities due to the martyrdom of the two mission workers. They were very serious when I met the authorities from various departments such as national defense, terrorist defense, national security, policemen, and religious affairs.

I would share their stories of martyrdom when the time comes. The authorities told me that they had been warning me many times in many years to stop the mission works but I did not listen. This time they would deport me out of the country and they would not let my family leave if I was not going to stop the mission works. This was not the first time they told me so, and every time, God gave me different words to respond to them.

I told them, "Do you prefer to monitor 1 person or do you want to monitor 100 persons, or 1000 persons or more?" They said, "Dr. (my name), what do you mean?" I said, "For years, you have been monitoring me. You can call me anytime you want, and you may come to my home any time you need. Whenever you arrange a meeting, I always follow your request. You know where I go and what I do."

"If I am still here, you can still monitor me but if I am not here anymore, I will be travelling and challenging churches to support 1000 mission workers, 10,000 mission workers, then you would not just be monitoring 1 person like me but many people. I think you would prefer to monitor only one person instead of many people". I was even surprised at what I said. They stared at me angrily because of what I said but I just kept smiling and praying.

They did not say directly anything about their choice of monitoring one or more person. They just told me the story of a businessman who owned a factory with a few hundred workers. That businessman also planted churches and they met him and warned him many times to stop the church services. Whenever they found and closed his church, he would open the church in a new place as my coworkers and I often did.

So they arrested him and as the result his factory was closed and he lost his business. And that was their direct answer of what they planned to do to my ministry and me. I also had about 200 full-time co-workers including staff, teachers, trainers, church planters and many volunteers to do church planting, mission mobilizations, various trainings, charities, evangelistic trips, mission and leadership conferences, crusades...

The authorities knew well that I planned to reach up to 300, then 600 and 1000 full-time co-workers and the goal is 10,000 to carry out Vision 20% and that there would be 20% of the population coming to know the Lord Jesus Christ as their Lord and Savior. They knew that if they did not take quick actions, my ministry and the mission networks would be able to accomplish the goal and the vision.

So they wanted to close down the operations and they have been working too hard to stop the ministries. Yet, the works of men can never prevail against the works of God. Though there are up and down moments, God has always been faithful to provide needs and expand His Kingdom. Global Missions Vision and China For World Missions are looking for generous donors so that the ministries could carry out Vision 20% and would be able to support: **2000 church planters in Gospel-restricted nations.**

Will You, Your Organization or Church Support 1 Church Planters or More with $50 or $100 or $200 per month and per Church Planter for a period of 3 years?

The strengths of Global Missions Vision (GMV) are in missions-orientation and partnership. GMV has been partnering with various ministries as an inter-denominational organization to pioneer more than 500 house churches in Gospel-restricted countries through supporting Church Planters. GMV has been training more than 700 young co-workers through Bible Schools.

GMV also trained more than 4000 leaders through its Seminary,

Leadership and Mission Training Centers. GMV also organized many evangelistic trips and mission conferences in many nations of the world. GMV is also called to organize Evangelistic Crusades in many African nations, Myanmar, Pakistan, Thailand and others. By the grace of God, the ministries of GMV are still growing in the midst of severe persecutions.

Global Missions Vision and China For World Missions are looking for speakers and trainers to minister to pastors, leaders and brethren in Gospel-restricted countries. Please send email to nationsrevivals@yahoo.com

Let us partner and pray together so that the Gospel-restricted nations would also reach their Vision 20% soon. They need your generous support to see the Gospel preached, lives touched, souls saved, and churches planted across the land.

For Donations and Partnership, Please Make Your Check Payable To And Send To:

China For World Missions
Address: 16027 Brookhurst St. Suite I-642. Fountain Valley. CA92708

Global Missions Vision.
Address: 16027 Brookhurst St. Suite I-642. Fountain Valley. CA92708
Paypal: gmvision7@gmail.com
For Wiring to Global Missions Vision: WELLS FARGO BANK
-Routing number: 122000247   -Account number: 3301902296

For More Information, Please Contact and Check Out Websites
Email: nationsrevivals@yahoo.com   www.globalmissionsvision.com
www.chinaforworldmissions.org   www.agapevisiontv.com

VISION 20% AND THE GLOBAL WORSHIP AND REVIVAL CONFERENCE

September 2021

Ask Me, and I Will Make The Nations Your Inheritance,
the Ends of the Earth Your Possession (Psalm 2:8)
Will You Not Revive Us Again,
that Your People May Rejoice In You? (Psalm 85:6)

Lord, We Ask You For The Vision 20%

Vision 20% Is The Call To The Body of Christ To Come Together:

* In Prayer, Intercessory and Spiritual Warfare.
* In Repentance, Confession and Declaration.
* In Unity, Missions and Revival.
* In Mission, Charity & Demonstrative Power of The Holy Spirit.

So That There Will Be An Increase of 20% of The Population In Our Villages, Districts, Counties, Cities and Nations To Come To Know The Lord Jesus As Lord and Savior.

I pray that Vision 20% would bring about the great move and the great awakening of God for this generation and that your churches, organizations, individuals and you would partner with GMV for the Unity, Missions and Revival of the Global Body of Christ. It was not my plan to be here in California, yet God has His plan and purpose to send a powerful revival here in California and this nation for His glory.

We are called to prepare for that great and powerful coming and the last outpouring of the Holy Spirit from this nation to the nations. Please pray and partner with my ministry and I, so that, together, we can accomplish the great things that God has in store for us here, and, praying that I will be faithful to commit my life to the realization of Vision 20%. Thank God for the healing, unity and revival for the many places I travelled to.

Now is the time for the Body of Christ to come together in prayer and repentance. Now is the great time for the Body of Christ to come together in unity and missions. Now is the high time for the Body of Christ to come together in boldness and in the empowerment of the Holy Spirit. Now is the significant time for the Body of Christ to come together in preaching and demonstration of His supernatural power.

Now is the historic time for the Body of Christ to come together in the great harvest of souls and the revival of the nations. It is not about our tasks, our talents or our territories, but, it is all about His Kingdom. It is not about our deeds, our dreams, or our denominations, but, it is all about His Power. It is not about our plans, our purposes, our passions, or our projects, but, it is all about His Call.

A couple was put into prison because they were very brave to talk about God and because they were not willing to deny their faith in God. The man was placed behind bars in male prison and his wife was placed in incarceration in a female prison. The two prisons were just steps away from each other. Every morning the wife and her husband could see each other from short distance as they went to work in the fields.

Every morning, the wife would shout calling her husband, "Old man, are you ready to go to heaven?" The husband was also quick in his response, "Old woman, have you prepared well to go to heaven?" Whether the day was rainy or sunny, they would repeat the same question and the same answer, "Yes, I am ready." The jailors stopped them from doing so and the authorities beat them for doing so.

Yet, they never gave up. Many times the prison guards threatened to shoot them dead with their guns at hands. Yet the couple never showed little fear of death. They told the prison guards, "I cannot commit suicide because that is a sin. Please execute me so that I can become a martyr and go to heaven soon. I am not of this world. Please send me to heaven." The prison guards gave up and saluted them.

The courage of this faithful couple and their faith in God and thousands of stories like that have been a great encouragement to many other Christians to stand firm in faith and to overcome their tough persecutions. It was with this determination, passion and desire to live for God that the Gospel is preached everywhere in the socialist nations. Millions of souls are saved and the Kingdom of God expanded.

I pray that their stories, their courage and their sacrifices would encourage you and I and churches to confirm our identity and our missions in Christ, again. Also, we must become more active to live out our faith and our callings regardless of the pains, challenges, failures, circumstances and obstacles or even death. Let us ask God together for His healings, deliverances, restorations, strengths and anointing.

As the Apostle Paul said, "Who shall separate us from the love of Christ? Shall trouble or hardship or persecution or famine or nakedness or danger or sword? [36]As it is written: For your sake we face death all day long; we are considered as sheep to be slaughtered. [37]No, in all these things we are more than conquerors through him who loved us. [38]For I am convinced that neither death nor life, neither angels nor demons, neither the present nor the future, nor any powers, [39]neither height nor depth, nor anything else in all creation, will be able to separate us from the love of God that is in Christ Jesus our Lord." (Romans 8:35-39)

We Ask Specifically That:

- Each Believer be Active In Outreach.
- Each Family Glorifies God in their Community.
- Each Church Department Is Mobilized For Missions.
- Each Church Supports 1 Missionary or More.
- Each Church Sends 1 Team or More for Missions.
- Each City Operates 1 Inter-Church House of Prayer or More.
- Each City Conducts 1 Revival Meeting or More.
- Each City Provides 20 Prayer Warriors or More.
- Each State Organizes The Annual Worship and Revival Congress.
- Each Nation Is Active In World Missions.

We Ask Further Lord That You Would Bring These Following Gideons To Come Together for Vision 20% and Global Worship and Revival Congress 2020:

- 300 Pastors, Leaders.
- 300 Ministry Team Leaders.

- 300 Prayer Warriors for Houses of Prayers.
- 300 Members for Worship, Dance, Banner Teams.
- 300 Speakers for Vision TV.
- 300 Financial Sponsors.
- 300 Volunteers to Serve.
- 300 Christian Business Men and Women.
- 300 Politicians and Government Officers.
- 300 Medical Doctors and Nurses.
- 300 Charity and Missions Organizations.
- 300 Educators and Teachers.
- 300 Christian Artists and Singers.
- And Others

If You Are Willing To Be One Of Those Gideons, Please Send Your Information (Name, Areas of Ministry or Works, Telephone Number and you Web page, if available) to: nationsrevivals@yahoo.com so we could be connected and pray together and take action together for Vision 20% and the revivals of the nations for His glory.

Rev. Dr. J.D. and Global Missions Vision are calling you and your ministry to be part of the different Gideon ministry groups to pray and to prepare for the coming great revival, as our great God is about to do so. Praying that you would come together at the 2nd Global Worship and Revival Conference 2020 and with one voice, one mind, one heart and one mission, we pray for the great revival to come.

You are invited to partner with Global Missions Vision and China For World Missions according to your callings and giftings. Kindly see the ministry opportunities in the coming pages and get involved in preaching, teaching, visiting, encouraging, praying, or supporting financially. The ministry opportunities are available in Asia, Africa and now North America and soon in South America.

We Also Ask for the Redemption of the 7 Mountains

Arts and Entertainment	(Through Inter-Cultural Shows).
Business	(Through Global Expo).
Education	(Through Educational Forum).
Family	(Through Family and Health Care).

Government	(Through Leadership Summit).
Media	(Through Media Forum).
Religion	(Through Charity and Mission Festival).

For the last three years, GMV has been in partnership with different ministries and partners to organize International Summer Fair in July 2018 at Westminster Mall, California and Global Expo 2019 in September 2019 at Anaheim Convention Center, California. The 1st Global Worship and Revival Congress and Charity & Missions Festival in 2019 was organized at the same time with Global Expo.

The purpose is to encourage Christian leaders and believers from various fields to come together to pray for the Unity, Missions and Revival of the global Body of Christ. It is also to challenge the Body of Christ to reach out to the 7 Mountains or 7 Spheres of Influences and people in those influences. The vision is clear and our experiences and networks are still at beginning stages.

Global Missions Vision invites ministries and organizations to partner with GMV to organize the conferences, cultural shows, forums and festival at the 3rd Global and Worship Revival Conference 2021. Let us partner together to accomplish His-given vision and that churches across the globe would pray, partner and take actions for Vision 20% in their respective villages, counties, cities, and nations.

For more information, please see the website at: www.GlocalExpo.org or send your concerns and partnership to: nationsrevivals@yahoo.com

We Ask for MORE:

That more believers and people would pray more for President Trump and that they would understand how God uses an imperfect person for His perfect plan to revive the U.S. economy and life stability, to bring about religious freedom and revival, and to protect Christians from persecutions, to restore morality, and to destroy atheists' anti-Christ agendas.

Thousands of pastors, leaders, ministry team leaders and worshippers and people from nations of the world would come together at the 2nd Global Worship and Revival Congress 2020 to Pray For The Great Awakening, To Take Actions for Missions, and To Exalt His Glorious

Name. This is the call for the global Body of Christ to come together for Repentance, Unity, Missions and Revival.

3ⁿᵈ Global Worship & Revival Congress
September 23-26, 2021 (In Planning)

VIP Free Tickets for Pastors & Leaders.
Kindly Send Your Name, Church,
Position and Contact Number to
Nationsrevivals@yahoo.com
For General Free Tickets and Information
Please Contact: Nationsrevivals@yahoo.com

Don't Forget To Register Your Business Booth For 2021 Global Expo or Charity and Mission Booths for Global Charity and Missions Festival Which Are Taking Place at the Same Time and Venue of Global Worship & Revival Congress 2020.

And Be Ready For:
Powerful God-Encountered Moments.
Supernatural Demonstration of The Power of The Holy Spirit.
Powerful Prayer, Praise and Worship.
Anointed Healing Evangelists and Powerful Speakers.
Great Teams from the Nations and Famous Artists, Singers, Celebrities.
Global Events: Expo, Health, Charity and Missions Festival...

SPONSORS FOR BOOK PUBLICATION AND CHRISTIAN LITERATURE DISTRIBUTION

Through the years, Global Missions Vision has been raising funds to provide Christian libraries to churches and underground Bible Schools, Bible School textbooks to leaders, and students in underground Bible Schools, and Christian literatures to different groups of people. GMV is looking forward to partnering with you and your organizations so that GMV continues to provide the many needs of Christian literatures.

Global Missions Vision is also looking for generous financial donors and partners to make the following new books available into the hands of millions of people so that at least Americans would be aware of the truth of socialism and its rise in this land of freedom.

GMV plans to have many of the books translated and published in various languages and to distribute these free books whenever funds are available to share the Gospels through current topics. People need God to walk with them through good and tough times.

Trump or Biden
The 12 Commandments of Socialism: Socialist Promises
The Boat of Destiny: Socialist Victims
Be Free Or Not Be Free: Socialist Freedom
Unbeatable: The Record Achievements of President Donald J. Trump.

Please Make Your Check Payable To:

Global Missions Vision
Address: 16027 Brookhurst St. Suite I-642. Fountain Valley. CA92708

Through PayPal:
GMvision@gmail.com

For Wiring to Global Missions Vision: WELLS FARGO BANK
-Routing number: 122000247
-Account number: 3301902296

For More Information Please See Our Websites
www.agapevisiontv.com
www.globalmissionsvision.com
www.chinaforworldmissions.org

Kindly send your feedbacks or recommendations to: nationsrevivals@
yahoo.com

SPEAKING APPOINTMENTS WITH AUTHORS

Dr. A. Y was a former university professor who was called to preach the Gospels to the nations as a Healing Evangelist. He is an anointed speaker for revival, leadership and mission conferences. He is also the organizer and speaker of many crusades, leadership, missions and revival conference. He is the Founder and President of underground Seminary, Missions organization, and TV Ministry.

Dr. A.Y is glad to be a guest speaker at your churches and conferences to inspire and challenge the Body of Christ for missions and ministries. Please contact Dr. J. D. to make arrangements for his speaking schedule and appointment at: nationsrevivals@yahoo.com

Dr. S.Y is a university professor who is gifted with prophetic words. She is called to bring His healing and restoration to families and challenging precious women and families to develop a strong and daily family devotion. God uses her stories of persecutions to inspire many people towards faith, prayer life, holiness, missions and revival. She is known for her dedication and love to God and peoples' inner beauty, fire and passion for God's Kingdom.

Dr. S.Y is also blessed to be your guest speaker at your churches, missions and women conferences to share her many experiences of ministry and life in Gospel-restricted countries. Please contact Dr. M. F. to make arrangements for her speaking schedule and appointment at: nationsrevivals@yahoo.com

ADOPTING CHURCH PLANTERS AND VISION 20%

The heart of Global Missions Vision is Vision 20% which calls for the many prayers and mission partnership so that there would be 20% or more of the population in socialist countries to come to know the Lord Jesus Christ as their Lord and Savior, GMV is looking for each of 2000 individuals, or churches, or organizations or businesses that is willing to support 1 church planter in the socialist nations.

By God's grace, in the last two decades, GMV has been able to train thousands of leaders, mission workers, church planters. Through the generous supports of GMV partners, more than 500 home churches were planted in Gospel-restricted countries in partnership with the local churches and various denominations.

Would You Support 1 Church Planter of the 2000 Church Planters?
Would You Connect GMV To 1 Donor or Church
To Support 1 Church Planter?

These church planters would reach out to the millions of the lost souls, pioneering thousands of churches, building up houses of prayer, organizing evangelistic events, sending out evangelistic teams, connecting churches, leaders and believers to pray and to take actions for Unity, Missions and Revivals, and being used by God to bring about soul saving, life changes and social transformation for His glory.

For Ministry Involvement and Partnership, Please Contact Joshua
Email: nationsrevivals@yahoo.com

For Joining Fund Raising Team, Please Contact Tiffany
Email: nationsrevivals@yahoo.com

For Joining Our Media Team, Please Contact Christine
Email: nationsrevivals@yahoo.com

For Sending Your Financial Support, Please Contact Henry
Email: nationsrevivals@yahoo.com

Please Make Your Check Payable to:

China For World Missions
Address: 16027 Brookhurst St. Suite I-642. Fountain Valley. CA92708

Global Missions Vision
Address: 16027 Brookhurst St. Suite I-642. Fountain Valley. CA 92708

Through Paypal: gmvision7@gmail.com
For Wiring to Global Missions Vision: WELLS FARGO BANK
-Routing number: 122000247   -Account number: 3301902296

For More Information, Please Contact and Check Out Websites
Email: nationsrevivals@yahoo.com
www.globalmissionsvision.com
www.chinaforworldmissions.org
www.agapevisiontv.com

PARTNERSHIP FOR CHARITY WORKS

Global Missions Vision also invites you, your churches, businesses or organizations to partner with GMV to reach out people and communities through social works. For Charity Works, GMV has been doing the following works:

1. Wheelchair Outreach: Providing wheelchair to disable people. We also invite their family members to come when we distribute the gift so we can get to know them and share the Gospel at the same time. Usually we can preach publicly and the team members also pray for people.

2. Clean Water: There are so many places in great needs of water. There are places that the local people must walk a long distance to fetch water. We have various ways to help the local people depending on the situations. There are places that we help them dig a well or thrill a well. There are places that we have to pup water from the river to the communities. Thus, we need to buy a water pump, build a water stellar, connecting water pipes from the river to water stellar. We may also provide the local people with water tank so they could fetch water from the newly build water stellar in their community and store water in the water tank at their home.

3. Scholarship: Providing scholarships to children that have excellent academic achievement from poor families so we could encourage the children to keep on studying and preparing them a better future

4. Vocational Training Center: so far we can only teach English, Music, Media, or teaching people how to do handcrafts so they can have better chances for better works.

5. Love Gift Distributions: This is given in various forms such as food distributions, school items to students, clothes and

daily-usage items, urgent cashes for families in need, motorbikes for pastors or church planters.... Love gifts are distributed to orphanages, elderly homes, families, schools...

6. Livelihood Projects: helping the needy people with start-up plan of 200 USD so they could support themselves. We do not give cash to the needy. Depending on the needs of people, we provide them chicks, ducklings, baby goats, piglets, rabbits, small fishes and then 3-6 month foods for these livestocks or animals. Other families may do farming or gardening so we can provide them seeds and fertilizer and they could do the jobs by themselves. This project has been transforming more than a thousand lives so far.

7. Gospel Bridges: There are many remote places where children and people must cross through rivers or bamboo sticks over the hill in order to go to schools or markets and it is dangerous for people and lives were lost because of the situations. We are now working on this project so we can bless the people and their communities and sharing His love to people

8. Daycare Centers: GMV also opened three daycare centers for children from 2 years-old to 6 years-old and after-class care for students as their parents could not come back home early due to the works. At our daycare centers, children and students are taught to pray, worship, read the Bible, develop godly characters.

May the Lord bless us so that we could invite more people and team to go to minister and bless needy people across our land. May God use everyone of us to reach out to people and to glorify God in all we are doing to bring the Good News and salvation to the people. Amen.

For Donations and Partnership, Please
Make Your Check Payable to:

China For World Missions
Address: 16027 Brookhurst St. Suite I-642. Fountain Valley. CA92708

Global Missions Vision
Address: 16027 Brookhurst St. Suite I-642. Fountain Valley. CA 92708

Through Paypal: gmvision7@gmail.com
For Wiring to Global Missions Vision: WELLS FARGO BANK
-Routing number: 122000247   -Account number: 3301902296

For More Information, Please Contact and Check Out Websites
Email: nationsrevivals@yahoo.com
www.globalmissionsvision.com
www.chinaforworldmissions.org
www.agapevisiontv.com

COMING AND ANNUAL EVENTS

Coming and Annual Events
Through Zoom Meeting ID: 793 812 3439 (Password: Jesus)

Weekly:	Friday Prayer, Worship, Healing and Testimonies @7pm, PST
January:	Global Intercessory Conference & Pray-For Vietnam Conference
February:	Global Children Conference
March:	Global Leadership and Pastoral Conference
April:	Vision Talent Contest
May:	Asia Missions and Revival Conference
June:	Global Marriage Conference
July 24-25:	Send Out Conference or Global Missions Conference
August:	Global Charity and Mission Festival
Sept. 4-6:	Global Worship and Revival Conference
Oct. 9-12:	Global Revival Conference
Oct. 30, 31 & Nov. 1-2:	Global Prayer and Prophetic Conference
Dec. 4-5:	Global Youth Conference

GMV is calling for various ministry teams such as Praise and Worship Teams, Prayer and Intercessory Teams, Dance Teams, Drama Teams, Choirs, Artists and Singers, Media Teams Business and Professional Teams to serve, to partner and co-organize the events to mobilize churches and the global body of Christ to come together in Unity, Prayer, Missions and Revival.

For Donation and Partnership, Please Make Your Check Payable to:

China For World Missions
Address: 16027 Brookhurst St. Suite I-642. Fountain Valley. CA92708

Global Missions Vision
Address: 16027 Brookhurst St. Suite I-642. Fountain Valley. CA 92708

Through Paypal: gmvision7@gmail.com
For Wiring to Global Missions Vision: WELLS FARGO BANK
-Routing number: 122000247   -Account number: 3301902296

For More Information, Please Contact and Check Out Websites
Email: nationsrevivals@yahoo.com   www.globalmissionsvision.com
www.chinaforworldmissions.org   www.agapevisiontv.com

Please Follow Us On Our Websites and Media Channels, Would You Please Connect and Subscribe Our YouTube and Facebook Channels

Chinese Vision TV: Mandarin YouTube and Facebook Channels

Vision TV: English YouTube and Facebook Channels

Viet Vision TV: Vietnamese YouTube and Facebook Channels

SOURCES

Alexe, Carmen. "I Grew Up In A Communist System. Here's What Americans Don't Understand About Freedom." *Intellectual Takeout*, Charlemagne Institute, 12 March 2018, https://www.intellectualtakeout. org/article/i-grew-communist-system-heres-what-americans-dont-understand-about-freedom/?fbclid=IwAR0jFZ9HSQ4-tzlCDijVp4NlA DECMmYbCNg2rikbSmZbbJOkoJ7ylEIl7FM

Amadeo, Kimberly. "Keynesian Economics Theory." *The Balance*, Dotdash Publishing Family, 19 December 2019, https://www.thebalance. com/keynesian-economics-theory-definition-4159776

Anirudh. "10 Major Accomplishments of Barack Obama." Learnodo-newtonic.com, *Turiya Infotainment Private Limited*, 30 May 2019, https:// learnodo-newtonic.com/obama-accomplishments#:~:text=10%20 Major%20Accomplishments%20of%20Barack%20Obama%20 1%20Barack,of%20Americans%20who%20lack%20insurance.%20 More%20items...%20

CFT Team. "Media Expose of Violent Antifa Ring Leader Joseph 'Chepe; Alcoff Fails to Mention He's a Jew." *Christians For Truth*, ChristiansForTruth.com, 20 December 2018, https://christiansfortruth. com/media-expose-of-violent-antifa-ring-leader-joseph-chepe-alcoff-fails-to-mention-hes-a-jew/

History.com Editors. "Eugene V. Debs." *History*, A&E Television Networks, LLC., 7 June 2019, https://www.history.com/topics/us-politics/ eugene-v-debs

Benko, Ralph. "Bernie Sanders And The Resurgence of Socialist Sentiment In America." *Forbes*, Forbes Media, LLC., 15 December 2017, https://www.forbes.com/sites/ralphbenko/2017/12/15/bernie-sanders-and-the-resurgence-of-socialist-sentiment-in-america/#2fcb8f0c32bd

"Capitalism vs. Socialism: A Soho Forum Debate." *Reason TV,* YouTube, 14 November 2019, https://www.youtube.com/watch?v=YJQSuUZdcV4

Chang, Samantha. "Trump Was Right Again: Travel Ban Praised After WHO Declares Europe 'Coronavirus Epicenter." *BPR,* BizPac Review, 14 March 2020, https://www.bizpacreview.com/2020/03/14/trump-was-right-again-travel-ban-praised-after-who-declares-europe-coronavirus-epicenter-897080

D'Antonio, Michael. "Obama's Successes, Failures and Impact On America." *Here & Now,* WBUR, 17 January 2017, https://www.wbur.org/hereandnow/2017/01/17/obama-consequential-president-michael-dantonio

Dobson, James. "Dr. Dobson's August Newsletter." *Dr. James Dobson's Family Talk,* James Dobson Family Institute, August 2019, https://drjamesdobson.org/news/commentaries/archives/2019-newsletters/august-newsletter-2019

DSA. "DSA Constitution & Bylaws." *DSA,* Democratic Socialists of America (DSA), https://www.dsausa.org/about-us/constitution/

DSA Ecosocialists. "National DSA Ecosocialists Support Bernie Sanders's Green New Deal." *DSA Ecosocialists,* DSA Ecosocialists, 23 August 2019, https://ecosocialists.dsausa.org/2019/08/23/national-dsa-ecosocialists-support-bernie-sanders-green-new-deal/

Editorials. "Media Trump Hatred Shows In 92% Negative Coverage of His Presidency: Study." *Investor's Business Daily,* Investor's Business Daily, Inc., 10 October 2018, https://www.investors.com/politics/editorials/media-trump-hatred-coverage/

Edwards, Lee. "What Americans Must Know About Socialism." *The Heritage Foundation,* The Heritage Foundation, 3rd December 2018, https://www.heritage.org/progressivism/commentary/what-americans-must-know-about-socialism

Faria, Miguel A. "A Brief History of Socialism in America." *Hacienda Publishing*, Hacienda Publishing, 28 September 2011, https://www.haciendapublishing.com/randomnotes/brief-history-socialism-america

FreedomHouse.org. "Freedom in the World 2018." *Freedom House*, Freedom House, https://freedomhouse.org/report/freedom-world/freedom-world-2018

Freedom House. "North Korea." *Freedom House*, Freedom House, https://freedomhouse.org/report/freedom-press/2016/north-korea

Graham, Jack. "What the Bible Teaches about Socialism and Capitalism." *Jack Graham,* Power Point, 4 July 2019, https://resources.jackgraham.org/resource-library/sermons/what-the-bible-teaches-about-socialism-and-capitalism

Graham, Tim. "MSNBC Producer Quits Because It's Liberal Fake News: We are a Cancer and There is No Cure." *LifeNews.com*, LifeNews.com 4 August 2020, https://www.lifenews.com/2020/08/04/msnbc-producer-quits-because-its-liberal-fake-news-we-are-a-cancer-and-there-is-no-cure/?fbclid=IwAR1b9Tdy5z1IWnPEXsXj80KqZke02MqxDv4saojaMTb58eElcHDCmrsY61Y

Greenberg, Jay. "Goodbye Antifa: AG Barr Creates Task Force To Take Down Far-Left Extemists." *Neon Nettle*, Neon Nettle, 27 June 2020, https://neonnettle.com/news/11794-goodbye-antifa-ag-barr-creates-task-force-to-take-down-far-left-extremists

H, Peter. "25 Countries with the Highest Murder Rates in the World." *List 25*, List25 LLC., 11 January 2019 https://list25.com/25-countries-with-the-highest-murder-rates-in-the-world/2/

Hanson, Victor Davis. "History Is Clear: Socialism Isn't the Cure. So Why Do Millennials Like It?" *PJ Media*, PJ Media, 7 November 2019, https://pjmedia.com/victordavishanson/history-is-clear-socialism-isnt-the-cure-so-why-do-millennials-like-it/?fbclid=IwAR2QJoKpEw5dTwrG0GSTiQn1qyyyFP_mtM4-UTuYsZNZ7n3DlekgiOoQeN4

Harvard T.H. Chan. "Nearly Half Of Americans Believe H1N1 Outbreak Is Over, Poll Finds." *Harvard T.H. Chan*, The President and Fellows of Harvard College, 5 February 2020, https://www.hsph.harvard.edu/news/press-releases/poll-half-of-americans-believe-h1n1-outbreak-over/

Hendricks, Scotty. "What Is Socialism Like in Scandinavia?" *Big Think*, Big Think, 11 February 2019, https://bigthink.com/politics-current-affairs/what-is-socialism-scandinavia

Hobson, Jeremy and Hagan, Allison. "What Democratic Socialism Means In The U.S." *Here & Now*, WBUR, 5 March 2020, https://www.wbur.org/hereandnow/2020/03/05/bernie-sanders-and-democratic-socialism

Hunter Moyler. "76 Percent of Democrats Say They'd Vote For a Socialist For President, New Poll Shows." *Newsweek*, Newsweek, 11 February 2020, https://www.newsweek.com/76-percent-democrats-say-theyd-vote-socialist-president-new-poll-shows-1486732?utm_term=Autofeed&utm_medium=Social&utm_source=Facebook&fbclid=IwAR37WKoztJyhRGkDvUPVvNjnLrUfNcCbfufyEIyUQnS1k4TO4cfWzhBrcXA#Echobox=1581436387

Kertscher, Tom. "Thinking Small: Why Bernie Sanders and other 2020 Candidates Seek Low-Dollar Campaign Contributions." *Politifact*, Poynter Institute, 15 July 2019, https://www.politifact.com/truth-o-meter/article/2019/jul/15/thinking-small-why-bernie-sanders-and-other-2020-c/

Langlois, Shawn. "More Than a Third of Millennials Polled Approve of Communism." *Market Watch*, Market Watch Inc., 2 November 2019, https://www.marketwatch.com/story/for-millennials-socialism-and-communism-are-hot-capitalism-is-not-2019-10-28?mod=mw_share_facebook&fbclid=IwAR3vZAGcY27Msp9D_LGAcN5JBQav3f-AE6E9xt0Clj935oEKpjBUCPePVi8

Law Enforcement Today. "Oklahoma Charging Anti-Police Rioters With Terrorism and Rioting: 'When you act like a terrorist, you will be treated like a terrorist.' *Law Enforcement Today*, Law Enforcement Today, 30 June 2020, https://www.lawenforcementtoday.com/ok-da-charging-anti-police-rioters-with-terrorism-and-rioting-when-you-act-like-a-terrorist-you-will-be-treated-like-a-terrorist/?fbclid=IwAR3b8G9g4IaGtokP2fUqcbC7aXyoQPU-eL5zb84xV2Y95gSvfmt5JKRt-e4

Leon Puissegur. "Obama: His Marxist/Communist Past Exposed & How It Continues." *Freedom Outpost*, Freedom Outpost, 4 September 2012, https://freedomoutpost.com/obama-his-marxist-communist-past-exposed/

Manning, Scott. "Communist Body Count." *Historian On The Warpath*, Scott Manning, 4 December 2006, https://scottmanning.com/content/communist-body-count/

McKern, Steve. "Why Do Democrats Hate President Trump So Much?" *Common Sense American Politics*, Common Sense American Politics, https://www.commonsenseamericanpolitics.com/why-do-democrats-hate-president-trump-so-much/?fbclid=IwAR0-vMsCqD8OobGut-pyDDj_gPMYnj1u1tkaJuqQnNbUi1Aw4hh6824q3BU

McQuillan, Karin. "Barack Obama Populated the US Government with Communists." Life Site, *Lifesitenews.com*, 3 June 2019, https://www.lifesitenews.com/opinion/barack-obama-populated-the-us-government-with-communists

Meredith, Sam. "10 Global Hotspots For Major Human Rights Violations in 2017." *CNBC*, CNBC LLC., 23 February 2018, https://www.cnbc.com/2018/02/23/amnesty-ten-global-hotspots-for-major-human-rights-violations-in-2017.html

Metzgar, Jayme. "30 Years Later, 3 Lessons From the Fall of Romanian Communism." *The Federalist*, FDRLST Media, 23 December 2019, https://thefederalist.com/2019/12/23/30-years-later-3-lessons-from-the-fall-of-romanian-communism/

Meyerson, Harold. "Why Are There Suddenly Millions of Socialists in America?" *The Guardian*, The Guardian, 29 February 2016, https://www.theguardian.com/commentisfree/2016/feb/29/why-are-there-suddenly-millions-of-socialists-in-america

Nammo, David. "Socialism's Rising Popularity Threatens America's Future." *National Review*, National Review, 18 March 2017, https://www.nationalreview.com/2017/03/socialism-poll-american-culture-faith-institute-george-barna-tradition-liberty-capitalism/

O'Neil, Tyler. "The Success of Socialist Candidates Would Mean a Return to Poverty and Tyranny." *PJ Media*, PJ Media, 27 June 2018, https://pjmedia.com/trending/socialists-like-ben-jealous-and-alexandria-ocasio-cortez-would-bring-back-the-dark-ages/

Patton, Julie Brown. "China's Largest Megachurch Ex-Pastor Arrested by Authorities for Supporting Religious Freedom." *The Gospel Herald Life*, The Gospel Herald, 13 January 2017, https://www.gospelherald.com/articles/69336/20170113/megachurch-ex-pastor-arrested-by-china-authorities-for-supporting-religious-freedom.htm

Paulson, Terry. "7 Reasons the Left's Hatred of Trump Is So Deep." Townhall, Townhall.com/Salem Media, 24 February 2020, https://townhall.com/columnists/terrypaulson/2020/02/24/7-reasons-lefts-hatred-n2561687?fbclid=IwAR2yDk6poKX2zvBT1DFCVBbojYldthjcVr09lW2IrS4ilbtEoVRURrK764I

Political Editors. "Communist Antifa Leader Unmasked." *The Patriot Post*, The Patriot Post, 20 December 2018, https://patriotpost.us/articles/60175-communist-antifa-leader-unmasked-2018-12-20

RT. "MSNBC Producer Quits In Scathing Letter: "We Are A Cancer And There Is No Cure." *Infowar.com*, Informar.com, 4 August 2020, https://www.infowars.com/msnbc-producer-quits-in-scathing-letter-we-are-a-cancer-and-there-is-no-cure/

Tracinski, Robert. "10 Ways Obama Has Failed as President." The Federalist, The Federalist, 16 September 2014, https://thefederalist.com/2014/09/16/10-ways-obama-has-failed-as-president/

Sanders, Jeff. "Democratic Socialists of America's Plan To Infiltrate America's Public Schools." *PJ Media*, PJ Media.com/Salem Media, 30 September 2018, https://pjmedia.com/culture/jeff-sanders/2018/09/30/

democratic-socialists-of-americas-plan-to-infiltrate-americas-public-schools-n173026

Smith, Scott. "Venezuela's Poorest Struggle to Take Care of Their Dead." *Yahoo News*, Yahoo, 26 December 2019, https://www.yahoo.com/news/venezuelas-poorest-struggle-care-dead-050029828.html

Spencer, Robert. "Rioters Attack Churches and Synagogues But No Mosques." *Jihad Watch*, Jihad Watch, 5 June 2020, https://www.jihadwatch.org/2020/06/rioters-attack-churches-and-synagogues-but-no-mosques

Stewart, Emily. "How Close Are We To Another Financial Crisis? 8 Experts Weigh In." *Vox*, Vox Media, LLC., 18 September 2018, https://www.vox.com/2018/9/18/17868074/financial-crisis-dodd-frank-lehman-brothers-recession

Suarez, Candie. "The Rise of Socialism In America." *The Daily Conspiracy*, The Daily Conspiracy, 5 May 2018, https://thedailyconspiracy.com/2018/05/05/the-rise-of-socialism-in-america/

Sunstein, Cass R. "Attention Sanders: Roosevelt Was No Socialist." *Boston Herald*, MediaNews Group, Inc., 9 February 2019, https://www.bostonherald.com/2019/02/09/attention-sanders-roosevelt-was-no-socialist/

Telzrow, Michael E. "Socialism's Broken Promises." *New American*, The New American, 25 December 2008, https://www.thenewamerican.com/culture/history/item/4687-socialisms-broken-promises

The Editors of Encyclopedia Britannica. "Eugene V. Debs: American Social and Labour Leader." *Encyclopedia Britannica*, Encyclopedia Britannica, https://www.britannica.com/event/United-States-presidential-election-of-1912

U-S-History.com. "Socialism in America." *U-S-History.com*, Online Highways LLC., https://www.u-s-history.com/pages/h1669.html

UShistory.org. "Eugene V. Debs and American Socialism." *U.S History*, Ushistory.org, https://www.ushistory.org/us/37e.asp

WBUR. "Obama's Successes, Failures and Impact On America." WBUR, WBUR, 17 January 2017, https://www.wbur.org/hereandnow/2017/01/17/obama-consequential-president-michael-dantonio

Wikipedia. "Democratic Socialists of America." *Wikipedia*, Wikimedia Foundation, Inc., 24 February 2020, https://en.wikipedia.org/wiki/Democratic_Socialists_of_America

Wikipedia. "History of the Socialist Movement In The United States." *Wikimedia*, Wikimedia Foundation Inc., 28 June 2020, https://en.wikipedia.org/wiki/History_of_the_socialist_movement_in_the_United_States

Wikipedia. "Human Rights In The Soviet Union." *Wikimedia*, Wikimedia Foundation Inc., 8 February 2020, https://en.wikipedia.org/wiki/Human_rights_in_the_Soviet_Union

Wikipedia. "Republics of the Soviet Union." *Wikimedia*, Wikimedia Foundation Inc., 16 May 2020, https://en.wikipedia.org/wiki/Republics_of_the_Soviet_Union

Wikipedia. "Socialism." *Wikimedia*, Wikimedia Foundation Inc., 12 June 2020, https://en.wikipedia.org/wiki/Socialism

Wikipedia. "Types of Socialism." *Wikimedia*, Wikimedia Foundation Inc., 15 June 2020, https://en.wikipedia.org/wiki/Types_of_socialism

"WORLD WATCH LIST 2019." *Open Doors*, Open Doors, https://www.opendoorsusa.org/wp-content/uploads/2019/01/WWL2019_FullBooklet.pdf

Your Dictionary. "Socialism." *Your Dictionary*, LoveToKnow, Corp., https://www.yourdictionary.com/socialism

Printed in the United States
By Bookmasters